THE SCIENCE OF DEATH

A Journey Through Life's Final Chapter

Dr Bhaskar Bora

A PERSONAL NOTE FROM THE AUTHOR

My journey, once marked by certainty and driven by purpose, has transformed in ways I could never have anticipated. It is no longer about grand achievements or the pursuit of external success, but about the quiet, tender moments that reveal the true essence of life—moments of love, care, and presence. What you hold in your hands is not just a collection of words, but a testament to resilience, a story woven from the delicate threads of struggle, acceptance, and ultimately, renewal.

There was a time when my life flowed with the grace of a symphony, every note in perfect harmony. As a doctor, my days were filled with the pulse of life itself—offering hope, easing suffering, and healing with steady hands. The white coat I wore wasn't just a symbol of my profession; it embodied my very identity; an outward reflection of the healer I believed I was destined to be. The lives I touched, the people I helped—it all gave profound meaning to my existence.

But life, in its mysterious and unpredictable ways, had other plans. In one swift, unforeseen moment, the world I knew unravelled. First came the spinal cord injury, stripping away the physical strength I had relied upon. Then, the shadow of cancer darkened the horizon, a stark reminder of life's fragility. The world of medicine, where I once found so much joy and purpose, suddenly slipped away, leaving a vast emptiness in its wake—a silence where once there had been meaning.

Gone were the bustling corridors of the hospital, replaced by the quiet solitude of my home. No longer a "Doctor," I found myself standing at the edge of an uncertain future, my hands—once so steady with the knowledge of healing—trembling with questions I wasn't ready to face. Without the title, without the work that had defined me for so long, who was I? What was left of me when everything I had known was no longer within reach?

In that silence, in the stillness of a life interrupted, I began to uncover something unexpected. The role of a disabled husband and father, once a distant concept, became my new reality—one that held unexpected grace. What began as an effort to nurture my relationships, to find solace in this new world, slowly evolved into a profound inward journey.

I found healing in the spiritual—a rhythm of meditation, reading, and reflection that allowed me to rediscover the parts of myself I thought were lost. As I immersed myself in books, audiobooks, and hours of research, I began to understand that this new chapter of my life was not an ending, but a rebirth. The solitude of these years, the quiet hours of writing and reflection, gave birth to the very pages you hold in your hands now.

It is with deep gratitude that I share these words with you, knowing that they carry with them not just knowledge, but a piece of my soul. I hope that these reflections and insights offer you a fresh perspective on life and perhaps some nourishment for your own journey.

That we cannot control what the universe throws at us but how we react to those curveballs define who we are and what we make of our lives.

TABLE OF CONTENTS

1. Chapter 1: The Moment of Death
2. Chapter 2: The Biology of Dying: Cell by Cell
3. Chapter 3: Post-Mortem: The Immediate Aftermath
4. Chapter 4: Understanding Decomposition
5. Chapter 5: The Role of Forensic Science in Death Investigations
6. Chapter 6: Embalming: Preserving the Dead
7. Chapter 7: The Body Farm: Where Science Meets Decay
8. Chapter 8: Cryonics: Freezing the Body After Death
9. Chapter 9: Cremation: The Science of Turning Bodies to Ash
10. Chapter 10: The Role of Insects: Forensic Entomology
11. Chapter 11: The Digital Afterlife: Death in the Internet Age
12. Chapter 12: Death Across Cultures: How Different Societies Handle Death
13. Chapter 13: Forensic Anthropology: Reading Bones
14. Chapter 14: Organ Donation: Life After Death
15. Chapter 15: Euthanasia: The Science and Ethics of Choosing Death
16. Chapter 16: The Future of Death: Emerging Technologies and Research

17. Chapter 17: Near-Death Experiences: What Science Says

18. Chapter 18: Dying in Space: The Science of Death in Extreme Environments

19. Chapter 19: The Brain After Death: What We Know So Far

20. Chapter 20: The Science of Autopsy: Revealing the Cause of Death

21. Chapter 21: Historical Plagues and Epidemics: Death on a Large Scale

22. Chapter 22: Mass Graves: Science and Discovery in Archaeology

23. Chapter 23: The Role of Religion and Science in Death

24. Chapter 24: The Legal Side of Death: Estates, Wills, and Rights

25. Chapter 25: Death by Poison: Chemical Causes of Death

26. Chapter 26: The Science of Autopsy: Revealing the Cause of Death

27. Chapter 27: Historical Plagues and Epidemics: Death on a Large Scale

28. Chapter 28: Mass Graves: Science and Discovery in Archaeology

29. Chapter 29: Euthanasia: The Science and Ethics of Choosing Death

30. Chapter 30: The Final Frontier: The Philosophical and Scientific Mystery of What Happens After Death

CHAPTER 1: THE MOMENT OF DEATH

Death, an event as inevitable as it is complex, represents the cessation of an organism's vital functions. Scientifically, the process of death begins well before the final breath is drawn. It is a gradual, systematic shutdown of physiological systems that are critical to sustaining life, culminating in what is referred to as clinical death—when the heart stops beating and respiration ceases. But what truly defines the moment of death? The answers lie in a detailed understanding of the body's biological processes and how they ultimately collapse.

Physiological Process of Death: An Overview

From a medical perspective, death is not an instantaneous event but rather a cascade of interrelated failures that result in the cessation of life. Key organs, especially the heart, brain, lungs, liver, and kidneys, work in unison to keep the body alive, and their eventual failure marks the decline toward death. These failures may be triggered by various factors such as trauma, disease, or natural ageing processes, but regardless of the cause, the physiological pathway to death shares several commonalities.

1. Cardiovascular System: The Heart's Final Beats

The heart, a muscular organ tasked with circulating blood throughout the body, plays a central role in the maintenance of life. Its primary function is to pump oxygenated blood from the lungs to the rest of the body, while simultaneously returning deoxygenated blood to the lungs for reoxygenation. When the heart stops pumping effectively—whether due to myocardial infarction (heart attack), arrhythmia, or circulatory collapse—oxygen and nutrient delivery to vital organs becomes compromised. This phenomenon is known as cardiac arrest.

In the moments leading up to cardiac arrest, the heart may struggle to maintain its rhythm, exhibiting abnormal electrical activity such as ventricular fibrillation, where the heart quivers instead of contracting effectively. This irregular rhythm can quickly lead to a drop in blood pressure and diminished perfusion of the brain and other critical organs, resulting in ischemia (a lack of oxygen to tissues). If untreated, cardiac arrest progresses to irreversible damage within minutes.

Without prompt intervention, death follows shortly after the heart ceases to function. The point at which blood flow halts completely is medically referred to as asystole—the flatline of cardiac electrical activity. In this state, the body is deprived of its ability to transport oxygen, and within minutes, the organs begin to deteriorate. This cessation of circulation marks one of the critical moments in the process of dying.

2. Respiratory System: The Final Breath

Simultaneous to the cardiovascular decline, the respiratory system begins to fail. The lungs, responsible for oxygenating the blood and expelling carbon dioxide, rely on the rhythmic contraction of the diaphragm and intercostal muscles to expand and contract the thoracic cavity. When respiration becomes compromised—whether due to direct injury, obstruction, neurological failure, or systemic disease—oxygen levels in the bloodstream plummet. This condition is known as hypoxia.

As hypoxia worsens, carbon dioxide accumulates in the blood, leading to a condition known as hypercapnia. This imbalance in gases triggers a cascade of physiological changes, including increased acidity in the blood (acidosis), altered brain function, and the eventual cessation of respiratory effort. In cases of sudden trauma or severe medical conditions such as acute respiratory distress syndrome (ARDS), the lungs can quickly lose their capacity to exchange gases, leading to respiratory arrest.

Agonal breathing is a characteristic sign seen during the final moments of life. It is a gasping, irregular respiratory pattern often witnessed in patients nearing death and reflects the body's desperate attempts to bring in oxygen despite failing physiological systems. These gasps may continue for several minutes after cardiac arrest but do not reflect meaningful or effective respiration. The moment of the last breath, though often seen as symbolic, is part of a larger cascade of failures that define death.

3. Central Nervous System: Brain Death and the Loss of Consciousness

While the cessation of heart and lung function is critical in the definition of death, the brain's failure marks a profound turning point in the dying process. The brain, as the control centre for all bodily functions, is highly sensitive to oxygen deprivation. Within seconds of anoxia (total lack of oxygen), brain cells—particularly neurons—begin to suffer irreparable damage.

A key indicator of irreversible brain failure is the loss of consciousness. Consciousness, regulated by the brainstem and higher cortical structures, depends on continuous oxygen and glucose delivery to function. When the oxygen supply is interrupted, as occurs during cardiac arrest or severe trauma, the patient rapidly loses awareness, and neurological activity declines.

If oxygenation is not restored within four to six minutes, neuronal death begins to occur on a significant scale. The brain's cortex, responsible for higher-order functions like thought, memory, and voluntary movement, is particularly vulnerable to this damage. In cases of brain death, defined as the irreversible cessation of all brain activity, the brainstem—the structure responsible for basic life-sustaining functions such as heartbeat and respiration—no longer signals the body to breathe or maintain homeostasis.

Brain death is considered the ultimate indicator of death in many medical and legal systems around the world. Once brain death has been diagnosed, even if the heart continues to beat or mechanical ventilation sustains oxygenation, the individual is declared deceased. This distinction is important because brain death signifies that the body can no longer sustain itself autonomously, despite the artificial support of machines.

The Mechanisms Leading to Death: Causes and Their Pathways

Though the physiological process of death follows a general sequence, the pathways that lead to this outcome vary widely depending on the cause. Several primary categories of death—each defined by its specific mechanism—are discussed below.

1. Cardiac Death: The Heart as the Focal Point

One of the most common pathways to death, particularly in older adults, is cardiac death, which is precipitated by the failure of the heart to pump blood effectively. Conditions such as coronary artery disease, hypertension, and cardiomyopathies place stress on the heart over time, leading to increased risk for myocardial infarction or heart failure.

In cases of myocardial infarction, commonly known as a heart attack, blood flow to a portion of the heart muscle is blocked, leading to ischemia and eventual tissue death. If the infarction is severe, it can cause electrical instability in the heart, resulting in arrhythmias such as ventricular fibrillation, which quickly progress to cardiac arrest.

Congestive heart failure, on the other hand, represents a more gradual decline in the heart's ability to pump blood. Over time, the heart weakens and can no longer meet the body's metabolic demands. While not as sudden as myocardial infarction, heart failure still leads to a slow and inevitable progression toward death, often complicated by fluid buildup in the lungs (pulmonary oedema), organ failure, and fatigue.

2. Respiratory Death: The Collapse of the Lungs

Respiratory failure is another common pathway to death, particularly in individuals with chronic lung diseases such as chronic obstructive pulmonary disease (COPD), asthma, or pneumonia. In respiratory failure, the lungs' capacity to take in oxygen and expel carbon dioxide is impaired, leading to hypoxia and hypercapnia. Over time, these imbalances become life-threatening.

In cases of acute respiratory distress syndrome (ARDS), often seen in sepsis or severe trauma, the lungs become inflamed and fill with fluid, rendering them unable to perform gas exchange. Without mechanical intervention, ARDS is rapidly fatal, as oxygen levels drop precipitously and organ systems begin to fail due to hypoxia.

3. Neurological Death: Stroke, Trauma, and Brain Haemorrhage

Neurological causes of death are varied but often involve catastrophic damage to the brain or spinal cord. Stroke, a leading cause of death worldwide, occurs when blood flow to the brain is interrupted, either by a blockage (ischemic stroke) or bleeding (haemorrhagic stroke). The resulting damage can be extensive, affecting the brain's ability to control vital functions like breathing, consciousness, and circulation.

Traumatic brain injury (TBI), often the result of accidents or violence, can cause significant swelling, bleeding, and pressure within the skull, leading to the compression of brain tissue and eventual brain death. When the brainstem is affected, the body can no longer sustain critical functions, leading to rapid deterioration.

In cases of brain haemorrhage, such as subarachnoid haemorrhage, the bleeding increases pressure within the skull, leading to herniation (displacement of brain tissue) and eventual brainstem failure. These conditions are frequently sudden and fatal without immediate medical intervention.

4. Sepsis and Multiorgan Failure: The Systemic Collapse

Sepsis, a life-threatening condition triggered by infection, leads to a cascade of inflammatory responses throughout the body. When unchecked, sepsis progresses to septic shock, where blood pressure plummets and multiple organs begin to fail due to inadequate perfusion. In severe cases, the combination of cardiovascular collapse, respiratory failure, and kidney or liver dysfunction leads to death despite aggressive treatment.

Sepsis represents a unique pathway to death in that it involves the failure of multiple systems simultaneously. Unlike cardiac or respiratory death, where one organ system may initially fail, sepsis overwhelms the entire body, triggering widespread dysfunction.

Medical and Biological Definition of the Moment of Death

Defining the exact moment of death remains a challenge, both medically and philosophically. Traditionally, death was defined by the cessation of heartbeat and breathing—criteria that marked clinical death. However, advances in resuscitation technology, such as cardiopulmonary resuscitation (CPR) and mechanical ventilation, have complicated this definition, as patients can be revived after several minutes without a heartbeat or breath.

Today, most medical professionals define death by the cessation of brain activity, known as brain death. Brain death is considered irreversible, as the brain cannot recover from prolonged oxygen deprivation, even if other organs are temporarily supported by machines. In cases of brain death, the absence of brainstem reflexes—such as the ability to breathe independently or respond to stimuli—serves as confirmation of death.

Clinical death occurs when both cardiac and respiratory functions cease, and the body can no longer sustain life autonomously. It is often seen as the precursor to biological death, where cellular functions irreversibly cease. Biological death typically occurs minutes after clinical death, once the body's organs and tissues begin to break down due to lack of oxygen and energy.

In summary, the moment of death is marked by the coordinated failure of the body's vital systems—primarily the cardiovascular, respiratory, and nervous systems. Although the exact definition of death has evolved with medical advancements, it remains a universal and unavoidable biological event. Whether death occurs due to trauma, disease, or age-related decline, the physiological processes leading to death reflect the delicate balance required to sustain life, and the inevitability of its end.

CHAPTER 2: THE BIOLOGY OF DYING: CELL BY CELL

Death is not an instantaneous event but rather a complex, gradual process that begins at the cellular level and culminates in the irreversible cessation of all bodily functions. To fully grasp the biology of dying, it is essential to understand how individual cells—tiny units of life—respond to the physiological challenges posed by oxygen deprivation, nutrient deficiency, and the cascade of biochemical events that lead to organ failure. In this chapter, we will explore the intricate mechanisms that govern cellular death, the specific pathways involved in apoptosis and necrosis, and how the failure of these processes leads to the systemic shutdown of organs, ultimately resulting in death.

The Cellular Framework of Life

Before delving into the processes that lead to cellular death, it is important to understand the basic structure and function of cells. Every human body is composed of approximately 37.2 trillion cells, each performing specialized tasks that contribute to the overall functioning of the organism. Cells are the fundamental units of life, enclosed by a lipid bilayer membrane that regulates the exchange of materials between the internal cellular environment and the external surroundings.

Within each cell, there are numerous organelles responsible for carrying out essential functions. The nucleus contains the genetic material (DNA) that dictates cellular activities, while mitochondria are the energy powerhouses that generate adenosine triphosphate (ATP), the cell's primary energy currency. The endoplasmic reticulum and Golgi apparatus are responsible for protein synthesis and modification, and lysosomes contain enzymes that break down cellular waste. This highly organized and interdependent system functions optimally under normal physiological conditions but begins to unravel when cells are deprived of the necessary substrates for survival—most notably oxygen.

Oxygen Deprivation: The Critical Factor

Oxygen is the single most vital resource for cellular function. It is required for aerobic respiration, the process by which cells produce ATP through the electron transport chain within mitochondria. Without oxygen, cells are unable to efficiently generate ATP, which is crucial for maintaining ion gradients, driving metabolic reactions, and ensuring the proper functioning of cellular organelles. In the absence of sufficient oxygen, cells shift to anaerobic metabolism, which generates far less ATP and produces lactic acid as a byproduct. This shift, while providing a temporary energy solution, is ultimately unsustainable and leads to cellular dysfunction.

The phenomenon of oxygen deprivation, known as hypoxia, can occur due to various factors, such as cardiac arrest, respiratory failure, or circulatory shock. Hypoxia triggers a cascade of biochemical events that disrupt cellular homeostasis, leading to energy failure and, eventually, cell death. Anoxia, a complete absence of oxygen, accelerates these processes, making cell death inevitable in a matter of minutes in oxygen-sensitive tissues such as the brain and heart.

Cellular Energy Crisis: ATP Depletion and Consequences

The depletion of ATP is one of the earliest and most critical steps in the pathway to cell death. ATP is required for numerous cellular processes, including maintaining the integrity of the cell membrane, regulating ion channels, and driving active transport mechanisms. When oxygen is no longer available to support oxidative phosphorylation (the primary ATP-producing mechanism in mitochondria), cells rapidly deplete their ATP stores.

As ATP levels drop, several key cellular functions begin to fail:

1. Failure of Ion Pumps: The sodium-potassium ATPase pump is essential for maintaining the electrochemical gradient across the cell membrane, which keeps intracellular sodium levels low and potassium levels high. This gradient is crucial for processes such as nerve impulse transmission and muscle contraction. When ATP is no longer available to fuel this pump, sodium begins to accumulate inside the cell, drawing water in through osmosis and leading to cellular swelling.

2. Loss of Membrane Integrity: As the cell swells, its membrane becomes more permeable, leading to the leakage of ions, proteins, and other cellular contents. This disruption of the membrane's integrity is a hallmark of necrosis, a form of uncontrolled cell death. In addition, intracellular calcium levels rise, activating destructive enzymes such as phospholipases, proteases, and endonucleases, which further degrade the cell's structural components.

3. Mitochondrial Dysfunction: Mitochondria, being the primary site of ATP production, are particularly vulnerable to the effects of hypoxia. Without oxygen, mitochondrial membranes become depolarized, impairing the electron transport chain and leading

to the generation of reactive oxygen species (ROS). These highly reactive molecules cause oxidative damage to lipids, proteins, and DNA, further exacerbating cellular injury.

The Pathways of Cell Death: Apoptosis and Necrosis

Cell death can occur through two primary mechanisms: apoptosis and necrosis. Both processes lead to the elimination of damaged or non-functional cells, but they differ significantly in their biochemical pathways and consequences.

1. Apoptosis: Programmed Cell Death

Apoptosis, often referred to as "programmed cell death," is a highly regulated and controlled process that allows cells to die in a manner that minimizes damage to surrounding tissues. It is an essential mechanism for maintaining tissue homeostasis, as it removes damaged, infected, or unwanted cells during development, immune responses, and tissue repair. Unlike necrosis, apoptosis does not elicit an inflammatory response, as apoptotic cells are neatly packaged into membrane-bound vesicles called apoptotic bodies, which are then phagocytosed by neighbouring cells.

The process of apoptosis is initiated through two main pathways:

- Intrinsic Pathway: The intrinsic (or mitochondrial) pathway is triggered by internal signals such as DNA damage, oxidative stress, or nutrient deprivation. These stressors lead to the activation of pro-apoptotic proteins such as BAX and BAK, which permeabilize the outer mitochondrial membrane. This permeabilization allows the release of cytochrome c from the mitochondria into the cytoplasm, where it binds to Apaf-1 and forms the apoptosome complex. The apoptosome activates caspase-9, an initiator caspase that triggers the cascade of proteolytic enzymes responsible for dismantling the cell.

- Extrinsic Pathway: The extrinsic pathway is activated by

external signals, such as the binding of Fas ligand or TNF-alpha to their respective death receptors on the cell surface. This interaction leads to the formation of the death-inducing signalling complex (DISC), which activates caspase-8, another initiator caspase that sets off the execution phase of apoptosis.

Once initiated, both pathways converge on the activation of executioner caspases (such as caspase-3 and caspase-7), which cleave key structural and regulatory proteins, ultimately leading to DNA fragmentation, cytoskeletal disassembly, and cell shrinkage. The remains of the apoptotic cell are then engulfed by neighbouring phagocytes, preventing the release of toxic intracellular contents and avoiding inflammation.

2. Necrosis: Uncontrolled Cell Death

In contrast to apoptosis, necrosis is an uncontrolled and chaotic form of cell death that occurs in response to acute injury, such as trauma, infection, or severe hypoxia. Necrotic cell death is characterized by the rapid breakdown of cellular structures, leading to the release of intracellular contents into the extracellular space. This release triggers an inflammatory response, as the immune system recognizes the leaked cellular components as signals of damage.

Necrosis typically involves several key features:

- Cell Swelling: As ATP is depleted and ion gradients collapse, water rushes into the cell, causing it to swell and eventually rupture.
- Membrane Rupture: The loss of membrane integrity is a hallmark of necrosis, leading to the leakage of cellular contents, including enzymes, proteins, and organelles.
- Inflammation: The release of intracellular contents, particularly molecules like high-mobility group box 1 (HMGB1) and heat shock proteins, acts as danger signals (or damage-associated molecular patterns, DAMPs) that activate immune cells and trigger inflammation. This inflammatory response can

cause further damage to surrounding tissues.

Necrosis is generally considered a pathological process and can have detrimental effects on the body, particularly when it occurs in large areas of tissue, such as in heart attacks, strokes, or severe infections.

Autophagy: The Cell's Last-Ditch Effort to Survive

In some cases, cells can attempt to stave off death through a process known as autophagy, a survival mechanism in which the cell degrades and recycles its components to generate energy and maintain essential functions during times of stress. Autophagy involves the formation of autophagosomes, double-membrane vesicles that engulf damaged organelles and proteins. These autophagosomes then fuse with lysosomes, where the contents are broken down and recycled.

While autophagy can initially help cells survive under conditions of nutrient deprivation or mild stress, prolonged or excessive autophagy can lead to autophagic cell death, a process in which the cell essentially digests itself. Autophagy plays a dual role in cellular biology, acting as both a protective mechanism and a potential pathway to cell death when other survival strategies fail.

The Role of Reactive Oxygen Species (ROS) in Cellular Damage

Reactive oxygen species (ROS) are highly reactive molecules that are generated as byproducts of normal cellular metabolism, particularly during oxidative phosphorylation in mitochondria. Under normal conditions, ROS are neutralized by antioxidant defences, such as superoxide dismutase (SOD), catalase, and glutathione peroxidase. However, during hypoxia, mitochondrial dysfunction, or exposure to toxins, ROS levels can increase dramatically, leading to a state of oxidative stress.

ROS cause extensive damage to cellular components,

including:

- Lipid peroxidation: ROS attack the unsaturated fatty acids in the cell membrane, leading to the formation of lipid peroxides. This process weakens the integrity of the membrane and makes it more susceptible to rupture.
- Protein Oxidation: ROS can modify the side chains of amino acids in proteins, leading to changes in their structure and function. This can impair enzymatic activity, disrupt cellular signalling, and cause protein aggregation.
- DNA Damage: ROS can induce breaks in the DNA strand, leading to mutations and chromosomal instability. If the damage is severe and cannot be repaired, it can trigger cell death through apoptosis or necrosis.

Systemic Organ Failure: The Macroscopic Consequence Of Cellular Death

As cells across different organs begin to die, the body's ability to maintain homeostasis collapses. This results in the failure of multiple organ systems, each contributing to the progression toward death.

1. Cardiovascular Failure

As cardiac myocytes (heart muscle cells) die, the heart's ability to pump blood effectively diminishes, leading to circulatory collapse. This manifests as a drop in blood pressure (hypotension), impaired perfusion of vital organs, and, ultimately, cardiac arrest. Without adequate blood flow, organs such as the brain, kidneys, and liver quickly succumb to hypoxia and nutrient deprivation.

2. Respiratory Failure

In the lungs, alveolar epithelial cells are critical for gas exchange. When these cells are damaged or die, the lungs lose their ability to oxygenate blood and remove carbon dioxide. This leads to acute respiratory distress syndrome (ARDS), characterized by fluid accumulation in the alveoli, decreased lung compliance, and hypoxemia. Without mechanical ventilation, respiratory failure progresses rapidly and is often fatal.

3. Renal Failure

The kidneys are responsible for filtering waste products from the blood and maintaining fluid and electrolyte balance. When renal tubular cells are damaged by ischemia, toxins, or oxidative stress, the kidneys lose their ability to perform these functions, leading to acute kidney injury (AKI). In AKI, the buildup of toxic metabolic waste products in the blood further exacerbates organ dysfunction and contributes to the overall progression toward death.

4. Hepatic Failure

The liver plays a central role in detoxification, metabolism, and the production of essential proteins such as clotting factors. When hepatocytes (liver cells) die, the liver can no longer perform these functions, leading to hepatic encephalopathy, coagulopathy (impaired blood clotting), and multi-organ failure.

The Gradual Dismantling Of Life At The Cellular Level

The biology of dying is a highly orchestrated process that begins at the cellular level and progresses toward the failure of entire organ systems. Cellular death, whether through apoptosis, necrosis, or autophagy, is the precursor to systemic organ failure and the eventual cessation of life. The mechanisms that govern these processes are tightly regulated under normal conditions but become disrupted in the face of injury, hypoxia, and disease.

As cells lose their ability to generate energy, maintain

homeostasis, and repair damage, the body enters an irreversible decline that culminates in death. Understanding the cellular and molecular pathways involved in this process is crucial for developing therapeutic interventions aimed at prolonging life or alleviating suffering in patients nearing the end of life. This deep dive into the biology of dying highlights the complexity of the human body and the delicate balance required to sustain life at the cellular level.

CHAPTER 3: POST-MORTEM: THE IMMEDIATE AFTERMATH

Upon the cessation of life, the human body embarks on a highly structured, scientifically understood process of degradation. This transition from living tissue to organic matter undergoing decomposition begins almost immediately following death. During the initial 24 hours, three primary post-mortem changes occur: algor mortis (the cooling of the body), rigour mortis (the stiffening of muscles), and livor mortis (the pooling of blood). These physiological markers provide critical insight into the timeline of death and are indispensable in forensic investigations. This chapter will methodically dissect the biology behind these early post-mortem changes and explore their significance in both medical and forensic contexts.

The Post-Mortem Interval (PMI)

The post-mortem interval (PMI) is a term used to describe the time that has elapsed since death. Estimating the PMI is one of the primary goals of forensic pathologists when investigating cases of unexplained or suspicious death. During the first 24 hours, the body undergoes changes that allow for a reasonably accurate estimation of the time of death. However, these estimates are not precise due to the influence of multiple environmental and physiological factors, which will be examined throughout this chapter. Still, the three key processes —algor mortis, rigour mortis, and livor mortis—provide vital clues in narrowing down the PMI within the first day after death.

Algor Mortis: The Cooling of the Body

Algor mortis refers to the gradual cooling of the body after death as it equilibrates with the surrounding environmental temperature. During life, the human body maintains a relatively constant internal temperature, averaging around 37°C (98.6°F), regulated by metabolic processes that produce heat. Upon death, these processes cease, and the body's temperature begins to drop.

The rate at which the body cools depends on several factors, but the general rule of thumb is a cooling rate of approximately 1 to 1.5°C per hour in a temperate environment, although this can be highly variable. Understanding the mechanics of algor mortis is crucial for investigators seeking to determine the PMI, especially when used in conjunction with other post-mortem signs.

Mechanism of Algor Mortis

The process of algor mortis is driven by the cessation of metabolic activity. In life, cells continually generate heat through biochemical reactions such as cellular respiration. The energy required for maintaining homeostasis—ion gradients, enzyme function, and intracellular reactions—produces heat as a byproduct, which is dissipated through the skin and respiratory system to maintain a stable body temperature.

Upon death, cellular metabolism halts, and the body's internal heat production ceases. The body's core temperature then begins to equalize with the temperature of the surrounding environment through a process governed by basic thermodynamic principles. Heat is lost through conduction, convection, radiation, and, to a lesser degree, evaporation from the body's surfaces.

The temperature gradient between the body and its environment is the primary determinant of the rate of cooling. In cooler ambient temperatures, heat loss is rapid, while in warmer environments, the body cools more slowly.

Factors Influencing Algor Mortis

1. Ambient Temperature: The external environment has the most significant impact on the rate of body cooling. In cold environments, the body cools rapidly, whereas in warm or humid conditions, the rate of cooling slows. For instance, bodies in cold water cool significantly faster than those in the air due to the greater heat conductivity of water.

2. Body Size and Composition: The surface area-to-volume ratio plays a critical role in heat loss. Smaller bodies cool faster than larger ones because they have a higher surface area relative to their volume. Additionally, fat acts as an insulator, meaning that individuals with higher body fat percentages may experience slower cooling.

3. Clothing and Coverings: Clothing and other materials covering the body can insulate and slow the rate of heat loss. The more insulated a body is, the slower the rate of algor mortis. Bodies exposed to the elements cool faster, whereas those wrapped in blankets or heavy clothing cool more slowly.

4. Environmental Conditions: Wind, humidity, and air circulation can either accelerate or decelerate body cooling. For example, in breezy conditions, heat loss through convection

increases, resulting in more rapid cooling.

Forensic Implications of Algor Mortis

In forensic pathology, the estimation of PMI using algor mortis requires precise temperature measurements, usually taken rectally or by inserting a probe into the liver. These temperatures are compared to environmental conditions and calculated using known cooling rates to provide a time of death estimate. However, because the rate of cooling is influenced by many variables, algor mortis is used alongside other post-mortem signs to corroborate the time of death.

Rigour Mortis: The Stiffening of the Body

Rigor mortis is the post-mortem stiffening of muscles due to biochemical changes within the muscle fibres. This phenomenon begins shortly after death and progresses predictably, providing valuable information about the time of death.

Biochemical Mechanism of Rigor Mortis

In living cells, muscle contraction is controlled by the interaction of actin and myosin filaments within the muscle fibres, a process regulated by calcium ions and powered by adenosine triphosphate (ATP). ATP is required for both the contraction and relaxation of muscles. After death, ATP production ceases, and as a result, calcium ions leak from the sarcoplasmic reticulum into the muscle fibres, binding to actin and allowing the actin-myosin cross-bridges to form. Without ATP to facilitate muscle relaxation, these cross-bridges remain locked in place, causing the muscles to stiffen.

Rigour mortis typically sets in within 2 to 6 hours after death, reaches its peak rigidity around 12 to 24 hours, and begins to dissipate after 24 to 48 hours as the muscle tissues begin to decompose. This process is both progressive and transient, with small muscle groups (such as the facial muscles) being affected first, followed by larger muscle groups in the limbs and torso.

Phases of Rigor Mortis

1. Onset: Rigor mortis begins in the smaller muscles, particularly in the face and neck, within 2 to 6 hours after death. During this phase, the body gradually stiffens as ATP depletion continues.

2. Peak: Maximum stiffness is reached within 12 to 24 hours post-mortem, depending on environmental conditions. By this point, all major muscle groups, including the limbs and torso, are in full rigour, with the joints becoming immobile.

3. Resolution: Rigor mortis begins to fade after 24 hours, as autolysis (self-digestion by cellular enzymes) and putrefaction start breaking down the muscle tissues. As decomposition progresses, the muscles relax, and the body returns to a flaccid state.

Factors Affecting the Progression of Rigour Mortis

The timeline of rigour mortis is affected by various intrinsic and extrinsic factors:

1. Ambient Temperature: As with algor mortis, temperature plays a critical role in the progression of rigour mortis. Higher temperatures accelerate the chemical reactions involved in muscle stiffening and decomposition, causing rigour to set in faster and dissipate more quickly. Conversely, in colder environments, rigour mortis may be delayed, with the stiffening process occurring more slowly and lasting longer.

2. Physical Activity Before Death: Vigorous physical activity before death can deplete ATP stores and cause an earlier onset of rigour mortis. For example, in cases of death following intense exertion or violent struggle, rigour mortis may set in more rapidly.

3. Muscle Mass: The size of the muscle groups involved affects

the progression of rigour mortis. Smaller muscles stiffen sooner than larger ones, while individuals with greater muscle mass may exhibit a delayed onset of rigour due to their higher ATP reserves.

4. Age and Condition of the Body: Rigor mortis may develop more quickly in infants, children, and the elderly due to their lower muscle mass and reduced ATP reserves. Additionally, individuals who are malnourished or suffering from chronic illness may experience a more rapid progression of rigour mortis due to weakened muscle tissue and depleted energy stores.

Forensic Applications of Rigour Mortis

In forensic investigations, the state of rigour mortis provides an important estimate of the PMI. Observing the location and intensity of muscle stiffening helps determine how long a body has been dead. Additionally, the pattern of rigour can offer insights into whether the body has been moved post-mortem. For instance, if rigour mortis is present in muscles that suggest a different position than the one in which the body is found, it may indicate post-mortem relocation.

Livor Mortis: The Pooling Of Blood

Livor mortis, also known as post-mortem hypostasis or lividity, refers to the gravitational pooling of blood in the lower, dependent portions of the body after circulation ceases. In life, the heart constantly pumps blood through the body's network of arteries and veins, maintaining an even distribution of blood. After death, the heart stops, and blood, no longer being actively circulated, begins to settle in the capillaries and small veins of the body, particularly in areas closest to the ground.

The result is a visible discolouration of the skin, ranging from red to purplish-blue, depending on the oxygenation level of the blood at the time of death. Livor mortis usually begins within 20 minutes to 3 hours after death, becomes fully visible after 6 to 12 hours, and eventually becomes "fixed" when the blood clots in place.

Mechanism of Livor Mortis

The mechanism of livor mortis is primarily governed by gravity:

1. Cessation of Circulation: After the heart stops beating, blood is no longer pumped through the body. Instead, it passively settles in the dependent (lower) portions of the body due to the pull of gravity.

2. Capillary Engorgement: As blood pools in the lower parts of the body, it engorges the capillaries and small veins, leading to a visible discolouration of the skin in those areas. The colour of the lividity depends on whether the blood is oxygenated (bright red) or deoxygenated (purplish blue). In cases of carbon monoxide poisoning, for example, lividity may appear cherry red due to the high levels of carboxyhaemoglobin in the blood.

3. Fixation of Lividity: Over time, the blood in the capillaries coagulates, or clots, and the pattern of lividity becomes fixed. Once this occurs, even if the body is moved, the areas of discolouration remain in their original locations, providing forensic investigators with clues about the body's position at the time of death.

Factors Influencing Livor Mortis

Several factors influence the appearance and progression of livor mortis:

1. Position of the Body: Livor mortis is influenced by the position of the body after death. For example, in a body lying on its back, lividity will typically be seen on the back, buttocks, and posterior surfaces of the limbs. In contrast, if the body is face down, lividity will appear on the front of the body.

2. Environmental Temperature: Colder environments slow the progression of livor mortis, while warmer environments accelerate the process. In cooler temperatures, lividity may take longer to become visible, and the blood may clot more slowly, delaying the fixation of livor mortis.

3. Pressure Points: Areas of the body that are in direct contact with a firm surface, such as the ground or a bed, may not display lividity due to the compression of the capillaries, which prevents blood from pooling in those areas. These areas may appear pale in contrast to the surrounding livid areas.

Forensic Significance of Livor Mortis

Livor mortis is a valuable tool in forensic pathology for several reasons:

1. Estimation of PMI: The timing of the onset, development, and fixation of livor mortis can be used to estimate the time of death. Lividity that is unfixed suggests a PMI of less than 6 hours, while fixed lividity indicates that death occurred more than 6 hours prior.

2. Determining Body Position: The location and distribution of lividity provide clues about the position of the body at the time of death. If the pattern of lividity does not match the current position of the body, it may suggest that the body was moved post-mortem.

3. Cause of Death Clues: The colour and intensity of livor mortis can provide hints about the cause of death. For example, cherry-red lividity may indicate carbon monoxide poisoning, while darker lividity may suggest asphyxiation or heart failure.

The Early Stages of Decomposition

While algor mortis, rigor mortis, and livor mortis provide important information about the immediate post-mortem changes, the body also begins to undergo the earliest stages of decomposition within the first 24 hours after death. Autolysis and putrefaction are the primary processes that initiate the breakdown of tissues.

1. Autolysis: Autolysis, or self-digestion, begins almost immediately after death as the cells' lysosomes—organelles containing digestive enzymes—rupture and release their contents into the cytoplasm. These enzymes break down cellular components, leading to the softening and eventual liquefaction of tissues.

2. Putrefaction: Putrefaction is the result of bacterial activity within the body. The gut's bacteria, no longer kept in check by the immune system, begin to proliferate and break down tissues. This process produces gases such as hydrogen sulphide, methane, and ammonia, which contribute to the characteristic bloating and odour associated with decomposition.

During the first 24 hours, these processes are relatively subtle, but they lay the foundation for the more advanced stages of decomposition that follow.

The immediate aftermath of death is marked by a series of physiological changes—algor mortis, rigor mortis, and livor mortis—that offer invaluable insight into the time and circumstances surrounding death. Each process follows a predictable timeline, influenced by both intrinsic factors (such as body composition) and extrinsic factors (such as environmental conditions). Understanding these processes is essential for forensic investigations, allowing pathologists to estimate the post-mortem interval, determine the position of the body, and infer potential causes of death. As the body continues to undergo autolysis and putrefaction, the initial signs of decomposition signal the irreversible transition from life to decay, marking the beginning of the body's return to the environment.

CHAPTER 4: UNDERSTANDING DECOMPOSITION

Decomposition is the process through which the human body, upon death, transitions from a complex, living organism to its elemental components. The breakdown of the body begins immediately after death and proceeds through a series of well-defined stages. These stages of decomposition—beginning with the fresh stage and culminating in the reduction of the body to skeletal remains—are driven by biological, chemical, and environmental factors. Central to this process is the activity of microorganisms, fungi, and insects, which work in concert to dismantle the human body after death.

In this chapter, we will explore the stages of decomposition in detail, including the pivotal role of bacteria, fungi, and insects in facilitating the breakdown of tissue. Furthermore, we will examine the external factors—such as temperature, humidity, environment, and the cause of death—that influence the rate and nature of decomposition. By understanding these processes, we gain critical insight into how the body returns to the environment after death and how forensic scientists utilize decomposition to estimate the post-mortem interval (PMI) and uncover details about the circumstances of death.

Stages of Decomposition: An Overview

The process of decomposition can be categorized into five primary stages: fresh, bloat, active decay, advanced decay, and skeletal remains. Each stage is characterized by distinct physical, chemical, and biological changes that reflect the breakdown of tissues and organs over time.

1. Fresh (Autolysis): This stage begins immediately after death and lasts until the body shows the first external signs of decomposition. Autolysis, or self-digestion, is the dominant process during this phase, driven by the release of digestive enzymes from the body's cells.

2. Bloat (Putrefaction): As microorganisms, particularly bacteria, begin to proliferate, the body enters the bloat stage. The production of gases, due to bacterial metabolism, causes the body to swell, or bloat, and distinctive odours begin to emerge.

3. Active Decay: During this stage, there is a significant loss of mass as the body undergoes rapid breakdown, fuelled by microbial activity and insect colonization. The liquefaction of tissues becomes apparent as the body collapses on itself.

4. Advanced Decay: With most of the soft tissues degraded, decomposition slows, and the remaining tissues begin to desiccate. By this stage, insect activity begins to decline.

5. Skeletal Remains: The final stage of decomposition is marked by the absence of soft tissue, leaving behind only bones, cartilage, and hair. The skeleton may undergo further degradation over time due to environmental factors.

Stage 1: The Fresh Stage (Autolysis)

The fresh stage of decomposition begins immediately upon death and is characterized by autolysis, or the self-digestion of the body's cells. This stage can last for hours or days, depending on environmental conditions. Although there are few visible external signs of decomposition during the fresh stage, significant changes are already occurring within the body at the cellular level.

Mechanism of Autolysis

Autolysis is initiated by the cessation of oxygen supply to the body's cells. During life, oxygen is delivered to cells via the bloodstream, enabling them to carry out aerobic metabolism. Upon death, blood circulation stops, and oxygen is no longer transported to the tissues. Without oxygen, cells switch to anaerobic metabolism, which produces acidic byproducts, such as lactic acid. The accumulation of these acids within the cells causes the breakdown of cellular membranes and organelles.

Lysosomes—membrane-bound organelles containing digestive enzymes—play a critical role in autolysis. When the cellular membranes become compromised, lysosomal enzymes are released into the cytoplasm, where they begin to digest the cell's internal components. Autolysis is most evident in tissues rich in enzymes, such as the liver, pancreas, and stomach lining. These organs typically undergo autolytic degradation before other tissues.

Internal Signs of the Fresh Stage

Although external changes may be minimal during the fresh stage, autolysis produces several internal signs of decomposition:

1. Tissue Softening: As cells break down, the tissue becomes increasingly soft and friable. The walls of blood vessels degrade, leading to the pooling of blood in dependent areas, a process known as livor mortis.

2. Colour Changes: The breakdown of red blood cells leads to the release of haemoglobin, which eventually permeates the

surrounding tissues. This results in greenish discolouration in the abdominal area due to the formation of sulfhemoglobin as haemoglobin reacts with hydrogen sulphide produced by bacteria.

3. Odor Development: The fresh stage is also the precursor to the development of decomposition odours. These odours become more prominent as bacteria begin to metabolize tissues, releasing volatile organic compounds (VOCs) such as putrescine and cadaverine.

Bacterial Role in the Fresh Stage

The gastrointestinal tract contains a vast number of bacteria, primarily anaerobic species that thrive in oxygen-deprived environments. After death, the body's immune system, which normally keeps these bacteria in check, is no longer functional. As a result, bacteria begin to migrate from the gastrointestinal tract to other parts of the body. This bacterial activity is responsible for initiating putrefaction, the next stage of decomposition.

Stage 2: The Bloat Stage (Putrefaction)

The bloat stage of decomposition is characterized by putrefaction, a process driven primarily by bacterial proliferation. Putrefaction is the microbial decomposition of organic matter, and it produces significant physical and chemical changes in the body. This stage is marked by the production of gases, which accumulate within the body, causing it to swell or bloat.

Bacterial Activity and Gas Production

The bacteria responsible for putrefaction are primarily anaerobic bacteria, which thrive in environments devoid of oxygen. These bacteria metabolize proteins, fats, and carbohydrates, producing gases such as hydrogen sulphide, methane, ammonia, and carbon dioxide as byproducts. These gases accumulate in the body's cavities, causing the body to expand and take on a distended, bloated appearance.

The characteristic foul odour associated with decomposition is due to the release of volatile organic compounds (VOCs), including putrescine and cadaverine, which result from the breakdown of amino acids. Hydrogen sulphide, produced by sulphate-reducing bacteria, contributes to the sulphurous odour often associated with decomposing bodies.

Physical Signs of Bloat

The bloat stage presents several noticeable physical changes in the body:

1. Swelling of the Abdomen: The abdomen is one of the first areas to show signs of bloating due to the accumulation of gases produced by intestinal bacteria. This swelling may cause the skin to stretch and become taut.

2. Protrusion of the Tongue and Eyes: As gas pressure increases within the body, internal organs are displaced, leading to the protrusion of the tongue and, in some cases, the eyes.

3. Marbling of the Skin: During the bloat stage, the blood vessels degrade, and blood begins to seep into the surrounding tissues. This creates a characteristic marbling pattern on the skin, particularly in areas where the skin is thinner, such as the face and limbs.

4. Skin Slippage: As the connective tissue between the skin and underlying structures degrades, the skin begins to detach, a phenomenon known as skin slippage. Blisters filled with gas or fluid may also form, and the skin can peel away in large sheets.

Insect Colonization During the Bloat Stage

Insects, particularly blowflies and flesh flies, play a significant role in the decomposition process, particularly during the bloat stage. Female blowflies are attracted to the odours released by putrefying tissues and will lay their eggs on the body, typically in natural orifices such as the mouth, nose, and eyes. Within hours, the eggs hatch into maggots, which begin feeding on the decomposing tissues. The presence of maggots accelerates the breakdown of soft tissues, as they consume large amounts of organic material.

Stage 3: Active Decay

The active decay stage is marked by a significant loss of mass as the body undergoes rapid breakdown. During this phase, the tissues liquefy and collapse, releasing large quantities of fluids into the surrounding environment. Active decay is often associated with the most rapid rate of decomposition and the most prominent odour production.

Tissue Breakdown and Liquefaction

By the time the body enters the active decay stage, much of the soft tissue has been compromised by autolysis, bacterial action, and insect activity. The liquefaction of tissues is a hallmark of this phase, with bodily fluids seeping from natural orifices and wounds. These fluids, known as purge fluids, are the result of the breakdown of cellular and connective tissues and can accumulate in the body's cavities or be expelled from the body.

The collapse of the body's structure during active decay is due to the extensive loss of tissue integrity. Muscles, fat, and internal organs are rapidly consumed by bacteria and maggots, resulting in the body's collapse itself. This stage is often referred to as wet decay because of the high moisture content of the tissues.

Insect Activity in Active Decay

Insects, particularly maggots, play a crucial role in the decomposition process during active decay. Blowfly maggots can consume large amounts of tissue, and their feeding activity creates an ideal environment for the proliferation of bacteria. As the maggots grow, they moult several times before entering the pupal stage. The presence of insects accelerates tissue breakdown and contributes to the liquefaction of tissues.

In addition to blowflies and flesh flies, beetles and ants may also become involved in the decomposition process during active decay. Dermestid beetles, for example, are known for feeding on the remaining dry tissues after the maggots have consumed most of the soft tissue.

Stage 4: Advanced Decay

The advanced decay stage is marked by a significant reduction in the rate of decomposition as most of the easily degradable tissues have already been consumed. By this stage, the body is primarily composed of bones, cartilage, hair, and small amounts of dried, desiccated tissue. The activity of insects and bacteria diminishes, and the body's mass is substantially reduced.

Desiccation and Drying

During advanced decay, the remaining tissues undergo desiccation or drying. This process is facilitated by exposure to air, which leads to the evaporation of moisture from the tissues. The skin and connective tissues become mummified, and the body takes on a leathery appearance.

The process of desiccation slows down the activity of bacteria and insects, as the lack of moisture creates an inhospitable environment for microbial and insect life. However, some insects, such as dermestid beetles, are adapted to feed on dry, desiccated tissues.

Reduced Insect Activity

By the time the body reaches advanced decay, the majority of insect activity has subsided. Most blowflies and flesh flies have completed their life cycles and left the body, and the maggot population has significantly decreased. Beetles and other scavengers may remain to feed on the remaining tissues, but their activity is much less pronounced than during the earlier stages of decomposition.

Stage 5: Skeletal Remains

The final stage of decomposition is the skeletal remains stage, during which all soft tissues have been removed, leaving behind only bones, cartilage, and hair. At this point, the body is no longer subject to rapid biological decay, and the remaining skeletal elements can persist for years or even decades, depending on environmental conditions.

Environmental Factors Affecting Bone Decomposition

While bones are highly resistant to decay, they are not immune to environmental influences. Factors such as soil acidity, moisture levels, and temperature can affect the rate at which bones degrade. In acidic soils, for example, bones may break down more rapidly due to the dissolution of hydroxyapatite, the mineral that gives bones their strength.

Additionally, the presence of scavengers, such as rodents and carnivores, can contribute to the degradation of bones by chewing and gnawing on the skeletal elements.

Bone Weathering and Degradation

Over time, bones that are exposed to the elements may undergo weathering, a process in which the bones become brittle and cracked due to repeated cycles of wetting and drying, freezing and thawing, and exposure to sunlight. Bones that are buried or protected from the elements may persist for much longer, depending on the conditions.

Factors Affecting the Rate of Decomposition

The rate of decomposition is influenced by several factors, including temperature, humidity, environment, and the cause of death. These factors play a critical role in determining how quickly the body progresses through the stages of decomposition.

1. Temperature: Higher temperatures accelerate the decomposition process by promoting bacterial and insect activity, while lower temperatures slow decomposition by inhibiting microbial growth.

2. Humidity: High humidity levels promote the growth of bacteria and fungi, leading to more rapid decomposition. Conversely, dry environments can slow decomposition by desiccating tissues and reducing microbial activity.

3. Environment: Bodies that are buried or submerged in water decompose at different rates than those left in open air. Burial slows decomposition by limiting access to oxygen and insects, while water immersion can either accelerate or decelerate decomposition depending on the temperature and oxygen content of the water.

4. Cause of Death: The cause of death can influence the rate of decomposition. For example, bodies that have sustained trauma or have been infected with certain pathogens may decompose more rapidly due to the presence of bacteria or damaged tissues.

Decomposition is a complex, multifaceted process driven by the interplay of biological, chemical, and environmental factors. From the initial stages of autolysis and bacterial putrefaction to the final reduction of the body to skeletal remains, decomposition follows a predictable sequence of events that provides critical information for forensic investigations. Understanding the stages of decomposition and the factors that influence them is essential for estimating the post-mortem interval, determining the circumstances of death, and uncovering the body's journey back to its elemental state. As research into decomposition continues to evolve, it enhances our ability to use these biological processes as a tool in the pursuit of justice and scientific knowledge.

CHAPTER 5: THE ROLE OF FORENSIC SCIENCE IN DEATH INVESTIGATIONS

Forensic science serves as a cornerstone in modern death investigations, bridging the gap between biological facts and legal conclusions. In the intricate and often ambiguous world of forensic pathology, the application of scientific methods enables investigators to establish the cause and manner of death with precision, ensuring justice is pursued correctly and comprehensively. The discipline encompasses a wide range of specialized techniques, from autopsies and toxicology to DNA analysis and trace evidence examination, each contributing to the overall picture of how, why, and when death occurred. This chapter delves deeply into the methodologies and technologies that form the foundation of forensic science, particularly in cases involving suspicious or unnatural deaths.

The Foundation of Forensic Science in Death Investigations

At its core, forensic science applies scientific principles to answer questions of legal relevance, with death investigations being a primary area of focus. Whether the investigation pertains to homicide, suicide, accidental death, or natural causes, forensic scientists play a critical role in providing objective, evidence-based answers to complex medical and criminal questions. The primary goal is to determine the cause of death—the medical reason the individual died—and the manner of death, whether it be natural, accidental, homicidal, or suicidal.

One of the key aspects of forensic science is its interdisciplinary nature. Forensic pathologists, toxicologists, DNA analysts, forensic anthropologists, and crime scene investigators all work in concert, each providing vital information based on their specialized knowledge. These experts rely on an extensive toolkit of investigative procedures, from examining physical injuries to performing molecular analyses, and their findings form the basis of conclusions that have far-reaching implications in both criminal and civil courts.

The Autopsy: The Cornerstone of Death Investigations

The autopsy, also known as a post-mortem examination, is perhaps the most recognizable and essential component of forensic death investigations. An autopsy is a systematic dissection of the body, conducted to ascertain the cause and manner of death. The forensic pathologist conducting the autopsy examines both the external and internal features of the deceased, documenting injuries, disease processes, and any other anomalies that may shed light on the circumstances surrounding death.

External Examination

The external examination provides crucial preliminary information that may guide the subsequent internal dissection. During this phase, the body is visually inspected for any signs of trauma, disease, or other external factors that may have contributed to death. The following are key components of the external examination:

1. Livor Mortis and Rigor Mortis: The pathologist examines the patterns of lividity (post-mortem blood pooling) and rigour

mortis (muscle stiffening) to estimate the time since death and determine whether the body has been moved post-mortem. Unusual patterns or inconsistencies in these post-mortem changes can suggest tampering or concealment.

2. External Injuries: Any bruising, lacerations, abrasions, or other injuries are carefully documented and photographed. The nature, location, and extent of these injuries can provide critical insight into the cause of death, as well as whether the death was violent or non-violent. For example, defence wounds on the hands or forearms may indicate a struggle, while ligature marks around the neck suggest strangulation.

3. Identification of the Deceased: Before proceeding with the internal examination, the forensic pathologist must establish or confirm the identity of the deceased. Methods of identification include visual recognition, fingerprints, dental records, or, in more complex cases, DNA analysis. In cases where decomposition or trauma obscures traditional identification methods, forensic anthropology or odontology may be employed.

Internal Examination

Once the external examination is complete, the pathologist proceeds with the internal dissection, which involves opening the body cavities to inspect the internal organs and tissues. This portion of the autopsy is critical in revealing medical conditions or trauma that are not externally visible. Key aspects of the internal examination include:

1. Examination of Organs: Each organ is systematically examined for signs of disease, trauma, or pathology. For example, in cases of suspected myocardial infarction (heart attack), the heart will be carefully dissected to look for evidence of ischemia or infarction. In cases of blunt force trauma, the internal organs will be inspected for lacerations, haemorrhages, or other injuries indicative of a violent death.

2. Collection of Biological Samples: During the internal examination, samples of bodily fluids—such as blood, urine, and vitreous humour—are collected for subsequent toxicological analysis. Additionally, tissue samples from various organs may be retained for histological examination under a microscope to identify microscopic changes, such as infection, malignancy, or degenerative disease.

3. Documentation of Findings: Throughout the autopsy, the pathologist meticulously documents all observations, including the weight, size, and appearance of each organ. Any abnormalities, injuries, or signs of disease are noted in detail, forming the basis of the final autopsy report. This report provides a comprehensive account of the pathologist's findings, offering a critical piece of evidence in determining the cause and manner of death.

Toxicology: Analysing the Chemical Contributions to Death

Toxicology is another pivotal branch of forensic science, particularly in cases where poisoning, overdose, or substance-related death is suspected. Forensic toxicology involves the identification and quantification of drugs, alcohol, poisons, and other chemicals in the body, helping to determine whether these substances played a role in the death. Toxicologists analyse blood, urine, and tissue samples collected during the autopsy to detect and measure the concentration of various substances.

Types of Substances Analysed in Toxicology

1. Drugs: Both licit and illicit drugs can contribute to death, either through overdose or as a contributing factor in accidents, homicides, or suicides. Toxicology screens are designed to detect common drugs of abuse, including opioids (e.g., heroin, fentanyl), stimulants (e.g., cocaine, methamphetamine), sedatives (e.g., benzodiazepines), and others. The identification of therapeutic drugs, such as antidepressants or antipsychotics,

can also provide context in cases of suicide or accidental overdose.

2. Alcohol: Alcohol is a frequent factor in accidental and intentional deaths. Blood alcohol concentration (BAC) levels are measured to determine whether alcohol intoxication was present at the time of death and whether it may have impaired judgment or motor skills, contributing to the fatal event.

3. Poisons: In cases of suspected poisoning, forensic toxicologists may screen for the presence of toxic agents such as cyanide, arsenic, carbon monoxide, and other hazardous substances. Certain poisons may leave telltale signs that guide toxicologists in their investigations—for example, cherry-red lividity in cases of carbon monoxide poisoning.

4. Metabolites: Toxicologists often look for metabolites—the byproducts produced when the body processes drugs or poisons—to confirm exposure and determine how long before death the substance was ingested. For example, morphine, a metabolite of heroin, may be detected in cases of heroin overdose, providing definitive evidence of opioid use.

Interpreting Toxicological Results

While detecting the presence of a drug or poison is a crucial step, forensic toxicologists must also interpret the significance of the findings. This involves understanding the pharmacokinetics and pharmacodynamics of the substance—how it is absorbed, distributed, metabolized, and eliminated by the body. Toxicologists assess the concentration of the substance in the blood or tissues to determine whether it is at a therapeutic, toxic, or lethal level.

For example, the presence of opioids in a decedent's system does not automatically indicate an overdose. The concentration must be high enough to cause respiratory depression, the mechanism of death in opioid toxicity. Similarly, in the case of alcohol, toxicologists must consider the BAC in conjunction with the individual's tolerance and potential for alcohol-related health conditions, such as cirrhosis or fatty liver.

DNA Analysis: Identifying Individuals and Establishing Links

The development of DNA analysis revolutionized forensic science, providing an unparalleled tool for identifying individuals and establishing links between suspects, victims, and crime scenes. DNA is highly specific to each individual, except identical twins, making it a powerful method for identifying deceased individuals, especially in cases of advanced decomposition or severe trauma.

Sources of DNA in Death Investigations

1. Blood and Tissue: DNA can be extracted from blood, tissue, and other biological materials collected during the autopsy. This is particularly important in cases where visual identification is impossible, such as in mass disasters, fires, or severely decomposed bodies.

2. Bone and Teeth: In cases where soft tissues have degraded, DNA can be obtained from bone marrow or dental pulp. These sources of DNA are more resistant to environmental degradation, making them invaluable in identifying skeletal remains or victims of long-term disappearance.

3. Hair and Nails: DNA can also be extracted from hair follicles or fingernails, although these sources may contain lower quantities of DNA than blood or tissue samples.

Applications of DNA in Forensic Science

1. Identification of the Deceased: In mass fatalities or cases of advanced decomposition, DNA profiling can be used to identify victims by comparing the DNA from the deceased with known reference samples, such as those from close relatives.

2. Linking Suspects to Crime Scenes: DNA evidence collected

from a crime scene—such as blood, saliva, or semen—can be compared to DNA profiles from potential suspects. A match provides strong evidence that the individual was present at the scene, although it must be corroborated by additional forensic or investigative findings.

3. Paternity and Familial Relationships: In cases of disputed identity, DNA analysis can also be used to establish familial relationships, such as paternity or sibling relationships.

This is particularly useful when a direct reference sample from the deceased is unavailable.

Forensic Anthropology: Analysing Skeletal Remains

When a body is reduced to skeletal remains, forensic anthropology becomes a critical tool in determining the cause and manner of death. Forensic anthropologists specialize in the analysis of bones, which can reveal a wealth of information about the decedent, including age, sex, ancestry, and any trauma or pathological conditions.

Age and Sex Determination

Forensic anthropologists can estimate the age of skeletal remains by examining the degree of bone ossification and the state of the epiphyseal plates. In children and adolescents, the epiphyseal plates, or growth plates, are still active, allowing for the estimation of age based on the degree of bone growth. In adults, the wear and degeneration of specific joints, such as the pubic symphysis, can provide clues to age at the time of death.

Sex determination is based on the examination of sexually dimorphic traits in the skeleton. The pelvis is the most reliable indicator of sex, as it differs significantly between males and females to accommodate childbirth. Skull features, such as the brow ridge and jawline, also exhibit sexual dimorphism and can aid in the determination of sex.

Analysis of Trauma and Pathology

Skeletal remains often bear evidence of traumatic injury or disease, which can provide critical insight into the cause of death. For example, perimortem fractures (those that occurred around the time of death) can indicate blunt force trauma, sharp force trauma, or gunshot wounds. The presence of healing or healed fractures may provide evidence of long-term abuse or previous injuries.

Forensic anthropologists also examine skeletal remains for signs of pathological conditions, such as osteoarthritis, tuberculosis, or malnutrition, which can inform investigators about the decedent's health and lifestyle. In some cases, skeletal pathology may be directly related to the cause of death, such as in cases of fatal infection or severe bone fractures.

Trace Evidence: Unseen Clues in Death Investigations

Trace evidence encompasses a broad range of materials—fibres, hair, glass, soil, and gunshot residue—that may be transferred between individuals, objects, or locations during a crime. Although often microscopic in size, trace evidence can provide crucial information linking a suspect to a crime scene or victim.

Hair and Fibre Analysis

Hair and fibre analysis involves the microscopic examination of hairs and fibres recovered from the crime scene or the deceased. Forensic scientists can compare hair samples from the deceased with those from suspects to determine whether a transfer occurred. Fibre analysis, particularly in cases involving violent crime, can establish whether the victim came into contact with certain fabrics or materials associated with a suspect or crime scene.

Gunshot Residue (GSR)

In cases of gunshot-related deaths, forensic scientists may test for gunshot residue (GSR) on the hands or clothing of the deceased. GSR consists of microscopic particles produced when a firearm is discharged. The detection of GSR can confirm that the individual was near the firearm at the time of discharge and may provide evidence in cases of suspected suicide or homicide.

Forensic science plays a pivotal role in death investigations, providing investigators and pathologists with the tools necessary to unravel complex medical and criminal mysteries. From the careful dissection of a body during an autopsy to the microscopic analysis of DNA, toxins, and trace evidence, each forensic technique contributes to the larger goal of establishing truth in the face of death. These scientific methods not only aid in determining the cause and manner of death but also serve to identify individuals, link suspects to crimes, and provide objective, legally admissible evidence in court. As forensic technology and methodologies continue to advance, they hold the promise of further improving the accuracy and efficiency of death investigations, ensuring that justice is both served and scientifically sound.

CHAPTER 5: THE ROLE OF FORENSIC SCIENCE IN DEATH INVESTIGATIONS

Forensic science plays a pivotal role in unravelling the complexities surrounding unexplained or suspicious deaths, bridging the gap between biological science and the legal process. Death investigations rely heavily on the meticulous application of various forensic techniques, which allow investigators to reconstruct the events leading to a person's demise, determine the cause and manner of death, and identify the individual involved. This chapter will explore the fundamental pillars of forensic science—autopsies, toxicology, DNA analysis, trace evidence examination, and other specialized methods—while illustrating their significance in the investigation of deaths, particularly in cases where foul play is suspected.

The Significance of Autopsies in Forensic Investigations

At the core of any forensic death investigation is the autopsy, a post-mortem examination that provides essential insights into the cause and manner of death. Autopsies are conducted by forensic pathologists, who are trained to recognize both the obvious and subtle signs of trauma, disease, or other underlying factors that contributed to the individual's death. This procedure is often indispensable, particularly in criminal cases where the circumstances of death are unclear.

Types of Autopsies

Autopsies fall into two primary categories: forensic autopsies and clinical autopsies. The former is conducted in cases of sudden, violent, suspicious, or unexplained deaths, often at the request of legal authorities. A forensic autopsy aims not only to determine the cause of death but also to document and collect evidence for criminal proceedings. Clinical autopsies, by contrast, are usually performed in hospital settings to understand disease processes or medical conditions, especially when a diagnosis is uncertain. In a forensic context, the autopsy serves as a crucial investigative tool, yielding information about the decedent's health, any external or internal injuries, and whether substances or toxins contributed to the fatality.

Steps in the Autopsy Procedure

A comprehensive autopsy consists of two phases: external examination and internal examination. Each stage is critical for constructing a complete forensic picture.

1. External Examination: This phase involves the visual and tactile inspection of the body's surface for injuries, abnormalities, or signs of disease. Pathologists meticulously document physical characteristics such as the presence of scars, tattoos, bruises, or lacerations. They also examine the body for external trauma, including gunshot wounds, stab marks, or signs of strangulation, all of which may indicate foul play. Special attention is given to the distribution of rigour mortis, livor mortis, and algor mortis, as these post-mortem changes provide essential clues regarding the time of death and whether

the body has been moved since the moment of death.

2. Internal Examination: After completing the external assessment, the pathologist proceeds with dissection, systematically opening the body's cavities to inspect the internal organs. Each organ is examined for evidence of trauma, disease, or other pathological conditions that may have caused or contributed to death. For instance, a detailed examination of the heart could reveal myocardial infarction as the cause of death, or an examination of the lungs might reveal pulmonary embolism. Additionally, injuries such as internal haemorrhages, fractured bones, or damage to vital organs are documented to determine if death resulted from violent trauma or natural causes.

3. Sample Collection: Biological samples, including blood, urine, and tissue specimens, are collected during the autopsy for further analysis. These samples are essential for subsequent toxicological and histological testing, which can detect the presence of drugs, toxins, or underlying diseases.

4. Forensic Documentation: Throughout the autopsy, detailed notes, photographs, and diagrams are generated to document findings. This information serves as the foundation of the autopsy report, which is a crucial piece of evidence in legal investigations, particularly in determining whether death was the result of homicide, suicide, accident, or natural causes.

Autopsy Outcomes and Legal Implications

Autopsies serve to clarify cause of death—the specific injury or disease that led to the individual's demise—and manner of death, which categorizes the death as natural, accidental, homicidal, or suicidal. The forensic pathologist's findings can significantly influence legal proceedings, especially in homicide cases, by providing objective evidence regarding the nature and mechanism of the fatal event.

Toxicology in Death Investigations

In many cases, determining the role of chemicals, drugs, or toxins is essential to understanding the circumstances surrounding death. Forensic toxicology is the scientific discipline that investigates the presence and concentration of foreign substances in the body, ranging from therapeutic drugs and alcohol to poisons and illicit drugs. Toxicologists work closely with forensic pathologists to ascertain whether these substances contributed to or directly caused death.

Key Substances Analysed in Toxicology

1. Alcohol: A leading contributor to accidental deaths, including those resulting from traffic accidents, drowning, and falls, alcohol's effects on the central nervous system can impair judgment and motor function. The measurement of blood alcohol concentration (BAC) is critical in understanding the extent of alcohol's influence at the time of death. Post-mortem ethanol production from microbial activity can also complicate analysis, necessitating careful interpretation by toxicologists.

2. Illicit Drugs: Substances such as cocaine, heroin, methamphetamine, and fentanyl are common contributors to overdose deaths. Toxicological analysis of blood, urine, and tissue samples can detect the presence and concentration of these drugs, helping to establish whether an overdose occurred. Opioids, for instance, act on the brain's respiratory centres, leading to respiratory depression and death at high concentrations.

3. Prescription Drugs: Overdose or improper use of prescription medications, including benzodiazepines, barbiturates, and antidepressants, can lead to fatal outcomes. Toxicologists assess therapeutic, toxic, and lethal levels of these drugs to determine whether they played a role in death. In cases where medications are prescribed, toxicology can help assess whether the patient adhered to the prescribed dosage or ingested lethal quantities.

4. Poisons: Intentional or accidental poisoning is rare but still relevant in forensic toxicology. Common poisons include cyanide, carbon monoxide, and arsenic. Toxicologists use advanced techniques such as mass spectrometry and chromatography to detect these poisons at trace levels, even long after death.

5. Toxins and Metabolites: The body metabolizes many substances, and toxicologists often look for the metabolic byproducts of drugs or poisons. For example, heroin rapidly breaks down into 6-monoacetylmorphine (6-MAM) and morphine, so identifying these metabolites can confirm heroin use.

Post-Mortem Toxicology Process

1. Sample Collection: During the autopsy, biological samples—including blood, urine, vitreous humour, and tissues from organs like the liver—are collected for toxicological analysis. Blood is typically the most useful matrix, as it reflects the concentration of substances circulating in the body at the time of death. Vitreous humour, the fluid from the eye, is less affected by post-mortem changes and is often analysed to confirm findings from blood samples.

2. Analytical Techniques: Forensic toxicologists utilize sophisticated instruments such as gas chromatography-mass spectrometry (GC-MS), high-performance liquid chromatography (HPLC), and immunoassays to identify and quantify substances. These techniques allow for the precise detection of both common drugs and rare toxic substances.

3. Interpreting Results: Detecting a substance in the body is only the first step; understanding its role in death requires careful interpretation. Toxicologists must consider pharmacokinetics (how the body processes the substance) and pharmacodynamics (how the substance affects the body) when determining

whether a drug or toxin contributed to death. For example, finding therapeutic levels of prescription medication may suggest that it did not play a direct role in the death, whereas finding high or lethal concentrations points to overdose.

DNA Analysis: Identifying Victims and Suspects

Since its first use in criminal cases in the 1980s, DNA analysis has become one of the most powerful tools in forensic investigations. The unique nature of each individual's DNA, aside from identical twins, allows forensic scientists to link biological material found at a crime scene with specific individuals, whether they be victims or suspects. In death investigations, DNA analysis is critical for both identification of the deceased and linking suspects to the crime scene.

Sources of DNA in Death Investigations

1. Blood, Semen, and Saliva: These bodily fluids are the most common sources of DNA in forensic cases. Blood found at a crime scene can link a suspect to an assault, while semen is critical in sexual assault cases. Saliva left on objects, such as cigarette butts or drinking glasses, is also a valuable source of DNA.

2. Tissue and Bone: In cases involving decomposition or severe trauma, soft tissues may be unsuitable for DNA analysis, but bone, especially from the teeth, can provide stable sources of genetic material. Bone marrow and dental pulp are commonly analysed in these situations.

3. Touch DNA: Advances in forensic science have made it possible to recover touch DNA, or DNA left behind on surfaces through skin contact. Although less abundant than DNA from bodily fluids, touch DNA can link suspects to weapons, clothing, or other objects involved in a crime.

DNA Profiling and Interpretation

DNA profiling involves analysing specific regions of the genome known as short tandem repeats (STRs). STRs are highly variable between individuals, making them ideal for distinguishing between different people. DNA samples are amplified using polymerase chain reaction (PCR), enabling even

trace amounts of DNA to be analysed. Once a DNA profile is generated, it is compared to known profiles, either from suspects, victims, or databases such as the Combined DNA Index System (CODIS), a national repository of DNA profiles used by law enforcement agencies.

In death investigations, DNA analysis can:

- Identify Victims: In cases of severe trauma, decomposition, or mass disasters, DNA analysis is critical in identifying human remains. Even when visual identification is impossible, DNA can link remains to family members by comparing their genetic profiles.

- Link Suspects to Crime Scenes: DNA recovered from crime scenes, such as from bloodstains or other biological materials, can directly link suspects to the scene. This evidence is often the strongest form of physical evidence in criminal trials, providing a near-certain connection between the suspect and the criminal act.

- Establish Familial Relationships: In cases where direct identification of remains is not possible, DNA testing can be used to establish familial relationships, linking unknown remains to close relatives for identification purposes.

Forensic Entomology: Estimating the Post-Mortem Interval

In cases where a body has been decomposing for an extended period, forensic entomology becomes an indispensable tool. Forensic entomologists study the insects that colonize a body after death, using their life cycles and species-specific behaviour to estimate the post-mortem interval (PMI), or time since death. This approach is particularly useful when traditional methods of determining the time of death, such as rigor mortis or livor mortis, are no longer applicable due to advanced decomposition.

Insect Succession in Decomposition

The process of decomposition attracts a predictable succession of insect species, beginning shortly after death. The most common insects found on decomposing bodies are blowflies and flesh flies, which lay eggs in natural orifices and open wounds. These eggs hatch into larvae, or maggots, that feed on the soft tissues of the body. Forensic entomologists can determine the PMI by examining the species present and the developmental stage of the insects.

1. Blowflies (Calliphoridae): Blowflies are typically the first insects to colonize a body, often arriving within hours of death. Their larvae undergo several moults before pupating, and forensic entomologists can estimate the time of death by examining the size and developmental stage of the maggots.

2. Flesh Flies (Sarcophagidae): These flies are also early colonizers of decomposing bodies, laying live larvae instead of eggs. The presence of flesh fly larvae, in conjunction with blowfly larvae, provides additional information about the timeline of decomposition.

3. Beetles (Coleoptera): As decomposition progresses, beetles, including Dermestid beetles, become more prominent. These insects feed on the drier remains and indicate a later stage of decomposition. The species of beetles present and their developmental stages can offer further insights into the PMI.

Forensic Applications of Entomology

Forensic entomologists collect and preserve insect samples from the body and surrounding environment during the investigation. By analysing the species present and their developmental stages, they can provide an estimate of the time since death, which is especially critical when other methods of determining PMI are no longer reliable.

Trace Evidence and its Role in Death Investigations

Trace evidence, which includes microscopic materials such as hair, fibres, soil, glass, and paint, plays a crucial role in linking individuals, objects, and crime scenes in death investigations. Although small and often invisible to the naked eye, trace evidence can provide powerful clues about the circumstances of death and the interaction between the victim and the perpetrator.

Hair and Fibre Analysis

Hair and fibre analysis is a staple of forensic trace evidence examination. Forensic scientists use microscopy to compare the physical and chemical properties of hair and fibres recovered from the scene or body with known samples. In death investigations, this evidence can establish contact between the victim and the suspect or place the suspect at the crime scene.

- Hair Analysis: Human hair can be identified by its characteristic structure, including the cuticle, cortex, and medulla. Forensic scientists can determine whether a hair sample originated from a specific individual by comparing it with a reference sample. Hair also contains DNA, which can be analysed for more conclusive identification.

- Fiber Analysis: Fibers from clothing, carpets, or other materials can transfer between individuals during a violent encounter. Fibres are examined under a microscope to identify their source, such as synthetic or natural fibres, and matched to items found at the crime scene or on suspects.

Soil and Glass Analysis

Soil and glass fragments are common types of trace evidence

in death investigations, particularly in vehicular homicides or crime scenes involving broken windows. Forensic scientists analyse the composition of these materials using techniques such as X-ray diffraction (XRD) or energy-dispersive X-ray spectroscopy (EDS) to match samples from the crime scene with those found on suspects or victims.

Forensic science forms the backbone of modern death investigations, providing investigators and legal professionals with the tools necessary to uncover the truth behind mysterious or suspicious deaths. From the systematic examination of the body in an autopsy to the detailed analysis of toxic substances, DNA, insects, and trace evidence, forensic techniques offer objective, scientifically validated insights that are critical for establishing the cause and manner of death. The precision and reliability of forensic science not only assist in solving criminal cases but also ensure that justice is administered based on robust, empirical evidence. As forensic technologies continue to evolve, their role in death investigations will only grow, offering deeper understanding and enhanced accuracy in the pursuit of truth.

CHAPTER 7: THE BODY FARM: WHERE SCIENCE MEETS DECAY

Forensic science depends heavily on empirical data to understand the processes of human decomposition, particularly in contexts relevant to crime scene investigations and death analysis. One of the most groundbreaking innovations in this field is the development of forensic body farms, research facilities designed to study human decomposition in a controlled environment. These facilities, scattered across various locations in the United States and elsewhere, provide essential data that helps forensic scientists and law enforcement agencies understand the temporal and environmental factors influencing decomposition.

The concept of the body farm—where donated human remains are exposed to different environmental conditions and studied over time—has revolutionized our understanding of death and decay. This chapter will explore the scientific methodologies employed at these research centres, the critical role body farms play in forensic research, and how the knowledge gained from these studies has contributed to advancements in crime scene investigations and the accurate estimation of the post-mortem interval (PMI).

The Origins of the Body Farm Concept

The first body farm was established in 1981 by Dr. William Bass at the University of Tennessee Anthropological Research Facility, in Knoxville. Dr Bass, a forensic anthropologist, recognized a significant gap in forensic science—there was little understanding of how human bodies decomposed under different conditions, and consequently, it was challenging to estimate the time of death with any degree of precision. The data available at the time were largely anecdotal or derived from animal studies, which did not accurately reflect the nuances of human decay.

Dr Bass founded the first body farm to systematically study human decomposition in real-time and under natural conditions. Since its inception, the facility has grown into an expansive outdoor research centre where forensic scientists, anthropologists, and law enforcement personnel work together to study the intricate processes of human decomposition. The success of this initial body farm led to the establishment of similar facilities at several other institutions in the United States, each contributing unique data sets based on their respective geographic and environmental conditions.

Scientific Objectives of Body Farms

The primary goal of body farms is to provide controlled, scientifically valid data on human decomposition, which can then be applied to forensic investigations. Several key research objectives underpin the work carried out at these facilities:

1. Understanding the Stages of Decomposition: Body farms enable researchers to observe and document the distinct stages of human decomposition—from fresh to skeletal remains—

in a variety of environmental settings. These observations are critical for developing timelines that assist forensic pathologists and investigators in estimating the PMI.

2. Studying Environmental Influences: Decomposition is highly dependent on environmental factors such as temperature, humidity, insect activity, and exposure to the elements. Body farms allow scientists to study the impact of these variables in controlled experiments, offering insight into how different climates and conditions accelerate or slow the decomposition process.

3. Developing Forensic Tools and Techniques: Data from body farms are used to develop new forensic tools and methodologies, including techniques for determining PMI, identifying the effects of scavenger activity, and understanding how factors like clothing, burial depth, and body positioning affect decay.

4. Training Law Enforcement and Forensic Professionals: Body farms serve as training grounds for law enforcement officers, forensic scientists, and medical examiners, offering hands-on experience in identifying human remains, estimating PMI, and collecting evidence from decomposing bodies.

Stages of Human Decomposition: Insights from the Body Farm

One of the fundamental contributions of body farms is the comprehensive understanding of the stages of human decomposition. The decomposition process can be divided into several well-defined stages, each characterized by specific physical, chemical, and biological changes. These stages provide a framework for analysing bodies found in various states of decay at crime scenes and serve as benchmarks for estimating the time of death.

1. Fresh Stage (0-3 Days)

In the first stage of decomposition, which begins immediately after death, visible changes to the body are minimal. However, internal processes are already underway. Autolysis is initiated as cells begin to break down due to a lack of oxygen. Digestive enzymes within the body's cells begin to degrade internal tissues, particularly in the liver and pancreas, which are rich in enzymatic activity. Externally, the body may begin to show signs of livor mortis (blood pooling) and rigour mortis (stiffening of muscles).

While the fresh stage exhibits little outward change, the groundwork is laid for the next stages of decomposition. Body farm researchers monitor factors such as temperature, humidity, and body mass to quantify the rate of internal tissue breakdown and how these factors influence the transition to the next stage.

2. Bloat Stage (3-7 Days)

During the bloat stage, the body undergoes a significant and visible transformation. This stage is primarily driven by the activity of anaerobic bacteria that proliferate in the gastrointestinal tract and tissues. These bacteria generate gases such as hydrogen sulphide, methane, and ammonia as they metabolize the body's tissues, causing the body to swell and become distended. The accumulation of gas leads to a pronounced bloat, especially in the abdomen, which is one of the first areas to show this effect due to bacterial activity.

Insect colonization begins during this stage, with flies laying eggs in the body's orifices and open wounds. Maggots (fly larvae) begin to consume soft tissues, accelerating decomposition. Body farm researchers meticulously document insect activity, as understanding the timing and behaviour of insect colonization is critical for estimating PMI.

At body farms, researchers study gas production and insect activity in controlled experiments, determining how variables such as body mass, exposure to sunlight, and burial depth influence the rate of decomposition. These findings contribute

THE SCIENCE OF DEATH

to forensic entomology, a field that uses insect life cycles to estimate the time of death in real-world investigations.

3. Active Decay Stage (7-21 Days)

The active decay stage marks a period of rapid tissue breakdown and mass loss. During this phase, maggots and other decomposers are highly active, consuming the body's soft tissues at an accelerated rate. As tissues liquefy, bodily fluids may seep from orifices or accumulate beneath the body, creating what is often referred to as a cadaver decomposition island (CDI), where fluids pool and affect the surrounding environment.

The distinctive odour of decay, caused by the release of volatile organic compounds such as putrescine and cadaverine, becomes strongest during active decay. Researchers at body farms collect and analyse these gases, which not only provide forensic scientists with clues about the stage of decomposition but have also led to the development of specialized detection tools, including cadaver-sniffing dogs and sensor technologies that can detect human remains in disaster or crime scenes.

The impact of environmental factors becomes particularly evident during active decay, as bodies exposed to different climatic conditions decompose at varying rates. Studies at body farms have shown that bodies in warm, humid climates undergo active decay much faster than those in cooler or arid environments. These findings are crucial for forensic pathologists working in diverse geographic regions, enabling them to adjust PMI estimates based on local conditions.

4. Advanced Decay Stage (3 Weeks to 2 Months)

By the advanced decay stage, most of the soft tissues have been consumed by insects, bacteria, and scavengers, leaving behind bones, cartilage, and other more resilient structures. The mass of the body is significantly reduced, and the decomposition process slows as fewer organic materials remain for decomposers to break down.

At this stage, researchers at body farms often study the effects of scavenger activity, such as predation by vultures, rodents, or other animals, on the decomposition process. Scavengers can significantly alter the decomposition timeline, and understanding their behaviour provides valuable forensic information. For instance, in some cases, scavengers may relocate body parts, which can complicate crime scene investigations.

Body farms also contribute to knowledge about soil interactions with decomposing remains. As fluids leach into the soil during advanced decay, the chemical composition of the soil changes. Researchers study these changes to better understand how long bodies have been decomposing and how cadaver decomposition impacts the surrounding environment.

5. Skeletal Stage (2 Months and Beyond)

The final stage of decomposition is characterized by the absence of soft tissues and the presence of bones, hair, and teeth. The skeletal remains are highly resistant to further decomposition, although they are still subject to weathering and environmental factors such as soil acidity, exposure to moisture, and ultraviolet light.

Research conducted at body farms has shown that skeletal remains can persist for years, although the bones undergo gradual degradation over time. The rate at which bones break down is influenced by factors such as soil composition, temperature fluctuations, and scavenger activity. Studies on bone degradation provide critical insight for forensic anthropologists tasked with determining the time since death in cases where only skeletal remains are recovered.

Environmental Variables Affecting Decomposition

One of the key contributions of body farm research is the understanding of how different environmental factors influence decomposition rates. Controlled experiments at these facilities allow researchers to isolate and manipulate variables such as temperature, humidity, and burial conditions to observe their impact on the decay process.

Temperature and Climate

Temperature is the most significant environmental factor affecting the rate of decomposition. Bodies decompose faster in warmer environments due to the accelerated metabolic activity of bacteria and insects. Conversely, cold temperatures can slow or even halt decomposition. Body farm researchers have established temperature-based models, known as accumulated degree-days (ADD), which allow forensic scientists to estimate PMI based on the temperature history of the crime scene.

In colder climates, bodies may remain in the fresh stage for extended periods before decomposition begins in earnest. Conversely, in tropical environments, bodies can progress through the early stages of decomposition in a matter of days. Body farm experiments have quantified these differences, providing forensic experts with data that help them make accurate PMI determinations across a range of environmental conditions.

Humidity and Moisture

Humidity also plays a critical role in decomposition. High humidity levels promote bacterial growth and insect activity, accelerating decay. In dry environments, the body may undergo mummification, where tissues desiccate and become leathery, slowing decomposition significantly. By controlling for moisture levels in body farm studies, researchers have developed predictive models that account for the effects of both high and low humidity on the decomposition process.

Burial Depth and Covering

Bodies buried underground or concealed in structures decompose at a slower rate than those exposed to open air. The lack of oxygen, lower temperatures, and reduced insect access in buried environments contribute to this deceleration. Body farms often include experimental burial plots, where researchers study how variables such as soil composition, burial depth, and coffin materials influence decomposition.

The presence of clothing or other coverings can also affect the rate of decay. Clothing slows insect access to the body and can trap moisture, altering the decomposition timeline. Body farm studies have demonstrated that bodies clothed in synthetic materials, such as polyester, decompose differently than those clothed in natural fibres like cotton.

The Impact of Body Farms on Forensic Investigations

The research conducted at body farms has profoundly impacted forensic science, particularly in the realm of death investigations. By providing empirical data on how human bodies decompose under various conditions, body farms have given forensic experts a powerful tool for estimating PMI, identifying post-mortem changes, and reconstructing the events surrounding death.

Post-Mortem Interval (PMI) Estimation

One of the most critical applications of body farm research is the development of accurate models for estimating the PMI. By documenting the rate of decomposition under different environmental conditions, researchers have created algorithms that forensic pathologists can use to estimate how long a body has been dead. These models consider factors such as temperature, humidity, insect activity, and body position, allowing investigators to make more precise PMI determinations.

In addition to temperature-based models like ADD, body farm researchers have developed tools for estimating PMI based on the succession of insect species colonizing a body. Forensic entomologists use data from body farms to determine which species of flies and beetles are present at various stages of decomposition, providing another layer of evidence for estimating PMI.

Forensic Training and Education

Body farms also serve as essential training grounds for forensic professionals, including medical examiners, law enforcement officers, and forensic anthropologists. These facilities offer hands-on experience in handling human remains, documenting decomposition, and collecting forensic evidence. By studying decomposition in real-time, trainees develop a deeper understanding of the complexities involved in death investigations.

Forensic anthropology students, in particular, benefit from body farm research, as they learn to identify skeletal remains and estimate time since death based on bone degradation and taphonomic changes. The knowledge gained from these training programs directly enhances the skills of forensic professionals tasked with solving complex death investigations.

Forensic body farms represent one of the most significant advancements in the study of human decomposition. By providing a controlled environment for the systematic study of decay, these facilities have transformed our understanding of the processes that occur after death. The data generated from body farm research have far-reaching applications in forensic science, particularly in estimating PMI, identifying post-mortem changes, and solving crime scene mysteries. As research continues, body farms will remain at the forefront of forensic science, offering new insights into the factors that influence decomposition and ensuring that investigators are better equipped to uncover the truth in death investigations.

CHAPTER 8: EMBALMING AND MODERN FUNERAL PRACTICES

Embalming, an age-old practice rooted in the preservation of the human body after death, has evolved into a sophisticated scientific process. It serves both aesthetic and practical purposes, preserving the deceased long enough for funeral rites to take place, while also delaying decomposition. Modern funeral practices, shaped by cultural, religious, and technological influences, have transformed how society handles death. The advent of embalming, chemical preservation, and cosmetic techniques has altered the traditional processes of decomposition, fundamentally changing our relationship with death. This chapter provides a comprehensive examination of embalming, from its historical origins to its contemporary application in the funeral industry, exploring the science behind the chemicals and techniques used, as well as the broader implications of these practices on the natural processes of decay.

The Historical Origins of Embalming

The practice of embalming can be traced back thousands of years, with its most famous origins in ancient Egypt. The Egyptians believed in an afterlife in which the soul required the preservation of the physical body to ensure eternal existence. The mummification process, which they perfected over centuries, was essentially an early form of embalming that sought to protect the body from decomposition. This technique involved the removal of internal organs, desiccation using natron (a naturally occurring salt), and the wrapping of the body in linen.

While Egyptian mummification is perhaps the most iconic, other ancient civilizations, including the Incas, the Chinese, and certain tribes in Papua New Guinea, practised their forms of body preservation. In these cases, the methods varied widely but often involved the removal of moisture from the body through drying, the application of natural preservatives, or submersion in specific substances like tar or honey.

In Europe during the Middle Ages, embalming was less common due to religious views on the integrity of the body. However, the Renaissance saw a revival of embalming, primarily for scientific and anatomical purposes. The development of chemical preservatives in the 18th and 19th centuries marked the shift from natural methods of preservation to modern embalming techniques, which were first widely adopted during the American Civil War for transporting soldiers' bodies long distances.

Modern Embalming: Purpose and Process

Modern embalming practices differ significantly from ancient methods, emphasizing the temporary preservation of the body to allow for public viewing and funeral ceremonies. The goal is not to indefinitely halt decomposition but to slow it significantly enough to ensure that the body remains presentable and intact for a set period. This process is typically conducted by licensed embalmers or morticians, professionals trained in the science and art of body preservation.

The Purpose of Modern Embalming

The primary purposes of embalming are:

1. Sanitation: Embalming helps prevent the spread of pathogens from the body to the environment or funeral attendees. While the risk of disease transmission from a deceased body is often minimal, particularly after the body's internal functions cease, embalming ensures that any lingering microorganisms are neutralized.

2. Preservation: Embalming slows the natural process of decomposition, which begins immediately after death due to autolysis (self-digestion) and bacterial activity. By treating the body with chemicals that retard this process, embalmers ensure the deceased remains in a suitable condition for viewing.

3. Restoration: In cases of traumatic death or illness, embalming is often necessary to restore the body to a lifelike appearance. The process can include the reconstruction of damaged tissue, cosmetic applications to improve skin tone, and the use of wax or prosthetics to replace missing or damaged features.

4. Presentation: Embalming provides the deceased with a dignified and presentable appearance for open-casket viewings or public funerals, which are common in many cultures. By maintaining the deceased's appearance, embalming allows mourners to say their final goodbyes in a manner that reflects the person's appearance during life.

The Embalming Procedure: Step by Step

The embalming process is both a chemical and physical intervention designed to preserve the body. It typically involves several steps, each of which is necessary to ensure effective preservation and sanitation.

1. Initial Preparation and Disinfection: The embalming process begins with the washing and disinfection of the body. The embalmer carefully cleans the skin using a disinfectant solution to remove any contaminants. During this stage, the body is positioned for presentation, usually with the arms folded or placed at the sides, and the facial features are set. The mouth is typically closed with either sutures or an adhesive, and the eyes are positioned using specialized caps or pads.

2. Arterial Embalming: Arterial embalming is the primary method of preservation. This procedure involves injecting a chemical solution into the arteries while simultaneously draining the body's blood. The embalmer typically accesses the carotid artery or femoral artery, inserting a tube through which the embalming fluid is pumped into the circulatory system. This solution replaces the blood, which is drained through a corresponding vein. The embalming fluid permeates the body's tissues, saturating cells and neutralizing enzymes and bacteria responsible for decomposition.

3. Cavity Embalming: After arterial embalming, the next step is cavity embalming, which focuses on the internal organs. Using a specialized tool called a trocar, the embalmer punctures the abdominal and thoracic cavities to remove gases and fluids from the internal organs. Once this is complete, a highly concentrated preservative solution is injected into the cavities to ensure complete preservation. This step is crucial because the internal organs are among the first to decompose due to their high moisture and enzymatic content.

4. Surface Embalming: In cases where the skin or other external areas have been damaged or decomposed, surface embalming is employed. This method involves applying preservative chemicals directly to the skin or tissues, sometimes using sprays or gels. Surface embalming is particularly useful in treating wounds, bedsores, or areas affected by trauma.

5. Cosmetic Application and Dressing: Once embalming is complete, the body is prepared for viewing. The embalmer applies cosmetics to restore a natural skin tone, correct discolouration, and enhance the overall appearance. The hair is styled, and any prosthetics or waxes needed to reconstruct damaged features are applied. The deceased is then dressed in clothes selected by the family, often reflecting the individual's personal style or cultural customs.

The Chemicals of Embalming

The success of modern embalming depends largely on the chemical solutions used in the preservation process. These solutions are composed of several key components:

1. Formaldehyde: The primary preservative in embalming fluid is formaldehyde, a powerful fixative that cross-links proteins, effectively "freezing" them in place and preventing decomposition. Formaldehyde denatures proteins by forming covalent bonds between their amino acids, thereby rendering them resistant to enzymatic breakdown. Its efficacy as a preservative is well-established, but formaldehyde is also a toxic and potentially carcinogenic compound, leading to debates about its environmental impact and health risks to embalmers.

2. Methanol: Methanol is often included in embalming fluids as a stabilizer and disinfectant. It inhibits bacterial growth and helps prevent the polymerization of formaldehyde, maintaining the fluid's stability over time.

3. Humectants and Moisturizers: These chemicals help retain moisture in the body's tissues, preventing the skin from becoming dry or shrivelled during the embalming process. Glycerine and lanolin are common humectants used in embalming solutions to ensure that the skin maintains a lifelike appearance.

4. Dyes and Colourants: To restore the natural colour of the

deceased's skin, dyes are often added to embalming fluids. These dyes, usually red or pink, mimic the flush of blood and help counteract the pallor that results from the cessation of circulation.

5. Water Conditioners and Buffers: In regions with hard water, conditioners are used to prevent the minerals in the water from reacting with the embalming chemicals. Buffers are also included to maintain the correct pH balance of the embalming fluid, which ensures optimal chemical reactions during preservation.

The Impact of Embalming on Decomposition

While embalming slows decomposition significantly, it does not halt it entirely. The preservatives used in the process create a temporary state of preservation, typically lasting from several days to weeks, depending on environmental conditions and the techniques employed. Eventually, the body will still undergo the stages of decomposition, although embalmed bodies often decompose more slowly than those not treated with preservatives.

Alteration of Natural Decomposition

In an unembalmed body, decomposition proceeds through well-documented stages: autolysis, putrefaction, active decay, and skeletonization. Embalming delays this process by neutralizing the enzymes and bacteria responsible for breaking down tissues. However, over time, even embalmed bodies will succumb to microbial activity, particularly if interred in a moist or warm environment.

The chemicals used in embalming, particularly formaldehyde, create an environment hostile to microbial life, but they are not permanent. The degree to which decomposition is slowed depends on factors such as burial conditions, temperature, and the quality of the embalming process. In cases where the body is exhumed after several years, embalmers often find that tissues have begun to degrade, particularly in areas where the embalming fluid may not have penetrated deeply.

Exhumation and Long-Term Preservation

Exhumations provide valuable insight into the effectiveness of embalming over long periods. In cases where bodies have been exhumed years or decades after burial, forensic scientists have observed varying degrees of preservation. Often, the body's soft tissues remain preserved, albeit desiccated and shrunken. However, in particularly moist environments, even embalmed bodies may decompose more quickly than expected, as water promotes bacterial activity and accelerates the breakdown of tissue.

The advent of refrigeration and cryopreservation offers alternative methods of delaying decomposition without the use of chemical preservatives. These methods are often employed in situations where embalming is not desired or where the body must be preserved for an extended period before burial or cremation. While effective in the short term, these techniques do not provide the same cosmetic or restorative benefits as embalming.

Modern Funeral Practices: Cultural and Technological Influences

Funeral practices have evolved considerably in the past century, shaped by advances in technology, changes in societal attitudes toward death, and the increasing diversity of cultural and religious customs. In many Western cultures, the embalming and presentation of the body in an open-casket funeral has become standard practice, though this is not a universal norm.

Cultural Perspectives on Embalming

In many cultures, embalming is seen as a way to honour the deceased, ensuring that the body is presentable for final goodbyes. Open-casket funerals allow mourners to view the deceased and offer a sense of closure, reinforcing the importance of physical presence in the grieving process.

However, there has also been a growing movement toward more natural, eco-friendly approaches to death care. Green burials, which eschew embalming and opt for biodegradable materials, have gained popularity among individuals concerned with the environmental impact of embalming chemicals and non-biodegradable caskets. Proponents of green burial argue that allowing the body to decompose naturally is a more sustainable and ecologically responsible choice.

Cremation and Alternatives

The rise in cremation as an alternative to traditional burial has also influenced modern funeral practices. Cremation bypasses the need for embalming and is often chosen for its convenience, cost-effectiveness, and reduced environmental footprint. The process of cremation, however, involves intense heat that reduces the body to bone fragments, which are then processed into ash. As cremation becomes more widespread, it has prompted discussions about alternative methods of body disposal, including alkaline hydrolysis (also known as water cremation) and promession (freeze-drying the body before it is broken down into organic powder).

Technological Innovations in Funeral Practices

The funeral industry has also embraced technological advancements to cater to the evolving needs of families and societies. Digital memorials, livestreamed funerals, and virtual reality tributes are becoming increasingly common, allowing distant relatives and friends to participate in funeral services without being physically present. These practices reflect the changing relationship between technology and the mourning process, offering new ways to honour the deceased while bridging geographical divides.

The Ethical and Environmental Considerations of Embalming

The widespread use of embalming has raised ethical and environmental questions, particularly regarding the use of formaldehyde and other chemicals. Formaldehyde is a known carcinogen, and repeated exposure to it poses health risks to embalmers and other funeral industry workers. Moreover, embalming chemicals can leach into the soil and groundwater when bodies are buried, raising concerns about environmental contamination.

Green Embalming and Alternative Preservation Methods

In response to these concerns, some funeral homes have begun offering green embalming alternatives that use non-toxic, biodegradable chemicals instead of formaldehyde. These alternatives, while not as long-lasting as traditional embalming fluids, provide a more environmentally friendly option for families seeking preservation without harmful chemicals.

The practice of embalming, deeply rooted in history and shaped by scientific advancement, remains a central feature of modern funeral practices. While it serves practical purposes in preservation, sanitation, and presentation, embalming also raises questions about its environmental impact and long-term effects on decomposition. Modern funeral practices continue to evolve, influenced by cultural shifts, technological advancements, and growing concerns about sustainability. As society's relationship with death changes, so too will the methods we use to care for the deceased, reflecting the diverse needs and values of the living. The exploration of embalming in this chapter illustrates both the scientific intricacies of the preservation process and the broader societal implications of how we approach death in the modern world.

CHAPTER 9: CREMATION: THE SCIENCE OF TURNING BODIES TO ASH

Cremation, a process that reduces the human body to bone fragments and ashes through the application of extreme heat, is an increasingly popular method of body disposal. Though it has been practised in various forms for thousands of years, modern cremation is a highly controlled, scientific process, utilizing advanced technologies to ensure efficient and respectful handling of the deceased. The process, often chosen for its practicality, cost-effectiveness, and environmental considerations, raises important scientific, cultural, and ethical questions about how societies manage death and the disposition of remains.

This chapter will provide a comprehensive examination of the science behind cremation, exploring the technological procedures used to transform a body into ashes, the environmental impact of the process, and the cultural contexts that have influenced the rise of cremation in the modern world. By understanding the mechanics and significance of cremation, we can gain insight into the choices made at the end of life and how they reflect evolving societal values and environmental concerns.

The History of Cremation

Cremation has a long and varied history, with evidence of its practice dating back to ancient times. Archaeological findings suggest that cremation was used in Europe as early as 3000 BCE. The method gained prominence in ancient Greece and Rome, where it was viewed as a noble way to honour the dead. In these societies, cremation was often reserved for military leaders, dignitaries, and those of high social standing, and the ashes were typically stored in urns and placed in elaborate tombs.

In contrast, other ancient cultures, such as those in Egypt and Mesopotamia, favoured burial, associating cremation with the destruction of the body and the disruption of the soul's journey to the afterlife. This divergence in practices reflects the profound influence of cultural and religious beliefs on how societies handle the dead. For example, in Hinduism, cremation is seen as an essential part of the soul's liberation, or moksha, from the physical body, a belief that continues to shape contemporary cremation practices in India.

The modern resurgence of cremation began in the late 19th century, fuelled by public health concerns during urbanization and the rise of infectious diseases. Advocates of cremation argued that it was a more sanitary alternative to burial, particularly in overcrowded cities where graveyards were often prone to contamination and poor conditions. Technological advancements, including the development of the crematorium —a facility specifically designed for the cremation process— enabled the method to become a widespread and accepted practice in many parts of the world.

The Cremation Process: From Body to Ash

Modern cremation is a meticulously regulated procedure, designed to ensure that the body is reduced to bone fragments and ashes in a safe, efficient, and respectful manner. The process typically takes place in a specialized facility known as a crematorium, where human remains are subjected to high temperatures within a cremation chamber. The steps involved in cremation are carefully controlled to meet both legal and environmental standards.

Preparation for Cremation

Before the cremation process can begin, certain preparations are made. The body is placed in a cremation container, which is often a simple coffin made of wood, cardboard, or another combustible material. This container serves two purposes: it protects the body during transport and handling, and it facilitates the burning process by providing additional fuel for combustion. In some cases, the container may be a more traditional coffin, depending on the preferences of the family or cultural practices.

Any materials that could interfere with the cremation process or pose safety risks are removed prior to cremation. This includes medical devices, such as pacemakers, which contain batteries that can explode at high temperatures, and metallic implants, which do not combust and can cause damage to the cremation equipment. Jewellery, prosthetics, and personal items are also typically removed to ensure a smooth cremation process.

The Cremation Chamber

The cremation chamber, also known as a retort, is the heart of the cremation process. It is a specially designed furnace lined with refractory bricks capable of withstanding extremely high temperatures. Once the body and cremation container are placed inside the chamber, the door is sealed, and the process begins.

The temperatures inside the cremation chamber typically range between 760°C and 980°C (1400°F to 1800°F), which is sufficient to vaporize the body's soft tissues and reduce the body to bone fragments. Modern cremation chambers use a combination of heat, air, and fuel (usually natural gas or propane) to maintain these temperatures, ensuring that the body is completely incinerated over the course of approximately two to three hours.

Stages of Combustion

Cremation is a process of controlled combustion that occurs in three distinct phases: primary combustion, secondary combustion, and cooling. Each phase plays a critical role in reducing the body to ash and ensuring that the process is environmentally safe.

1. Primary Combustion: In the initial stage, the body and cremation container are exposed to the intense heat of the retort. The organic components of the body—comprising mostly water, fat, muscle, and connective tissue—are vaporized and converted into gases. The high temperatures cause the soft tissues to combust rapidly, leaving behind only the denser, inorganic components, primarily the bones.

During this phase, water vapor, carbon dioxide, and other gases are released into the cremation chamber. To prevent these gases from escaping into the atmosphere, modern cremation chambers are equipped with secondary burners and filtration systems that reduce emissions and ensure compliance with environmental regulations.

2. Secondary Combustion: In the secondary combustion phase, the gases and particles produced during the primary combustion process are subjected to additional heat and air, which oxidizes them further. This phase ensures that any remaining organic material is fully incinerated and

that emissions are minimized. The secondary burners in the cremation chamber help achieve complete combustion, reducing smoke, soot, and other pollutants.

The gases are typically passed through filters before being vented from the crematorium. This step is critical for adhering to environmental standards, as it helps reduce the release of harmful substances such as mercury from dental fillings or particulate matter into the atmosphere.

3. Cooling: After the combustion process is complete, the retort is allowed to cool before the next stage of cremation can proceed. This cooling period is essential to ensure the safe handling of the remaining bone fragments, which are still at high temperatures immediately following combustion. Once the temperature has dropped to a manageable level, typically after several hours, the cremated remains are collected.

Collection and Processing of Ashes

After the cremation process, the remaining materials consist primarily of bone fragments, which are too dense to be completely incinerated by the heat of the retort. These fragments are carefully collected from the cremation chamber using specialized tools. Metal implants or other non-combustible materials, such as surgical pins or dental prosthetics, are separated and discarded or recycled.

The bone fragments are then placed into a cremulator, a machine designed to pulverize the bones into a fine, uniform powder, commonly referred to as "ashes." This process takes only a few minutes and results in the smooth, sand-like texture that is familiar to families receiving cremated remains. The ashes are then transferred into an urn or container chosen by the family.

The amount of ashes produced by cremation typically ranges between 1.8 to 2.7 kilograms (4 to 6 pounds) for an adult, depending on the individual's body size and bone density. These ashes are composed primarily of calcium phosphate and trace elements that remain after the combustion of organic material.

Environmental Impact of Cremation

Although cremation has long been promoted as an environmentally friendly alternative to traditional burial, it still carries environmental costs, particularly in terms of energy consumption and emissions. As cremation becomes more popular, understanding its environmental footprint has become increasingly important for both the funeral industry and those seeking more sustainable options for body disposal.

Energy Consumption

The cremation process requires significant amounts of energy to maintain the high temperatures necessary for complete combustion. Most crematoriums rely on natural gas or propane to fuel their retorts, and the energy consumption per cremation can vary depending on the efficiency of the equipment and the duration of the process. On average, a single cremation consumes approximately 200 to 400 kilowatt-hours of energy, equivalent to the amount of electricity used by a household in one month.

Efforts to improve the energy efficiency of crematoriums have led to advancements in retort design and the development of more efficient burners. For example, some modern crematoriums are equipped with heat recovery systems that capture excess heat generated during the cremation process and use it to preheat the next cycle, thereby reducing overall fuel consumption.

Emissions and Pollutants

Cremation generates a variety of emissions, including carbon dioxide (CO_2), nitrogen oxides (NO_x), particulate matter, and trace amounts of other pollutants such as mercury from dental amalgam fillings. Of particular concern are the emissions of CO_2, a greenhouse gas that contributes to climate change. It is estimated that a single cremation releases between 150 to 200 kilograms of CO_2, which adds to the global carbon footprint.

To mitigate the environmental impact of cremation, crematoriums are increasingly adopting filtration systems and scrubbers that capture harmful pollutants before they are released into the atmosphere. These systems use activated carbon and other materials to trap particles and gases, reducing the emission of mercury and other toxic substances. In some regions, regulatory bodies have implemented strict limits on crematorium emissions, requiring facilities to install advanced filtration technologies to comply with environmental standards.

Mercury Emissions

One of the most significant environmental concerns associated with cremation is the release of mercury from dental fillings. When a body is cremated, the high temperatures vaporize the mercury, allowing it to enter the atmosphere as a gas. Mercury is a neurotoxin that can accumulate in the environment, particularly in water bodies, where it converts into methylmercury—a toxic compound that poses serious risks to wildlife and human health.

Some countries and regions have introduced legislation to address mercury emissions from crematoriums. For example, in the United Kingdom, crematoriums are required to install mercury abatement systems, which can capture up to 95% of mercury emissions. Additionally, some funeral directors offer the removal of dental amalgam fillings before cremation to further reduce the environmental impact.

Cremation vs. Traditional Burial: Environmental Considerations

When comparing the environmental impact of cremation and traditional burial, both methods present certain challenges. Traditional burial often involves the use of chemically treated wood or metal coffins, non-biodegradable materials, and embalming fluids containing formaldehyde, a toxic chemical that can leach into the soil and groundwater over time. Additionally, cemeteries require large amounts of land, and the maintenance of burial plots, including mowing and irrigation, can contribute to environmental degradation.

Cremation, while eliminating the need for land use, embalming, and non-biodegradable coffins, still generates emissions and consumes significant amounts of energy. As awareness of the environmental impact of both methods grows, alternatives such as green burial, alkaline hydrolysis, and natural burial have gained popularity as more sustainable options.

Cultural and Religious Perspectives on Cremation

The practice of cremation is deeply influenced by cultural and religious beliefs, which shape how different societies view the disposition of the dead. While cremation has become more widespread in the modern era, particularly in the West, attitudes toward the practice vary significantly across regions and religious traditions.

Hinduism and Cremation

In Hinduism, cremation is considered a fundamental rite, known as antyeshti or "the last sacrifice." Hindus believe that cremation is essential for the liberation of the soul, or atman, from the physical body, allowing it to continue its journey toward reincarnation or moksha (spiritual liberation). The ritual of cremation is imbued with religious significance, and it is traditionally performed on the banks of a sacred river, such as the Ganges, which is believed to purify the soul.

The ashes of the deceased are often scattered in a body of water, following the belief that the soul will be cleansed and freed from earthly attachments. Cremation in Hindu culture is viewed not merely as a method of body disposal, but as a sacred ritual that facilitates the soul's transition to the next phase of existence.

Buddhism and Cremation

Buddhism, like Hinduism, generally supports cremation, with the practice seen as a reflection of the impermanence of the physical body and material existence. The Buddha himself was cremated after his death, and his ashes were divided among his followers and placed in stupas (sacred monuments). Many Buddhist communities continue the practice of cremation, particularly in countries like Thailand, Sri Lanka, and Japan, where it is the most common form of body disposal.

However, Buddhists may differ in their approach to cremation based on local customs and sectarian beliefs. Some Buddhists opt for burial instead, particularly in regions where burial has traditionally been more common.

Western Attitudes Toward Cremation

In Western cultures, cremation has gained acceptance as a practical and flexible alternative to burial. While burial was historically the preferred method of body disposal in Christian communities, cremation has become more common, particularly in secular contexts or among individuals concerned with the environmental impact of burial. The shift toward cremation has also been influenced by changes in family structures, the increasing cost of land for cemeteries, and a growing emphasis on personal choice in end-of-life planning.

Religious views on cremation in the West have also evolved. For example, while the Roman Catholic Church once prohibited cremation, it has since softened its stance, allowing cremation as long as it is not chosen for reasons that contradict Christian beliefs in the resurrection of the body.

Alternatives to Traditional Cremation

As concerns about the environmental impact of cremation grow, alternative methods of body disposal have emerged, offering more sustainable and eco-friendly options. These alternatives seek to reduce energy consumption, emissions, and the overall environmental footprint of the process.

Alkaline Hydrolysis (Water Cremation)

Alkaline hydrolysis, also known as water cremation or resomation, is an alternative to traditional flame-based cremation. This method uses water, heat, and an alkaline solution (usually potassium hydroxide) to break down the body's tissues into a liquid solution and bone fragments. The process takes place in a pressurized chamber, where the body is submerged in the solution and subjected to temperatures of approximately 160°C (320°F). Over several hours, the body's organic components dissolve, leaving behind a sterile liquid and the inorganic bone fragments.

Alkaline hydrolysis is considered a more environmentally friendly option than traditional cremation, as it consumes less energy and produces fewer emissions. The sterile liquid produced during the process can be safely discharged into the wastewater system, and the bone fragments are returned to the family like the ashes from traditional cremation.

Promession (Freeze-Drying)

Promession is another emerging alternative that uses freeze-drying to reduce the body to a biodegradable powder. The process involves freezing the body using liquid nitrogen, which makes the tissues brittle. Once the body is frozen, it is subjected to vibrations that cause it to break apart into small particles. The resulting powder is then dried in a vacuum chamber to remove moisture.

The advantage of promession is that it produces no harmful emissions and the remains are fully biodegradable, allowing for natural decomposition if buried. This method is still in the experimental stage and has yet to be widely adopted, but it offers an innovative approach to body disposal that aligns with growing interest in sustainable and eco-friendly practices.

Cremation is a scientifically complex process that transforms the human body into ashes through the controlled application of extreme heat. It offers a practical and increasingly popular alternative to traditional burial, reflecting societal shifts in how death and body disposal are managed. However, as awareness of the environmental impact of cremation grows, it is clear that both cremation and burial present challenges in terms of sustainability. The rise of alternative methods such as alkaline hydrolysis and promession highlights the ongoing search for more environmentally conscious approaches to the disposition of human remains. As these alternatives develop, they may provide new options that better align with both ecological concerns and personal or cultural preferences, shaping the future of death care practices.

CHAPTER 10: THE ROLE OF INSECTS: FORENSIC ENTOMOLOGY

Forensic entomology, the scientific study of insects as they relate to criminal investigations, plays a crucial role in modern forensic science, particularly in determining the post-mortem interval (PMI), or the time since death. Insects, especially flies and beetles, are among the first organisms to colonize a decomposing body, and their predictable life cycles make them invaluable in estimating PMI, reconstructing the circumstances of death, and even linking suspects to crime scenes. This chapter explores the fundamental principles of forensic entomology, the specific types of insects involved in decomposition, and the methods forensic scientists use to analyse insect evidence.

In addition to understanding the biological processes at play during insect colonization, forensic entomologists must consider various environmental and situational factors that influence insect behaviour. These include temperature, humidity, body location, and accessibility. Through meticulous analysis of insect activity, entomologists can provide insights that are often critical in solving cases involving decomposition, delayed discovery of remains, or concealed bodies.

The History and Evolution of Forensic Entomology

Although forensic entomology is a relatively modern scientific discipline, the use of insects in investigations dates back centuries. The first recorded instance of using insects in a criminal investigation occurred in 13th-century China, documented in the Chinese legal text "The Washing Away of Wrongs" by Song Ci. In this early case, the presence of flies on a sickle led to the identification of a murderer in a rural village, marking a primitive form of forensic entomology.

The formal scientific study of insects in forensic contexts began in the 19th century, when pioneering entomologists like Jean Pierre Mégnin published seminal works on the stages of insect colonization during human decomposition. Mégnin's research outlined how insects arrive at bodies in predictable waves, with each group playing a specific role in breaking down tissues. This work laid the foundation for modern forensic entomology, which today uses highly advanced techniques, including DNA analysis and computerized modelling, to estimate PMI with increasing precision.

Insect Succession and Decomposition: A Biological Overview

The process of human decomposition is a complex interplay of biological and chemical changes that begins almost immediately after death. Insects, primarily flies and beetles, are key agents in this process, colonizing the body in distinct waves, known as insect succession. Each species contributes to the breakdown of the body's tissues, and the predictable nature of their life cycles allows forensic entomologists to estimate PMI with a high degree of accuracy.

Insect Succession: Stages of Colonization

Insects are attracted to decomposing bodies by volatile organic compounds (VOCs) released during the early stages of decomposition. These compounds, produced by bacteria and the breakdown of body tissues, act as olfactory cues for insects, signalling the availability of a food source and an ideal environment for egg-laying.

1. Initial Colonizers – Blowflies (Calliphoridae): Blowflies, also known as bluebottle flies and greenbottle flies, are typically the first insects to arrive at a decomposing body. They can detect the scent of decomposition from great distances and often arrive within hours of death, particularly in outdoor settings. Blowflies lay their eggs in natural orifices (eyes, nose, mouth) or open wounds, providing a food source for their larvae (maggots) upon hatching. The development of blowfly larvae is temperature-dependent, and forensic entomologists can use the age and stage of these larvae to estimate how long a body has been decomposing.

2. Flesh Flies (Sarcophagidae): Flesh flies are another group of early colonizers, often arriving shortly after blowflies. Unlike blowflies, flesh flies deposit live larvae rather than eggs, accelerating the decomposition process. These flies are particularly attracted to bodies in advanced stages of bloat and active decay, where large amounts of exposed flesh are available.

3. Beetles (Coleoptera): Various beetle species arrive later in the decomposition process, typically during the active decay stage when the body's soft tissues have been significantly broken down by maggots and bacteria. Carrion beetles (Silphidae), rove beetles (Staphylinidae), and skin beetles (Dermestidae) feed on the remaining tissue, hair, and other organic material. Dermestid beetles, in particular, are known for feeding on dried tissues, cartilage, and bone fragments, and are often found on bodies in advanced decay or mummification stages.

4. Scavenging Insects: Insects such as ants, wasps, and mites

may also play a role in the decomposition process, though they are not primary decomposers. These insects often feed on the eggs or larvae of blowflies and beetles, potentially altering the natural progression of decomposition by removing colonizers.

Decomposition Stages and Insect Activity

Insect colonization is closely tied to the stages of decomposition, and forensic entomologists must understand how each stage influences insect behaviour. There are five primary stages of decomposition, each characterized by specific insect activity:

1. Fresh Stage (0-3 Days Post-Mortem): The fresh stage begins immediately after death and is marked by autolysis, or self-digestion, where cells break down due to internal chemical changes. Insects begin to colonize the body during this stage, with blowflies being the first to arrive. Egg-laying often begins within hours of death, and maggots hatch and start feeding on the soft tissues of the body.

2. Bloat Stage (3-7 Days Post-Mortem): During the bloat stage, anaerobic bacteria within the body produce gases that cause the body to swell, resulting in skin distension and an increase in pressure. The strong odour of decomposition attracts additional flies, particularly flesh flies and other carrion-eating species. Maggot activity accelerates, as larvae consume the tissue and fluids released from the body.

3. Active Decay Stage (7-21 Days Post-Mortem): The active decay stage is marked by the rupture of the body's cavities and the release of fluids, as the skin and tissues break down under the pressure of gas buildup. At this point, maggots have consumed much of the body's soft tissue, and beetles begin to arrive, feeding on both the decaying flesh and the maggots themselves. This stage represents the most rapid period of decomposition, with insect activity reaching its peak.

4. Advanced Decay Stage (3 Weeks to 2 Months Post-Mortem):

As the majority of soft tissue has been consumed, insect activity diminishes, and the body enters the advanced decay stage. Beetles such as dermestids continue to feed on the remaining tissue, hair, and bones, while maggots complete their development and begin to pupate.

5. Dry/Skeletal Stage (2 Months and Beyond Post-Mortem): In the final stage of decomposition, only bones, hair, and some dried skin remain. Insects such as dermestid beetles may continue to feed on any remaining organic material, but activity is minimal compared to earlier stages. The skeleton may undergo weathering and degradation over time due to environmental factors.

The Forensic Value of Insect Evidence

Forensic entomology plays a pivotal role in death investigations, particularly in estimating the post-mortem interval (PMI) and reconstructing the circumstances surrounding death. Insects provide a reliable timeline of decomposition due to their predictable life cycles, and by analysing the species present, their developmental stages, and environmental conditions, forensic entomologists can offer crucial insights into how long a body has been exposed to the elements.

Estimating the Post-Mortem Interval (PMI)

The primary application of forensic entomology is the estimation of PMI, which is often critical in criminal investigations. Determining how long a body has been deceased can help establish timelines, alibis, and the sequence of events leading to death. Insect evidence is particularly useful when other methods of estimating PMI, such as rigour mortis or body temperature, are no longer applicable due to advanced decomposition.

Forensic entomologists estimate PMI by examining the species of insects present on the body and analysing their developmental stages. The most reliable method for determining PMI involves calculating the accumulated degree days (ADD) or accumulated degree hours (ADH), which account for the time and temperature required for insect development. By comparing the life cycle stages of collected insects with temperature data from the crime scene, entomologists can estimate the time since colonization and, by extension, the time of death.

1. Life Cycle Analysis: The development of insect larvae, particularly blowfly maggots, is highly dependent on ambient temperature. Forensic entomologists use data on the average developmental time of blowfly larvae at specific temperatures to estimate PMI. For example, if blowfly maggots are found in the third instar (larval stage), and the ambient temperature has remained consistent, the entomologist can calculate how many days it has taken for the maggots to reach that stage, thus providing an estimate for how long the body has been decomposing.

2. Species Identification: Identifying the species of insects present on a body is crucial for accurate PMI estimation. Different species of blowflies and beetles have varying colonization patterns and temperature requirements, and their presence can provide additional information about the time since death. Some species, such as Lucilia sericata (the common greenbottle fly), are early colonizers, while others, such as dermestid beetles, arrive later in the decomposition process.

3. Environmental Factors: Temperature is the most critical factor affecting insect development, but other environmental conditions—such as humidity, sunlight, and access to the body—also influence colonization. Bodies left in direct sunlight decompose more quickly than those in shaded areas, and bodies covered with clothing or buried may attract different species of insects or delay colonization altogether.

Insect Evidence in Crime Scene Reconstruction

In addition to estimating PMI, insect evidence can provide valuable insights into crime scene reconstruction, including whether a body has been moved after death or whether trauma occurred before death.

1. Body Relocation: If insects associated with a particular environment are found on a body located in a different environment, it may indicate that the body was moved post-mortem. For example, the presence of aquatic insects on a body found in a forest suggests that the body was originally in or near water and was later relocated. Forensic entomologists can identify such discrepancies by analysing the species composition and the habitats typically associated with those species.

2. Wound Analysis: Insects are attracted to open wounds, and forensic entomologists can use insect colonization patterns to determine whether wounds were inflicted before or after death. For example, blowflies preferentially lay their eggs in moist areas such as wounds, natural orifices, or decomposing tissues. If maggots are found in a wound, it may suggest that the wound was present before death, as maggots tend to avoid freshly created post-mortem injuries. This information can help establish whether a victim was assaulted or injured before death.

3. Toxicology and Insect Larvae: In some cases, forensic entomologists can extract chemical residues from insect larvae to perform entomotoxicology, the study of toxins in decomposing remains. When human tissue is no longer available for toxicological testing due to decomposition, the maggots feeding on the body's tissues may retain traces of drugs, poisons, or other substances ingested by the victim before death. For example, maggots can absorb barbiturates, cocaine, or heavy metals, and analysing these substances in the

larvae can provide insight into the cause of death or whether the victim was exposed to toxic substances.

Challenges and Limitations in Forensic Entomology

While forensic entomology provides invaluable information in death investigations, the discipline is not without its challenges and limitations. The accurate application of entomological evidence requires careful consideration of environmental factors, insect species identification, and the potential for contamination or misinterpretation.

Environmental Variables

Temperature is the most significant variable influencing insect development, but other environmental factors—such as humidity, precipitation, wind, and body location—can complicate PMI estimation. For example, extreme weather conditions, such as heavy rain or freezing temperatures, can delay insect colonization or alter the rate of decomposition. Forensic entomologists must account for these factors when analysing insect evidence and adjust their PMI estimates accordingly.

Species Misidentification

Accurate species identification is critical for reliable PMI estimation, but it can be challenging in cases where insect specimens are damaged, incomplete, or in early developmental stages. Misidentification of species can lead to incorrect conclusions about the time of death or the conditions surrounding decomposition. Forensic entomologists must be highly skilled in insect taxonomy and have access to reference collections and identification keys to ensure accurate species identification.

Contamination and Forensic Integrity

Insect evidence can be subject to contamination or tampering, particularly if a body is moved or if the crime scene is disturbed. Forensic entomologists must work closely with crime scene investigators to ensure that insect evidence is collected, preserved, and analysed properly. Failure to maintain the integrity of insect evidence can result in unreliable conclusions or the exclusion of entomological evidence in court.

Forensic entomology is a critical component of death investigations, offering insights that are often unobtainable through other forensic methods. By analysing the life cycles of insects, forensic entomologists can estimate PMI, reconstruct crime scenes, and provide valuable information about the circumstances surrounding death. The predictable patterns of insect colonization and the precision of temperature-dependent development models make insect evidence an indispensable tool in solving crimes involving decomposition. However, the discipline's success relies on careful consideration of environmental factors, accurate species identification, and rigorous forensic methodology. As the field of forensic entomology continues to evolve, its contributions to the pursuit of justice in criminal investigations will undoubtedly grow, further enhancing our understanding of death and decomposition.

CHAPTER 11: NATURAL BURIAL: RETURNING TO THE EARTH

Natural burial, often referred to as green burial, is a method of interment that seeks to return the body to the earth in an environmentally responsible and minimally invasive way. It is based on the principle of allowing the body to decompose naturally, without the use of chemicals, concrete vaults, or metal caskets, thus enabling it to nourish the soil and contribute to the ecological cycle. The practice of natural burial, while not a new concept, has gained renewed attention in recent years due to growing environmental awareness and the desire to reduce the ecological footprint of death.

This chapter explores the scientific and ecological processes involved in natural burial, examining how bodies decompose in natural environments and how natural burial practices differ from conventional burial and cremation. It also considers the resurgence of green burial as a movement, the factors driving its popularity, and the potential for natural burial to provide an alternative to the more resource-intensive practices that dominate contemporary funeral services.

The Science of Decomposition in Natural Burials

Natural burial allows the body to follow the same decomposition processes that occur in nature but in a controlled setting designed to minimize environmental disruption. The body, typically buried in a biodegradable shroud or coffin, is placed directly in the soil at a depth that facilitates decomposition through natural microbial and environmental processes. This approach avoids the introduction of embalming chemicals, metal caskets, and concrete vaults, all of which can hinder decomposition and contribute to environmental degradation.

The Biological Process of Decomposition

Decomposition is a natural biological process that breaks down organic material into its elemental components. The body, like all organic matter, is composed of proteins, fats, carbohydrates, and water, all of which provide the nutrients necessary for microbial activity. Decomposition occurs in several stages, each characterized by specific biological and chemical processes that transform the body into simpler organic and inorganic substances.

1. Autolysis: The process of decomposition begins immediately after death with autolysis or self-digestion. In life, cells are tightly regulated by enzymes and cellular membranes. When death occurs, these regulatory mechanisms cease, and the enzymes within cells begin to break down the cell walls. This causes the release of cellular fluids and the breakdown of tissues, particularly in organs with high enzymatic activity such as the liver, pancreas, and stomach.

2. Putrefaction: Following autolysis, bacteria that are normally present in the body, especially those found in the gastrointestinal tract, begin to proliferate and further

decompose the tissues. This stage, known as putrefaction, is marked by the production of gases such as methane, hydrogen sulphide, and ammonia, which are byproducts of bacterial metabolism. These gases cause the body to bloat, and the characteristic odours of decomposition become evident.

3. Active Decay: During active decay, bacteria, fungi, and other microorganisms break down the body's proteins, fats, and carbohydrates. This process releases nutrients into the soil, where they are absorbed by plants and other organisms. In a natural burial, these nutrients contribute to the surrounding ecosystem, supporting the growth of trees, grasses, and other vegetation.

4. Skeletonization: Over time, the soft tissues of the body are fully decomposed, leaving behind the bones and teeth, which take much longer to degrade. The rate at which bones break down depends on environmental factors such as soil composition, moisture, and temperature. In an acidic environment, bones may degrade more quickly, while in dry, alkaline soils, they may persist for decades or even centuries.

Environmental Factors Influencing Decomposition

The rate of decomposition in natural burial is influenced by several environmental factors, including temperature, moisture, oxygen availability, and soil composition. Understanding these factors is crucial for ensuring that natural burials are conducted in a way that promotes efficient decomposition and minimal environmental impact.

1. Temperature: Warmer temperatures accelerate the rate of decomposition by increasing microbial activity and enzymatic reactions. In temperate climates, decomposition occurs more rapidly during the warmer months, while colder temperatures slow down the process significantly. In cold or frozen ground, decomposition may halt altogether until temperatures rise again.

2. Moisture: Moisture is essential for microbial life, and the availability of water in the soil can significantly influence the rate of decomposition. In arid environments, decomposition may proceed more slowly due to the lack of moisture, leading to desiccation or mummification of the body. In contrast, waterlogged soils may inhibit the oxygen needed for aerobic decomposition, leading to anaerobic conditions that slow down the process and produce different byproducts, such as methane.

3. Oxygen: Aerobic decomposition, which requires oxygen, is the most efficient way for the body to break down in a natural burial. Oxygen facilitates the activity of aerobic bacteria and fungi, which rapidly decompose organic material into carbon dioxide, water, and nutrients. In oxygen-poor environments, such as deep burial or waterlogged soil, anaerobic decomposition may occur, which is slower and results in the production of different gases like methane and hydrogen sulphide.

4. Soil Composition: The chemical composition and pH of the soil play a significant role in the decomposition process. Acidic soils, such as those found in peat bogs or certain forested areas, can slow decomposition and lead to the preservation of soft tissues, as seen in some archaeological discoveries of well-preserved bodies in bog environments. Alkaline or neutral soils, on the other hand, support more rapid decomposition by providing a hospitable environment for microbes and scavengers.

Natural burial practices are designed to optimize these environmental factors by selecting sites that promote efficient decomposition. Burial at shallow depths, for instance, ensures that the body is exposed to aerobic conditions, allowing for faster breakdown of tissues and the recycling of nutrients into the surrounding ecosystem.

The Practice of Natural Burial

Natural burial stands in contrast to conventional burial methods, which typically involve the use of embalming fluids, metal or hardwood caskets, and concrete vaults. These materials, designed to preserve the body or protect it from the elements, often impede the natural processes of decomposition and introduce harmful chemicals into the environment.

Key Features of Natural Burial

1. Biodegradable Materials: In natural burial, the body is interred in a biodegradable shroud or coffin made from materials such as untreated wood, wicker, cardboard, or cotton. These materials decompose alongside the body, ensuring that no synthetic or non-degradable substances remain in the soil.

2. No Embalming: Natural burial prohibits the use of embalming fluids, particularly those containing formaldehyde, a chemical commonly used in conventional embalming to preserve the body temporarily. Formaldehyde is a known carcinogen that can leach into the soil and groundwater, posing environmental and health risks. In natural burial, the body is allowed to decompose naturally, without the use of chemical preservatives.

3. Shallow Grave Depth: Unlike conventional burials, which often place the body six feet underground, natural burials typically involve shallower graves, usually between three and four feet deep. This depth ensures that the body remains in the aerobic zone, where oxygen is available to support microbial activity and decomposition. Shallower graves also allow the body to interact more directly with the soil and surrounding plant life, facilitating the recycling of nutrients.

4. Conservation Burial Grounds: Many natural burials take place in conservation burial grounds, which are designated areas of land set aside for ecological preservation. These burial grounds are often integrated into forests, meadows, or other natural landscapes, and the burial sites are left in their natural state

without headstones or other traditional markers. Instead, GPS coordinates or small, biodegradable markers may be used to locate graves. The goal of conservation burial is not only to provide a resting place for the deceased but also to protect and restore natural habitats.

Cultural and Religious Contexts of Natural Burial

Natural burial is not a new practice; it has been the predominant method of body disposal for much of human history. Many ancient and Indigenous cultures practised forms of natural burial, often based on religious or spiritual beliefs about the cyclical nature of life and death. The resurgence of natural burial in modern times reflects a return to these older traditions, as well as a growing awareness of the environmental impact of contemporary funeral practices.

In some religious traditions, natural burial is seen as a way to honour the body's return to the earth. For example, in Islam and Judaism, burial practices traditionally involve interring the body in a simple shroud without embalming or caskets. Both faiths emphasize the importance of allowing the body to decompose naturally, in accordance with the belief that the body belongs to the earth.

The modern green burial movement has drawn inspiration from these traditions, as well as from environmental ethics. For many, natural burial is seen as a final act of environmental stewardship, a way to reduce the ecological footprint of death and contribute to the health of the planet.

Environmental and Ecological Benefits of Natural Burial

The primary appeal of natural burial lies in its environmental benefits. By avoiding the use of embalming chemicals, non-biodegradable materials, and resource-intensive burial practices, natural burial offers a sustainable alternative that minimizes the impact on ecosystems.

Reduction of Chemical Pollution

Conventional embalming fluids, which contain formaldehyde and other chemicals, are widely recognized as environmental hazards. These chemicals can leach into the soil and contaminate groundwater, posing risks to both human health and wildlife. According to the U.S. Centres for Disease Control and Prevention (CDC), formaldehyde is a known carcinogen, and its widespread use in embalming contributes to the release of toxic substances into the environment.

Natural burial eliminates the need for embalming and its associated chemicals, allowing the body to decompose without introducing harmful substances into the soil. This reduces the overall pollution load on the environment and ensures that burial sites remain free from chemical contaminants.

Conservation of Resources

Traditional burial practices often involve the use of resource-intensive materials such as hardwood caskets, steel vaults, and polished stone headstones. The production and transportation of these materials require significant energy inputs, contributing to deforestation, carbon emissions, and the depletion of natural resources.

In contrast, natural burial emphasizes the use of biodegradable materials that decompose naturally and leave no lasting environmental footprint. By forgoing metal caskets, concrete vaults, and other resource-intensive materials, natural burial conserves natural resources and reduces the environmental costs associated with conventional burial practices.

Land Conservation and Habitat Restoration

Conservation burial grounds are often established on land that is set aside for ecological preservation, such as forests, meadows, or wetlands. These burial grounds serve dual purposes: they provide a final resting place for the deceased while also protecting and restoring natural habitats. Burial fees may be used to fund land conservation efforts, including reforestation, invasive species removal, and habitat restoration projects.

In some cases, conservation burial grounds are integrated into larger nature preserves, ensuring that the land is protected from development and preserved for future generations. By choosing natural burial, individuals can contribute to the preservation of ecosystems and the protection of biodiversity.

The Resurgence of Green Burial Practices

The growing interest in natural burial reflects a broader societal shift toward environmental consciousness and sustainability. As concerns about climate change, resource depletion, and pollution continue to mount, more people are seeking eco-friendly alternatives in all aspects of life, including death care.

Public Interest and Environmental Advocacy

Environmental advocacy groups have played a key role in raising awareness about the environmental impact of conventional funeral practices and promoting green burial as a sustainable alternative. Organizations such as the Green Burial Council and the Natural Death Centre have developed certification programs for funeral homes and burial grounds that meet environmental standards for green burial.

These organizations have also worked to educate the public about the benefits of natural burial and to dispel common misconceptions about the practice. For example, some people believe that natural burial poses a public health risk by allowing the spread of disease from decomposing bodies. However, research has shown that the risk of disease transmission from natural burial is minimal, as most pathogens do not survive long after death, and the decomposition process itself helps to neutralize any remaining microorganisms.

Legislative and Regulatory Changes

In recent years, there has been a growing movement to revise laws and regulations governing burial practices to accommodate natural burial. In many jurisdictions, outdated laws require the use of concrete vaults, metal caskets, or embalming, even when these practices are not necessary for public health or safety. Environmental advocates have worked to change these regulations, allowing for more flexibility in burial practices and making natural burial more accessible.

Some states and countries have already made significant progress in this area. For example, the United Kingdom has seen a rapid increase in the number of natural burial sites, with more than 300 green burial grounds now operating across the country. In the United States, several states have passed laws that explicitly permit natural burial, and many more are considering similar legislation.

Challenges and Future Directions

Despite its growing popularity, natural burial still faces several challenges. One of the primary obstacles is the lack of awareness and understanding among the general public and within the funeral industry. Many people are unfamiliar with the concept of natural burial or may mistakenly believe that it is illegal or impractical.

Additionally, the availability of natural burial grounds is limited in some areas, particularly in urban regions where land is scarce and expensive. Expanding access to natural burial will require ongoing efforts to educate the public, revise regulations, and develop new burial grounds that prioritize environmental sustainability.

Natural burial represents a return to a more eco-conscious approach to death, offering a sustainable alternative to conventional burial and cremation practices. By allowing the body to decompose naturally and contribute to the ecosystem, natural burial not only reduces the environmental impact of death but also aligns with a growing societal desire for sustainability. As awareness of the environmental consequences of conventional funeral practices continues to grow, natural burial is likely to become an increasingly popular option, offering individuals a way to make their final act on earth one of ecological responsibility.

CHAPTER 12: DEATH ACROSS CULTURES: HOW DIFFERENT SOCIETIES HANDLE DEATH

Introduction to Cultural Perspectives on Death

Death is a universal certainty, an event that every individual will ultimately face, yet how societies understand, respond to, and ritualize death varies dramatically across the globe. The rituals surrounding death serve a myriad of purposes: to honour the deceased, to provide solace for the living, and to guide the soul into the next realm, whatever form that may take according to the belief system. While death itself is unchanging, the customs and practices that accompany it are deeply influenced by cultural, spiritual, and philosophical contexts. How societies handle death reflects their collective values, their relationship with the physical body, and their interpretations of the afterlife.

Across cultures, death is viewed not simply as a biological cessation but often as a passage—a transformative moment that links this life with something beyond. Whether that next stage is conceptualized as reincarnation, eternal life, or spiritual transcendence, rituals help mediate the fear, uncertainty, and grief that accompany this profound event. From the sky burials in the mountains of Tibet to modern embalming practices in the West, humans have developed intricate ways to address both the emotional and physical realities of death.

One of the most fascinating aspects of death rituals is how they balance deeply rooted traditions with scientific and practical advancements. In some regions, ancient customs have remained largely untouched for centuries, while in others, modernization and medical science have redefined how death is managed. This chapter will explore the diversity of these death practices, examining how science and tradition interact in different cultural contexts.

Asian Traditions

Tibetan Sky Burial: Spirituality Meets the Sky

In the high, rugged landscapes of the Tibetan plateau, the practice of jhator, or sky burial, remains one of the most unique and spiritually significant rituals associated with death. This practice, grounded in the Tibetan Buddhist belief in the impermanence of the physical body, serves both a symbolic and ecological function. Central to this ritual is the idea that the body is merely a vessel, and after death, it becomes an empty shell that must return to nature. For Tibetan Buddhists, the soul continues its journey through cycles of rebirth, and the body's fate is inconsequential to this spiritual progression.

The sky burial process begins soon after death. A designated person, called a rogyapa or body-breaker, prepares the deceased's body by disassembling it into manageable parts. This work is done with precision and deep reverence, as the body is laid out on a mountaintop to be consumed by vultures, which are seen as sacred creatures. The offering of the body to these scavengers is considered an act of generosity, allowing the deceased to give back to the natural world in their final act.

Beyond the symbolism, sky burials also fulfil practical needs. Tibet's harsh terrain, with its rocky soil and freezing temperatures, makes traditional burial or cremation nearly impossible. Firewood for cremation is scarce, and the frozen ground is too hard for digging graves. Thus, the sky burial not only aligns with spiritual beliefs but also suits the environmental limitations of the region.

The scientific rationale behind this practice complements its spiritual roots. The exposure of the body to vultures and the elements allows for a natural form of decomposition. This aligns with modern ecological principles, as it reduces the environmental footprint associated with traditional burial practices, which can require significant resources like wood, land, and embalming chemicals. Moreover, the practice of sky burial also highlights the Tibetan approach to mortality—there is no attachment to the body, only an acknowledgement of the ongoing cycle of life and death.

Japanese Funerary Practices: The Synthesis of Shinto, Buddhism, and Modernity

In Japan, death rituals are influenced by a blend of Shintoism, Buddhism, and increasingly, Western practices. Japanese funerals are complex, multi-stage events that reflect the nation's deep spiritual connection to death as well as its respect for ritual and tradition.

Historically, Shintoism, Japan's indigenous belief system, viewed death as an impurity, something to be distanced from the living. As a result, the responsibility for handling the dead traditionally fell to the burakumin, a caste tasked with death-related occupations. Over time, however, Buddhism's teachings on reincarnation and the impermanence of life became deeply ingrained in Japanese death rituals, shifting attitudes toward the treatment of the deceased.

Modern Japanese funerals, known as soshiki, typically follow Buddhist customs, with cremation being the most common practice. The process begins with a wake, known as otsuya, where the family gathers to pay respects to the deceased. This is followed by the cremation itself, during which close family members often participate in a solemn ritual of bone-picking, using chopsticks to place fragments of the cremated remains into an urn. The use of cremation reflects a long-standing Buddhist influence, as it symbolizes the release of the soul from its earthly vessel and its journey into the afterlife.

In contemporary Japan, funerals have also become sites of technological innovation. Urbanization has led to a shortage of burial spaces, particularly in major cities like Tokyo. As a response, modern columbariums—structures that house urns—have been developed, with some utilizing digital displays to allow family members to visit and pay respects through virtual means. Robotic priests are even being employed in some ceremonies to lead Buddhist rites, reflecting a striking intersection of tradition and modern technology.

Despite these technological shifts, the heart of Japanese funerary practices remains tied to Buddhist and Shinto values. Ritual purification, ancestor worship, and the honouring of the deceased's spirit continue to play central roles. Japan exemplifies how a society can maintain its deeply rooted cultural beliefs about death while adapting to the practical challenges of modernity.

African Funeral Traditions

Ghanaian Fantasy Coffins: Artistry in Death

In the West African nation of Ghana, particularly among the

Ga people, funerals are seen as a celebration of life, and this philosophy is nowhere more evident than in the tradition of fantasy coffins. These elaborately designed coffins are crafted to reflect the personality, occupation, or aspirations of the deceased. From fish-shaped coffins for fishermen to aeroplanes for pilots, these artistic creations symbolize the individuality of the person and the community's desire to honour their life in a memorable and meaningful way.

The construction of these coffins is not merely a decorative effort but is deeply intertwined with the Ga people's spiritual beliefs. The afterlife is viewed as a continuation of life on Earth, and thus, the deceased must enter this new phase in a style befitting their earthly existence. These coffins also serve as a way for families to display their respect and love for the deceased, while the elaborate nature of the designs reflects the status and wealth of the family.

While fantasy coffins are deeply tied to cultural expression, they also highlight an important interaction between art, tradition, and modern craftsmanship. Skilled artisans known as abebuu adekai specialize in crafting these coffins, using modern tools and techniques to create highly personalized tributes. This practice blends cultural symbolism with contemporary artistry, showcasing how death rituals in Ghana continue to evolve while staying rooted in long-standing traditions.

South African Burial Practices: The Blend of Tradition and Christianity

In South Africa, burial practices reflect the country's complex socio-cultural landscape, where indigenous customs coexist with Christian rituals introduced during colonial times. Among the Xhosa and Zulu communities, death is viewed as a time when the spirit of the deceased transitions to become an ancestor. Maintaining good relationships with the ancestors is crucial, as they are believed to influence the well-being of the living.

Traditional funerals among these groups are elaborate affairs, often lasting several days. The deceased is prepared and buried in a way that reflects their social standing and ensures their proper transition to the afterlife. Animal sacrifices are common, as they are seen as a way to honour the ancestors and seek their blessings. The burial is followed by a homecoming ceremony, in which the spirit of the deceased is invited back to the family home to continue watching over the living.

Christianity has also significantly influenced burial practices in South Africa. Many families now hold church services in conjunction with traditional rites, blending Christian hymns, prayers, and scripture readings with indigenous rituals. This syncretism allows families to maintain their cultural heritage while embracing the spiritual teachings of Christianity. The result is a rich tapestry of customs that honour both the physical and spiritual aspects of death.

CHAPTER 13: MUMMIFICATION: A HISTORICAL PRESERVATION

Introduction to Mummification

Mummification is one of the most enduring and scientifically intriguing methods of body preservation practised across various civilizations throughout history. The term "mummification" originates from the Persian word mummiya, meaning "bitumen," referring to the dark resinous substances initially believed to be used in preserving bodies. However, mummification, in its broader sense, refers to any method that arrests the decomposition of a corpse, preserving it through either natural or artificial processes. While most commonly associated with ancient Egypt, mummification has been a global phenomenon, with evidence of its practice found in various forms across cultures as diverse as the Chinchorro people of South America and the Inca civilization, as well as the frozen bodies discovered in Arctic regions.

The practice of mummification holds dual significance: it is both a scientific process and a cultural ritual. Historically, mummification was often intertwined with religious beliefs, aiming to secure the deceased's passage to the afterlife by preserving the body for eternity. This cultural objective frequently aligned with scientific principles, whether or not practitioners at the time understood the underlying biological mechanisms. By halting or significantly slowing the decomposition process, mummification methods allowed for remarkable preservation, often maintaining the physical features, skin, and even internal organs of the deceased. In modern times, these preserved bodies provide critical insights into the ancient world, offering a window into the health, disease, diet, and cultural practices of past societies.

Contemporary scientists, particularly in fields like archaeology, forensic anthropology, and biology, study mummified remains to understand the conditions that allow for such preservation. The study of mummies goes beyond the physical body —it extends into areas such as the analysis of ancient pathogens, environmental conditions, and even insights into the microbiome. Mummification is thus a nexus where science and history converge, revealing how ancient peoples managed to both preserve their dead and provide modern scholars with invaluable information about life in past millennia.

Ancient Egyptian Mummification: The Gold Standard of Preservation

Among all civilizations, ancient Egypt is perhaps the most renowned for its sophisticated and ritualistic approach to mummification. Egyptian mummification, which spanned over three millennia, was not only a method of body preservation but also an elaborate spiritual practice. The Egyptians believed that the preservation of the physical body was essential for the deceased to achieve immortality. This belief stemmed from the Egyptian concept of the ka, ba, and akh, three components of the soul. For these elements to reunite in the afterlife, the body needed to remain intact, thus giving rise to the meticulous practice of mummification.

The Process of Egyptian Mummification

The science behind Egyptian mummification combined both the mechanical removal of decaying elements and the chemical preservation of the remaining body. The process evolved over time, but by the New Kingdom period (circa 1550–1070 BCE), the standard procedure involved several well-defined steps.

1. Evisceration: One of the first tasks was the removal of the internal organs, which are the first parts of the body to decay after death due to bacterial activity. The ancient Egyptians would extract the stomach, intestines, lungs, and liver through an incision in the abdomen. These organs were preserved separately in canopic jars, each protected by one of the Four Sons of Horus. The heart, considered the seat of intelligence and emotion, was typically left in place, as it was believed to be weighed in the afterlife to determine the deceased's fate.

2. Desiccation: The body was then desiccated using a naturally occurring salt compound called natron, which was abundant in the dry lake beds of Egypt. Natron is a mixture of sodium carbonate and sodium bicarbonate, with small amounts of sodium chloride and sodium sulphate. The application of natron was the most crucial step in mummification, as it drew moisture from the body tissues, preventing bacterial growth and enzymatic reactions that would otherwise lead to decomposition. The body was packed inside and out with natron and left to dry for 40 days.

3. Wrapping: Once fully desiccated, the body was wrapped in multiple layers of linen. This wrapping served both a practical and symbolic function. From a practical standpoint, the linen helped maintain the body's structural integrity, especially after the removal of the organs. From a religious perspective,

the wrappings were often accompanied by amulets placed strategically between the layers, each serving to protect the deceased on their journey to the afterlife. Resins and oils were used to seal the layers of linen and to further preserve the body.

4. Resin Application: The application of resin to the body served as an additional barrier to decay. Recent studies on Egyptian mummies have shown that resins used in the process had antibacterial properties, further aiding in the preservation of the body. The use of these substances demonstrates the ancient Egyptians' understanding—whether by trial and error or practical knowledge—of the role of chemicals in halting decomposition.

5. Final Rites and Burial: After wrapping, the mummy was placed in a sarcophagus or wooden coffin, adorned with protective spells and images meant to guide the deceased into the afterlife. The funerary rites, such as the "Opening of the Mouth" ceremony, were performed to reanimate the deceased's senses so they could experience the afterlife fully.

Scientific Insights into Egyptian Mummification

Modern studies of Egyptian mummies have provided significant insights into ancient preservation techniques. Recent advances in bioarchaeology and chemistry have allowed researchers to analyse the materials used in mummification with remarkable precision. For example, the use of natron as a desiccant has been scientifically validated as an effective method for drawing out moisture and halting decay. Additionally, the resin used in the wrappings has been found to contain compounds like myrrh and frankincense, which possess antimicrobial properties, explaining their use in preservation.

Interestingly, studies have also revealed that different techniques were employed depending on the period and the status of the deceased. For example, more affluent Egyptians, such as pharaohs and nobles, were given the most elaborate treatment, while commoners received simpler and less expensive mummifications, often with varying success in preservation.

In some cases, modern science has uncovered the imperfections of the mummification process. For instance, despite the best efforts of embalmers, some organs would still decay, leaving behind only traces of their original form. This has been a rich source of information for modern scientists studying ancient Egyptian health and disease. The bodies, though preserved, sometimes show signs of ailments like tuberculosis, arthritis, and parasitic infections. The examination of such preserved bodies offers an unparalleled opportunity to study the diseases that affected ancient populations, providing valuable context for the evolution of modern health conditions.

Mummification in Other Cultures

Chinchorro Mummies: The Oldest Known Mummification

The Chinchorro culture of present-day northern Chile and southern Peru is credited with practising the earliest known form of mummification, predating the Egyptians by several millennia. Unlike the Egyptians, who primarily mummified their elite, the Chinchorro mummified all members of their society, including infants and children. This egalitarian approach to mummification is unique and speaks to the cultural significance placed on the deceased in Chinchorro society.

The Chinchorro method of mummification was strikingly different from the Egyptian process. Rather than focusing solely on drying the body, the Chinchorro embalmers removed the skin, muscles, and internal organs, leaving only the skeleton. The bones were reinforced with sticks or clay to maintain the body's structure. Once the frame was stable, it was stuffed with various materials like earth or straw, and the body was reassembled. The final step involved covering the body in clay and painting it with pigments, often red or black.

This labour-intensive process suggests that the Chinchorro placed a significant emphasis on the appearance of the deceased, not merely on preserving their remains for the afterlife. The desire to maintain a lifelike appearance stands in contrast to other mummification traditions, where the goal was more functional—preserving the body for religious or spiritual reasons. While the motivation behind Chinchorro mummification is still debated, it is clear that this culture viewed death as an event that required continued attention to the physical form, even in death.

Recent archaeological studies have allowed scientists to better understand the materials and methods used by the Chinchorro people. Analysis of the pigments used in painting the mummies has revealed that the black pigment was derived from manganese, a naturally occurring element in the region, while the red pigment came from hematite, an iron oxide. These findings highlight the local resources used in the preservation process and offer insights into the Chinchorro's technological capabilities.

Natural Mummification: The Role of the Environment

While many mummification processes were intentionally designed to preserve the body, some of the most well-preserved remains from ancient times are the result of natural environmental conditions. Natural mummification occurs when the body is subjected to extreme environmental factors, such as freezing temperatures, arid climates, or acidic peat bogs, which significantly slow down the decomposition process. These environments act as inadvertent preservers, maintaining the physical integrity of the corpse for centuries or even millennia.

Freezing: The Arctic Mummies

One of the most well-known examples of natural mummification through freezing is the body of Ötzi the Iceman, discovered in 1991 in the Alps near the Austrian-Italian border. Ötzi, who lived around 3300 BCE, was naturally preserved by the freezing temperatures of the high-altitude environment where he died. His body, along with his clothing and tools, was found almost intact, offering an unprecedented glimpse into life during the Copper Age.

The preservation of Ötzi's body has been attributed to the stable, low temperatures in the Alps, which prevented microbial activity, thereby arresting the process of decay. His internal organs, stomach contents, and even tattoos were remarkably well-preserved. Subsequent scientific studies have yielded a wealth of information about Ötzi's life, including his last meal, his health condition (including traces of heart disease and arthritis), and even insights into the weapons he carried.

Other examples of natural freezing mummification include the Siberian mummies of the Pazyryk culture. These mummies, found in the permafrost of the Altai Mountains, were buried in large kurgans (burial mounds) and preserved by the sub-zero temperatures. Like Ötzi, the Pazyryk mummies provide critical information about ancient cultures, including their burial rituals, clothing, and diet. The cold environment acts as a natural barrier to decomposition, preserving not only the bodies but also the organic materials buried with them.

Desert Mummification: The Dry Heat of Egypt and Beyond

Arid climates are another natural preserver of bodies. The combination of dry heat and low humidity creates conditions that desiccate the body rapidly, preventing the growth of bacteria that would normally lead to decomposition. This type of natural mummification was common in ancient Egypt, where the desert climate played a significant role in preserving corpses even before the development of artificial mummification techniques.

The pre-dynastic Egyptians, who lived long before the elaborate mummification processes associated with the pharaohs, buried their dead in shallow graves in the desert sand. The hot, dry sand acted as a natural desiccant, drying out the bodies and preserving them remarkably well. It was likely the observation of these naturally mummified bodies that inspired the later, more sophisticated mummification techniques of ancient Egypt.

Desert mummification has also been observed in other parts of the world, including the Atacama Desert in South America, where the naturally mummified bodies of the Chinchorro people were found. In this case, the dry desert environment worked in tandem with their intentional mummification techniques, enhancing the preservation of the bodies over millennia.

Bog Mummies: The Chemical Preservation of Northern Europe

In contrast to the drying and freezing methods seen in desert and Arctic environments, bog mummies are preserved through a unique chemical process that occurs in waterlogged, acidic peat bogs. These mummies, primarily found in Northern Europe, are the result of the highly acidic, low-oxygen environment of peat bogs, which prevents bacterial growth and the normal processes of decay.

The most famous of these bog bodies is Tollund Man, discovered in a peat bog in Denmark in 1950. Dating back to the 4th century BCE, Tollund Man was so well-preserved that he was initially mistaken for a recent murder victim. His skin, facial features, and even the stubble on his chin remained intact due to the tannins in the bog, which preserved the soft tissues while dissolving the bones.

The preservation of bog bodies is particularly fascinating to scientists because it preserves not only the physical features of the deceased but also details about their diet, clothing, and even the circumstances of their death. Many of these bog bodies, such as the Tollund Man, appear to have been victims of ritual sacrifice, providing archaeologists with valuable insights into the spiritual beliefs and practices of ancient peoples.

The science of bog mummification reveals how the interplay of environmental factors can create conditions for near-perfect preservation, offering modern researchers a rare opportunity to study ancient individuals in incredible detail.

Modern Mummification and Preservation Techniques

Mummification is not confined to the ancient world; modern techniques of body preservation have evolved considerably and are used for both medical and ceremonial purposes. While modern embalming differs significantly from ancient methods, the goal remains the same: to preserve the body by preventing or slowing down the natural process of decomposition.

Embalming in Contemporary Societies

Modern embalming, particularly in Western societies, developed during the 19th century, reaching its zenith during the American Civil War when soldiers' bodies were preserved for transportation back to their families. Today, embalming is commonly used in funeral homes to temporarily preserve the body for viewing during funerals.

The process involves replacing the body's fluids with a preservative solution, typically formaldehyde-based. Formaldehyde acts as a disinfectant and preservative by cross-linking proteins in the body, which makes it more difficult for bacteria to break down tissues. Modern embalming also includes the removal of blood and the injection of embalming fluids into the arteries, while the body is aspirated to remove gases and liquids from the internal organs.

Although embalming slows decomposition, it is a temporary measure. Unlike the ancient Egyptians, who aimed for long-term preservation, modern embalming is designed to preserve the body for a short period, typically until burial or cremation. Nonetheless, embalming serves as a modern continuation of the ancient human desire to maintain the physical form of the deceased, at least for a time.

Plastination: Preservation for Science

In the late 20th century, a new form of body preservation known as plastination was developed by Dr Gunther von Hagens. This process involves replacing the water and fat in tissues with plastic polymers, which results in a dry, odourless, and durable specimen. Plastination preserves the body for educational and scientific purposes, allowing for detailed anatomical studies without the decomposition and decay associated with traditional cadaver use.

Plastination has gained significant popularity in medical schools and museums, providing a more permanent and accessible way to study human anatomy. The preserved specimens are often displayed in exhibitions, such as von Hagens' famous Body Worlds series, which showcases plastinated human bodies in lifelike poses, providing the public with a deeper understanding of human anatomy.

While plastination serves a different purpose from mummification, it continues the tradition of body preservation by using modern technology to create specimens that can be studied indefinitely.

What Modern Science Learns from Mummies

The study of mummies offers modern scientists a wealth of information, not only about the individuals themselves but also about the cultures, health, and environments of ancient civilizations. Advances in technology, particularly in fields like DNA analysis, radiology, and microbiology, have transformed mummy research, allowing scientists to uncover details that were previously inaccessible.

Ancient DNA and Pathology

One of the most significant breakthroughs in mummy studies is the extraction and analysis of ancient DNA (aDNA). Mummified bodies offer a unique opportunity to study genetic material from ancient populations, which can provide insights into ancestry, migration patterns, and even genetic diseases. Studies of ancient Egyptian mummies, for example, have revealed their genetic connections to populations in the Near East, highlighting the region's historical role as a crossroads for trade and migration.

Pathological studies of mummies have also shed light on the health conditions of ancient peoples. For example, X-ray and CT scans of mummified bodies have revealed the presence of diseases such as arthritis, tuberculosis, and atherosclerosis, conditions that were previously thought to be modern afflictions. The discovery of hardened arteries in mummies as old as 3,500 years suggests that cardiovascular disease may have been influenced by factors beyond modern diet and lifestyle.

Mummified remains also provide clues about ancient medical practices. Evidence of trepanation (the surgical removal of part of the skull) has been found in several mummies, indicating that ancient civilizations practiced rudimentary forms of brain surgery. Studying these remains helps modern scientists trace the development of medical knowledge and practices over time.

The Microbiome of Mummies

Recent research into the microbiome of mummified remains is providing new insights into the health and diets of ancient peoples. By analysing the bacteria and other microorganisms found in the guts of mummies, scientists can reconstruct ancient diets and identify the pathogens that plagued these populations.

For example, the study of Ötzi's stomach contents revealed that he had consumed a meal of deer and grains shortly before his death, while DNA analysis of his microbiome showed that he was infected with Helicobacter pylori, a bacterium that causes stomach ulcers. This discovery has provided valuable information about the prevalence of H. pylori in ancient populations and its role in human health over millennia.

The Enduring Legacy of Mummification

Mummification, whether achieved through intentional human practices or natural environmental conditions, offers a unique window into the past. The preservation of bodies over thousands of years provides modern scientists with unparalleled opportunities to study ancient civilizations, their health, and their environments. From the meticulous procedures of the ancient Egyptians to the natural mummification of bodies in deserts and bogs, these preserved remains continue to shape our understanding of history.

Mummification's enduring legacy is evident in the continued fascination with preserved bodies, both ancient and modern. Whether through the religious and cultural motivations of ancient peoples or the scientific advancements of modern embalming and plastination, the desire to preserve the human body reflects a deep-seated human need to remember and honour the dead. For researchers and scientists, these preserved bodies are invaluable resources that will continue to inform and enlighten us for generations to come.

CHAPTER 14: FORENSIC ANTHROPOLOGY: READING BONES

Introduction to Forensic Anthropology

Forensic anthropology, a specialized field within anthropology, is the study of human skeletal remains in the context of legal investigations. The work of forensic anthropologists is essential in cases where decomposed, burned, or otherwise unrecognizable remains are discovered. By analysing the structure, composition, and modifications of bones, forensic anthropologists can determine critical details about the deceased, such as age, sex, ancestry, stature, and sometimes the cause of death. This information can be pivotal in identifying individuals and providing insight into the circumstances of their death.

The term "forensic" refers to any scientific work applied to the law. Forensic anthropologists are often called upon to assist in criminal cases where skeletal remains are involved, such as in cases of homicide, mass disasters, or historical investigations of unmarked graves. Their work is particularly crucial when there is little soft tissue left, and traditional methods of identification—such as fingerprints or dental records—are not feasible.

Forensic anthropology is a multifaceted discipline, combining elements of biology, anatomy, archaeology, and even history. Skeletal remains can hold the key to unlocking the stories of the dead, revealing not only who the individual was but also how they lived, what they ate, and what might have caused their death. The skeleton, far from being an inert structure, is a dynamic and living record of an individual's life. By carefully reading this record, forensic anthropologists can provide valuable evidence that may help solve forensic cases, identify missing persons, or shed light on ancient populations.

The Science of Bones: Structure and Composition

The human skeleton, composed of 206 bones in adults, serves as the support structure for the body, providing protection for vital organs, facilitating movement, and acting as a reservoir for minerals such as calcium and phosphorus. From a forensic perspective, understanding the basic anatomy and physiology of bones is the first step in decoding the information they hold.

Bone Anatomy and Function

Bones are made up of two types of tissue: compact (cortical) bone and spongy (trabecular) bone. Compact bone is dense and forms the outer layer of bones, providing strength and protection. Spongy bone, found inside bones, has a porous structure and is filled with bone marrow, where blood cells are produced.

Each bone has a specific shape and function. For example, long bones such as the femur (thigh bone) and humerus (upper arm bone) are designed to support weight and facilitate movement. Flat bones, like the skull and ribs, protect vital organs, while irregular bones, such as the vertebrae, provide structural support for the body.

Bones are also highly vascular, meaning they have a good blood supply, which is essential for bone growth and repair. Throughout life, bones are constantly remodelled, a process regulated by cells known as osteoblasts (which build new bone) and osteoclasts (which break down old bone). This remodelling allows bones to adapt to stress, repair damage, and maintain mineral homeostasis.

Bone Formation and Growth

The formation of bones, or ossification, begins in the embryo and continues throughout childhood and adolescence. Bones grow in length at the growth plates, or epiphyseal plates, located at the ends of long bones. These plates remain open until an individual reaches adulthood, at which point they fuse and the bone stops growing in length.

The timing of epiphyseal closure is a key marker for estimating age in forensic cases. In general, growth plates close between the ages of 18 and 25, but this can vary based on sex and genetics. Forensic anthropologists can examine the state of these growth plates to estimate the age of the deceased, particularly in individuals who died during adolescence or early adulthood.

Post-Mortem Changes and Bone Degradation

After death, bones undergo a series of post-mortem changes, collectively known as taphonomy. Taphonomy includes all the processes that affect a body after death, including decomposition, scavenging, and environmental exposure. Understanding these processes is essential for forensic anthropologists, as they must be able to distinguish between changes that occurred during life, those that happened at the time of death, and those that occurred post-mortem.

Over time, bones lose organic material and become more brittle, particularly in environments with high acidity or moisture. In dry environments, bones may become desiccated and well-preserved, while in acidic soils, they may degrade rapidly. Forensic anthropologists use knowledge of these environmental factors to estimate the post-mortem interval (PMI)—the time that has passed since death.

Determining Age, Sex, and Ancestry from Skeletal Remains

One of the primary objectives of forensic anthropologists is to construct a biological profile of the deceased. This profile includes estimations of the individual's age, sex, ancestry, and stature, which can narrow down potential matches in missing persons databases and help identify the deceased. Each of these characteristics leaves distinctive markers on the skeleton, which anthropologists analyse using established methods.

Estimating Age at Death

Determining the age of an individual from skeletal remains involves analysing changes in bone structure that occur throughout life. In subadults (individuals who have not reached skeletal maturity), age estimation is relatively straightforward due to the predictable stages of bone growth and development.

1. Dental Development: Teeth are one of the most reliable indicators of age, particularly in children and adolescents. The timing of tooth eruption and the formation of tooth roots follow a well-documented schedule, allowing forensic anthropologists to estimate age with a high degree of accuracy. For example, the appearance of the first molars typically occurs around age six, while the third molars (wisdom teeth) erupt between ages 17 and 21.

2. Epiphyseal Fusion: As mentioned earlier, long bones grow in length through the process of epiphyseal fusion, where the growth plates gradually close as a person reaches maturity. By

examining which growth plates are still open and which have fused, forensic anthropologists can estimate the age of the deceased, particularly in individuals between the ages of 10 and 25.

In adults, age estimation becomes more challenging because there are fewer clear markers of skeletal growth. Instead, forensic anthropologists rely on degenerative changes that occur in the skeleton over time, such as:

1. Pubic Symphysis: The pubic symphysis, where the two halves of the pelvis meet at the front of the body, undergoes distinct changes with age. As an individual age, this joint shows signs of wear, which can be used to estimate the age of the deceased, particularly in middle-aged and older adults.

2. Auricular Surface of the Ilium: Another useful marker is the auricular surface of the ilium, a part of the pelvis that changes with age. These changes include increased porosity and granularity of the surface, which can provide clues about the individual's age at death.

Determining Sex

Sex determination from skeletal remains is based on the observation that certain bones, particularly the pelvis and skull, exhibit sexually dimorphic traits—morphological differences between males and females. The pelvis is the most reliable bone for determining sex due to its role in childbirth.

1. Pelvic Differences: The female pelvis is typically broader and has a wider subpubic angle, larger pelvic inlet, and more flared iliac bones, all of which facilitate childbirth. In contrast, the male pelvis is narrower and more robust. Forensic anthropologists examine these features to estimate sex with a high degree of accuracy.

2. Skull Features: The skull also exhibits sex-specific traits. Male skulls tend to have more pronounced brow ridges, a larger

mastoid process (the bony protrusion behind the ear), and a square jaw. Female skulls are generally smaller, with a more rounded chin and less prominent brow ridges. By examining these traits, forensic anthropologists can determine sex with considerable confidence.

However, it is important to note that sex estimation from skeletal remains is not always straightforward. Individuals who fall near the biological averages for male and female traits can be difficult to categorize, and forensic anthropologists must use multiple traits in combination to make accurate determinations.

Ancestry Estimation

Ancestry estimation involves identifying traits in the skeleton that are associated with specific populations. While it is important to recognize that ancestry is a complex and socially constructed concept, certain skeletal features can provide clues about an individual's genetic background.

1. Cranial Traits: The shape and structure of the skull vary among different populations. For example, individuals of African descent tend to have wider nasal apertures, more pronounced alveolar prognathism (forward projection of the jaw), and a more rounded forehead. Individuals of European descent often have narrower nasal apertures, flatter faces, and a more pronounced nasal bridge. East Asian populations typically show characteristics such as a flatter face and more rounded orbits (eye sockets).

2. Metric and Non-Metric Traits: Forensic anthropologists use both metric (measurable) and non-metric (observable) traits to estimate ancestry. Metric traits involve taking precise measurements of the skull and other bones and comparing them to established databases of skeletal measurements from different populations. Non-metric traits are observable features, such as the shape of the eye orbits, the form of the nasal opening,

and the prominence of certain cranial features.

Ancestry estimation is not an exact science, and forensic anthropologists must be cautious when interpreting these traits, as human populations have considerable overlap in their skeletal features due to migration and interbreeding. Nonetheless, when combined with other data, ancestry estimation can provide valuable information in forensic cases.

Trauma and Pathology: What Bones Reveal About Injury and Disease

Bones can reveal not only information about an individual's biological profile but also details about their health, injuries, and cause of death. Trauma analysis is a critical component of forensic anthropology, as it can help distinguish between injuries sustained during life (antemortem), injuries sustained at or around the time of death (perimortem), and damage that occurred after death (post-mortem).

Identifying Fractures and Trauma

Fractures and other injuries leave telltale marks on bones that can provide forensic anthropologists with insights into the events leading up to an individual's death. For example:

1. Blunt Force Trauma: Blunt force trauma occurs when a body is struck by a blunt object, causing fractures, depression in the bone, or even the shattering of the skull. The pattern and location of these injuries can reveal information about the type of weapon used and the circumstances of the injury.

2. Sharp Force Trauma: Sharp force trauma, caused by sharp objects such as knives or swords, leaves distinct marks on bones, including cuts, incisions, and punctures. The depth, direction, and placement of these marks can help forensic anthropologists determine the weapon used and the manner of attack.

3. Projectile Trauma: Projectile trauma, such as gunshot wounds, often leaves distinct entry and exit wounds on bones. The size and shape of the bullet hole, as well as the presence of radiating fractures, can provide information about the calibre of the bullet and the trajectory of the shot.

Perimortem and Post-Mortem Damage

A key challenge in trauma analysis is distinguishing between injuries that occurred at or around the time of death (perimortem) and those that occurred after death (post-mortem). Perimortem fractures tend to have smooth, sharp edges, and the bone may exhibit signs of bending or splintering, as the bones were still fresh and pliable at the time of injury. In contrast, post-mortem damage usually results in jagged, brittle breaks, as the bones have become dry and fragile after death.

Forensic anthropologists use these distinctions to determine whether injuries were sustained as part of the cause of death or if they occurred after death, perhaps due to scavengers, environmental factors, or human activity.

Forensic Case Studies: How Bones Solve Mysteries

Forensic anthropology has played a crucial role in solving some of the most challenging forensic cases, often providing the key evidence needed to identify victims and bring perpetrators to justice. From cold cases to mass disasters, forensic anthropologists have been instrumental in reconstructing the events surrounding death.

Historical and Cold Cases

In cases where bodies have been buried for many years, forensic anthropologists are often called upon to provide insights that cannot be gained through traditional forensic methods. For example, in the case of unidentified soldiers from World

War II, forensic anthropologists have used skeletal remains to determine the age, sex, and ancestry of the individuals, helping to match them with missing soldiers' records.

Similarly, in cold cases involving unidentified bodies, forensic anthropologists can use skeletal evidence to estimate the age, sex, ancestry, and stature of the deceased, narrowing down potential matches in missing persons databases.

Mass Graves and War Crimes

Forensic anthropologists have also played a vital role in the investigation of war crimes and genocide. In the aftermath of conflicts in places like Rwanda, the former Yugoslavia, and Iraq, forensic anthropologists have been involved in the excavation of mass graves. By analysing the skeletal remains, they can identify victims, document evidence of torture and execution, and provide testimony in war crimes tribunals.

The Future of Forensic Anthropology

The field of forensic anthropology continues to evolve, driven by advances in technology and an increasing demand for expertise in legal and historical cases. Techniques such as 3D imaging, isotope analysis, and DNA extraction from bones have revolutionized the way forensic anthropologists work, allowing for more precise and detailed analyses of skeletal remains.

Looking ahead, forensic anthropology will continue to play a crucial role in the investigation of criminal cases, human rights abuses, and historical research. As our understanding of human biology and the skeleton deepens, forensic anthropologists will remain at the forefront of unlocking the stories that bones can tell.

CHAPTER 15: THE MYSTERY OF IDENTIFYING THE UNIDENTIFIED

Introduction to Identifying the Unidentified

Throughout history, one of the most challenging tasks for forensic scientists has been identifying unknown human remains. Whether the individuals are victims of crime, accidents, natural disasters, or even war, the imperative to return a name to the body is both a scientific and moral obligation. Unidentified remains—referred to in forensic circles as John or Jane Does—represent a puzzle that involves multiple scientific disciplines working together. Each body carries clues that, if properly interpreted, can unlock the mystery of the individual's identity and the circumstances surrounding their death. However, the process of identification is often hindered by various factors, including decomposition, fragmentation, or a lack of prior records, making the identification of some individuals a monumental challenge.

Identifying the unidentified is more than a forensic exercise; it is about restoring humanity to those whose lives were abruptly interrupted, often under tragic circumstances. Families of missing persons endure immeasurable grief and uncertainty, waiting for answers that, in some cases, take years or even decades to materialize. Forensic identification offers these families closure, bringing an end to their liminal state between hope and despair. This chapter explores the scientific methods used to solve the mystery of unidentified human remains, focusing on the role of DNA profiling, dental records, facial reconstruction, and the challenges associated with identifying bodies in diverse contexts.

The methods of identification discussed here are essential in various settings, from cold cases to mass disasters. Whether working on a single victim or attempting to identify hundreds of individuals from a disaster site, forensic teams rely on a combination of biology, technology, and human insight to reconstruct an identity and restore dignity to the deceased. Identifying the unidentified is a painstaking process but one that continues to evolve with advancements in forensic science.

DNA Profiling: The Gold Standard for Identification

Deoxyribonucleic acid (DNA) has revolutionized forensic science since its introduction in the 1980s. DNA is the blueprint for every living organism, encoding genetic information that is unique to each individual, save for identical twins. DNA profiling has become the most reliable and widely used method for identifying unknown remains, particularly when other methods, such as visual recognition or fingerprinting, are impossible due to decomposition or other post-mortem changes.

The Science Behind DNA in Forensics

DNA is found in nearly every cell of the human body. The two primary types of DNA used in forensic identification are nuclear

DNA and mitochondrial DNA. Nuclear DNA is housed in the nucleus of each cell and is inherited equally from both parents, making it highly individualistic. Mitochondrial DNA, on the other hand, is inherited only from the mother and is found in the mitochondria, the cell's energy-producing structures. While nuclear DNA is the most precise for individual identification, mitochondrial DNA is often used when nuclear DNA is too degraded to be recovered, as mitochondrial DNA is more abundant and resistant to degradation.

Forensic scientists extract DNA from remains and amplify specific regions of the DNA using a technique called polymerase chain reaction (PCR). This allows scientists to create a DNA profile from even a small or degraded sample. Once the profile is generated, it can be compared to the DNA profiles of living relatives or entered into national and international DNA databases, such as the Combined DNA Index System (CODIS) in the United States, to search for matches.

Matching DNA Profiles in National Databases

CODIS is a national repository of DNA profiles that contains samples from convicted offenders, arrestees, and unidentified human remains. When a DNA profile is uploaded to CODIS, it is compared against millions of profiles in the system. If a match is found, it can provide an immediate link between the unidentified remains and a missing person or known individual. CODIS also allows for familial searching, which looks for partial matches that might indicate a genetic relationship between the unidentified individual and a living relative whose DNA is already in the system.

Even in cases where no direct match is found, DNA analysis can still yield valuable information. For example, DNA can provide information about an individual's ancestry, which can narrow down the search in missing persons cases by suggesting a particular ethnic background or geographic origin. Advances in

DNA analysis now allow scientists to predict certain physical traits, such as eye colour or hair colour, based on genetic markers, providing further clues to an unidentified individual's appearance.

Case Studies: DNA Solving Identification Mysteries

The power of DNA profiling is illustrated in numerous high-profile identification cases. For instance, in 2001, after the September 11 attacks on the World Trade Centre, DNA was one of the key tools used to identify victims. Given the extreme conditions at Ground Zero, where fire, debris, and time had severely compromised most of the remains, traditional methods such as fingerprinting and dental records were often ineffective. Instead, forensic scientists collected thousands of bone fragments and tissue samples, extracting DNA and comparing it to profiles from family members and personal items (like hair from a hairbrush) to identify the victims.

Another striking case of DNA's potential occurred in 2018 when investigators solved the decades-old cold case of the Golden State Killer by using familial DNA. Although the DNA of the perpetrator did not exist in any criminal database, genealogical DNA from a relative who had submitted a sample to an ancestry website led authorities to the killer. This case marked a significant moment in forensic science, showing the power of DNA not only in identifying remains but also in identifying living perpetrators of crime.

Dental Records and Forensic Odontology

When DNA is not available or is too degraded to provide a clear profile, forensic odontologists—specialists in dental science—step in to help identify unknown individuals. Teeth, being one of the most durable structures in the human body, often survive even in cases where the rest of the skeleton has deteriorated. Teeth resist decomposition and environmental damage, making them critical in forensic investigations, especially in scenarios involving fire, decomposition, or skeletal remains.

The Structure and Durability of Teeth

Teeth are composed of three main layers: enamel, dentin, and pulp. Enamel, the outermost layer, is the hardest substance in the human body, even stronger than bone. This durability allows teeth to endure extreme conditions, from high temperatures in fires to long periods of burial. The unique patterns in a person's teeth—such as dental work, restorations, fillings, crowns, and even alignment—form a "dental fingerprint" that can be used to match remains to a person's dental records.

How Forensic Odontologists Use Dental Records

Forensic odontologists compare post-mortem dental records with ante-mortem records to identify an individual. These comparisons involve examining unique dental characteristics such as missing teeth, fillings, root canal treatments, crowns, or braces. Even subtle details, such as wear patterns from chewing or evidence of past dental injuries, can help confirm an identification.

In mass disasters, where remains may be severely fragmented or burned, dental records often provide the best means of identification. This was notably the case after the 2004 Indian Ocean tsunami, where thousands of victims were identified through their dental records, which had survived where soft tissue and fingerprints had not.

Challenges in Dental Identification

While dental identification is often highly effective, it is not without challenges. In many cases, individuals may not have detailed dental records on file, especially in less developed regions where access to dental care may be limited. Moreover, in mass disaster scenarios, where hundreds or thousands of individuals are involved, matching post-mortem dental remains to antemortem records can be time-consuming and resource-intensive.

In cases of missing persons or long-term unidentified remains, dental identification relies on whether a person has significant dental work or distinct dental features. For those without detailed records or substantial dental treatments, identification via dental analysis becomes more complex, requiring careful analysis of any existing features.

Facial Reconstruction and Forensic Art

When DNA or dental records fail to provide a match, forensic anthropologists and artists may turn to facial reconstruction to recreate the appearance of unidentified individuals based on their skeletal remains. This process involves rebuilding the face using the underlying bone structure as a guide. Facial reconstruction has solved numerous cases by producing a lifelike image of the person, which can then be circulated to the public or missing persons agencies.

The Science Behind Facial Reconstruction

Facial reconstruction begins with the skull, which provides important clues about an individual's facial features, including the shape of the nose, eyes, and jawline. Forensic anthropologists study the skull's proportions, using statistical data about average tissue depths at various points on the face to recreate soft tissue features. This process can be done manually with clay or digitally using advanced software that generates a three-dimensional image of the face.

Key features that guide reconstruction include:
- The nasal aperture: The shape and width of the nasal cavity can suggest the size and shape of the nose.
- The zygomatic arches: These cheekbones influence the width of the face.

- The mandible: The shape and robustness of the lower jaw suggest the overall jawline and chin shape.

Forensic artists also consider population-specific traits in the skull, such as whether the individual likely belonged to a certain ancestral group, which can affect characteristics like eye shape or nose width.

Technological Advances in Facial Reconstruction

Advances in computer modelling have improved the accuracy of facial reconstructions, making it possible to generate highly realistic digital images from skulls. These images can be adjusted for factors such as age, weight, and ethnicity, providing a more precise depiction of how the individual may have looked in life. In some cases, forensic anthropologists use photos or descriptions from relatives to refine the reconstruction further, enhancing the chances of identification.

Case Studies in Successful Facial

Reconstruction

One of the most famous cases of facial reconstruction was the identification of "The Boy in the Box," a young boy whose body was found in Philadelphia in 1957. Despite multiple attempts to identify him over the years, it wasn't until a facial reconstruction was created that renewed public interest led to more tips, though he remains unidentified to this day.

In another case, facial reconstruction led to the identification of a young woman known as "The Lady of the Dunes," whose mutilated remains were found in Provincetown, Massachusetts, in 1974. The reconstruction created a lifelike image that was shared with the public, leading to new clues about the case.

Challenges in Identifying Unidentified Bodies

Despite the advances in forensic science, identifying

unidentified bodies remains a complex and challenging task. Several factors can hinder the identification process, including the condition of the remains, the availability of antemortem records, and the resources available for investigation.

Environmental Degradation and Incomplete Remains

The condition of the remains is one of the most significant challenges in forensic identification. Environmental factors such as heat, moisture, and scavengers can significantly degrade human remains, making it difficult to extract usable DNA or identify features from the bones. In cases where only partial remains are recovered, forensic anthropologists must rely on limited evidence to construct a biological profile and attempt identification.

Lack of Ante-Mortem Data

The absence of antemortem data, such as dental records or medical history, can also complicate the identification process. In many parts of the world, comprehensive medical or dental records are not readily available, making it difficult to compare post-mortem findings to known individuals. In these cases, forensic teams must rely on public databases or attempt to generate new leads through techniques like DNA phenotyping or facial reconstruction.

The Continuing Evolution of Forensic Identification

Forensic science continues to evolve, and with it, the methods for identifying unidentified remains are becoming increasingly sophisticated. Advances in DNA technology, computer modelling, and data analysis have opened new possibilities for solving cases that once seemed unsolvable. As technology continues to develop, forensic identification will become more accurate and efficient, bringing hope to families waiting for closure and contributing to the resolution of cold cases.

However, the quest to identify the unidentified is more than just a scientific challenge—it is a humanitarian effort to restore names and stories to those who have been lost. As forensic science advances so too does our ability to honour the dignity of the deceased and provide answers to those left behind.

CHAPTER 16: DEALING WITH THE DIGITAL AFTERLIFE: DEATH IN THE INTERNET AGE

The advent of the digital age has revolutionized nearly every facet of modern life, and death is no exception. In centuries past, death was primarily a physical and spiritual event, attended by rituals and legalities tied to the tangible remains of a person's life. However, as technology has woven itself into the fabric of our daily existence, it has created an entirely new dimension: the digital afterlife. With the proliferation of social media accounts, online data, emails, cloud storage, and various digital footprints, the question of what happens to these virtual legacies after death has become increasingly relevant. The digital footprint—once left inadvertently in scattered remnants online—has evolved into a substantial, often meticulously curated, record of one's life.

The complexity of dealing with the digital afterlife reflects the ongoing integration of technology into our identity. No longer confined to physical assets such as properties or heirlooms, a modern individual's estate may also include personal emails, social media profiles, blogs, digital photo albums, cryptocurrency holdings, and much more. Handling these intangible assets requires a nuanced understanding of the legal, ethical, and cultural implications of managing data postmortem. As the boundaries between the physical and the virtual worlds continue to blur, society faces unprecedented challenges in determining how to handle the digital presence of those who are no longer living.

The exploration of death in the context of the Internet age touches upon several areas of concern. First, there is the issue of ownership and privacy: who controls a deceased person's digital assets? This question has sparked legal debates across jurisdictions, as courts and governments grapple with how to regulate access to digital data after death. Second, there is the emotional impact on those left behind, particularly in the context of social media profiles, where a deceased individual's account often lingers as a digital memorial, offering a space for grief, remembrance, and even interaction. Finally, there are the technical and ethical challenges of managing vast amounts of data, some of which may hold personal or sensitive information, raising questions about security and long-term storage.

The digital afterlife represents a new frontier in the human experience of death, where technology intersects with tradition, and where personal identity is preserved not only in memories and legacies passed down but in the data streams we leave behind. The implications of this shift are profound, with both practical and philosophical questions emerging about how we manage the transition from life to death in an era defined by connectivity.

Changing Concepts of Death in the Internet Age

The concept of death has traditionally been rooted in the physical cessation of life and the subsequent processes of mourning, burial, and remembrance. Rituals surrounding death vary across cultures, but the emphasis has historically been on tangible elements: the body, the will, and the belongings left behind. In contrast, the digital age introduces a new paradigm where death does not mark the immediate end of an individual's presence. A person's digital footprint continues to exist, sometimes indefinitely, after their physical death, complicating how we understand the finality of death.

The persistence of digital identities challenges age-old notions of closure. Social media accounts remain active unless intentionally deactivated, allowing the deceased to maintain a posthumous presence online. This phenomenon is exemplified by platforms like Facebook, which offers memorialization options for deceased users' profiles. These accounts can become virtual shrines where friends and family members leave messages, often years after the person has passed away. While this practice can provide comfort and an ongoing sense of connection for the bereaved, it also raises ethical questions about consent and control. Should the dead maintain a digital voice? Who has the authority to manage these accounts, and for how long should they remain accessible?

In many ways, the internet has disrupted the traditional boundaries between life and death. The ease with which people can access and interact with a deceased person's social media profile—viewing their posts, sharing memories, or even tagging them in photos—blurs the line between the living and the dead. Unlike physical mementoes, which are typically archived and carefully curated by loved ones, digital remains are widely accessible, often lacking the same level of intentional preservation. This raises new questions about the durability of online legacies and the role of digital spaces in the mourning process.

As more individuals spend increasing amounts of time online, cultivating personal brands, and sharing intimate details of their lives, the posthumous management of digital identities has become a pressing issue. For many, their online persona is an extension of themselves, encompassing not only public-facing content like social media profiles but also private data stored in emails, cloud drives, and other digital services. The task of managing this information after death is no longer a simple matter of inheritance—it involves navigating complex digital ecosystems where privacy laws, terms of service agreements, and evolving social norms intersect.

Legal and Privacy Implications of Digital Assets

The legal framework governing digital assets after death remains murky and inconsistent, with significant variation across jurisdictions. Unlike physical property, which is generally subject to well-established inheritance laws, digital assets occupy a nebulous legal space. Most digital platforms and service providers operate under terms of service agreements that grant users access to their services during their lifetime but provide little clarity on what happens after death. In many cases, these agreements prohibit anyone other than the account holder from accessing their data, leaving families and executors struggling to retrieve essential information from the deceased's accounts.

In the United States, for example, the Revised Uniform Fiduciary Access to Digital Assets Act (RUFADAA) has been adopted in some states to address the question of access to digital assets by fiduciaries, such as executors or trustees. This law allows account holders to designate who can access their digital assets upon death, provided the service provider offers such an option. However, if no provision is made, the fiduciary may have to rely on court orders or petition the service provider to gain access. This patchwork approach often leaves grieving families in legal limbo, particularly if the deceased did not leave explicit instructions regarding their digital assets.

Internationally, the picture is even more complex. The General Data Protection Regulation (GDPR) in the European Union emphasizes the protection of personal data, making it difficult for families or executors to access a deceased person's online accounts without explicit consent. Under GDPR, service providers are bound to uphold the privacy of the deceased's data unless otherwise directed by the individual before their death. This creates significant barriers to accessing critical information, such as passwords, personal correspondence, or financial data stored online.

The issue of privacy also looms large when considering digital legacies. With so much personal information stored in digital form—ranging from private emails and messages to photos and videos—the question of who accesses this information after death is not easily resolved. In many cases, the deceased may have wanted certain data to remain private, while family members might feel entitled to access everything in the interest of preserving the memory of their loved one. This tension between privacy and remembrance creates ethical dilemmas for those tasked with managing digital estates.

Another layer of complexity arises from the sheer volume of data involved. Many people accumulate vast digital archives throughout their lives, including emails, social media posts, digital photos, videos, and files stored in the cloud. Sorting through and managing this data can be a daunting task for executors, particularly if there are no clear instructions left behind. The prospect of managing digital estates in a world where data accumulation continues to grow exponentially raises important questions about the future of digital inheritance and the role of technology in estate planning.

Digital Memorials and the Emotional Impact on the Bereaved

One of the most visible aspects of the digital afterlife is the emergence of online memorials, particularly through social media platforms like Facebook, Twitter, and Instagram. These platforms allow friends and family to interact with the deceased's digital presence, sharing memories, posting comments, and tagging the deceased in photos long after their death. For many, these digital memorials provide a sense of continuity and a way to keep the memory of the deceased alive.

However, the presence of digital memorials is not without emotional complexities. Some bereaved individuals find solace in continuing to interact with their loved one's online profile, while others may find the experience unsettling. The ability to leave public messages on a deceased person's profile creates a form of "social grieving" that is both unprecedented and challenging to navigate. Unlike physical memorials, which are typically private spaces for reflection, digital memorials are often open to the public, allowing anyone with access to the profile to engage in the grieving process.

This phenomenon has raised important questions about the etiquette of digital grieving. Should there be limits on how long a social media profile remains active after death? Should family members have the right to control or delete the deceased's account, even if it holds sentimental value for others? The role of social media companies in managing these memorials has become a focal point, with some platforms offering specific services for memorializing accounts, while others leave these decisions largely in the hands of the families.

The emotional impact of digital memorials is further complicated by the way algorithms interact with online profiles. For example, on Facebook, a deceased person's account might continue to appear in friends' suggested contacts, or their memories might be triggered by "On This Day" notifications, which can lead to distress for the bereaved. These unintentional reminders of loss are a byproduct of platforms designed to keep users engaged with content, highlighting the disconnect between the technical and emotional realities of managing death in the digital age.

Another consideration is the permanence of digital memorials. Unlike physical memorials, which may be visited infrequently or fade over time, digital memorials exist in a state of constant accessibility. This can create an environment where grieving never fully concludes, as the deceased's digital presence is continually revisited and maintained. The notion of "digital immortality," where a person's online persona remains indefinitely, has sparked philosophical debates about the nature of death and remembrance in the 21st century.

The Challenges of Managing Digital Legacies

Managing digital legacies presents a range of practical, legal, and ethical challenges that differ significantly from traditional estate management. A digital legacy encompasses a wide variety of assets, including social media profiles, email accounts, financial information, and personal data stored on various platforms. The task of organizing, preserving, and distributing these assets is often complicated by the lack of standardized procedures for handling digital estates.

One of the most pressing challenges in managing digital legacies is the issue of access. Without proper planning, family members or executors may be unable to retrieve important information from the deceased's digital accounts. This can be especially problematic in cases where the deceased managed critical aspects of their life, such as financial accounts or personal records, exclusively online. Passwords, security questions, and two-factor authentication protocols can make accessing these accounts nearly impossible without prior arrangements.

To address these challenges, legal and financial experts have increasingly advocated for digital estate planning. This involves creating a comprehensive inventory of digital assets and providing instructions for how they should be managed after death. Many individuals now choose to designate a "digital executor"—someone who is tasked with managing their online accounts and digital assets in the event of their death. Some online services also allow users to set up legacy contacts, who can take over their accounts or request the deletion of the account after the user's death.

Despite these advancements, digital estate planning is still a relatively new concept, and many people are unaware of the steps necessary to ensure that their digital assets are properly managed after death. This has led to a growing demand for legal and financial professionals who specialize in digital estates, as the complexity of navigating multiple platforms and service agreements requires specialized knowledge.

The Future of the Digital Afterlife

As technology continues to evolve, so too will how we manage the digital afterlife. The increasing integration of artificial intelligence, virtual reality, and data storage technologies raises new questions about how we will handle digital legacies in the future. Will people leave behind digital avatars that continue to interact with loved ones after their death? Will artificial intelligence play a role in maintaining a person's digital presence indefinitely? These questions push the boundaries of what it means to die in the digital age and what it means to live on—virtually—after death.

The digital afterlife is a frontier where technology and humanity intersect in unexpected ways. As society grapples with the implications of living more of our lives online, the management of digital legacies will become an increasingly important aspect of estate planning and personal identity. The questions raised by the digital afterlife are not merely legal or technical; they touch upon the very nature of death, remembrance, and what it means to leave behind a legacy in an era defined by connectivity. In this evolving landscape, the digital afterlife stands as both a challenge and an opportunity, offering new ways to memorialize the dead while confronting the complexities of managing a legacy that transcends the physical world.

CHAPTER 17: DEATH BY POISON: CHEMICAL CAUSES OF DEATH

The use of poison as a method of causing death has a long and infamous history, stretching from ancient times to modern criminal cases. It is a practice that blends science, secrecy, and subtlety. Poisons are lethal agents that, when introduced into the body in sufficient quantities, disrupt physiological processes, leading to illness and often death. From a forensic perspective, poisonings present unique challenges because of the variety of toxic substances and the often delayed effects of their action, allowing perpetrators time to escape detection. The discipline of toxicology, the study of the effects of chemicals on living organisms, plays a critical role in uncovering the causes of these deaths, making it a cornerstone of forensic science.

The science of toxicology is complex, involving the analysis of how specific chemicals interact with the body to cause harm or death. Toxic substances can be ingested, inhaled, injected, or absorbed through the skin, each pathway affecting how quickly and severely the poison acts on the body. Some poisons attack specific organs or disrupt particular biochemical pathways, while others may cause general systemic failure. The severity of the poisoning depends on the dose, the individual's health, and the nature of the poison itself. The work of forensic toxicologists is crucial in determining not only the presence of a toxic substance but also understanding how it contributed to the death.

Throughout history, certain poisons have gained notoriety for their use in high-profile murders and assassinations. Arsenic, cyanide, strychnine, and more recently, nerve agents such as Novichok, have all been employed with deadly intent. These substances have shaped toxicology's evolution as forensic scientists have developed increasingly sophisticated methods to detect and analyse them, even in trace amounts. Historical poisoning cases are often pivotal moments in the development of forensic toxicology, as each case has driven advancements in detection techniques and the understanding of how poisons operate in the human body.

Poison is often considered the weapon of the subtle and calculated criminal, as it leaves no immediate visible wounds or overt signs of violence. However, the physiological damage inflicted by poison can be profound, targeting critical systems within the body, from the central nervous system to the cardiovascular system. This chapter explores the mechanisms by which various poisons cause death, the historical significance of famous poisoning cases, and the techniques forensic scientists use to uncover the often hidden truth behind toxic deaths.

The Science of Poisons and Their Effects on the Body

Poisons, by definition, are substances that cause harm or death when introduced to a living organism. The study of how these substances interact with the human body, known as toxicokinetics and toxicodynamics, is essential to understanding how poisoning occurs. Toxicokinetics refers to the absorption, distribution, metabolism, and excretion (ADME) of toxic substances, while toxicodynamics focuses on the interaction between the toxic substance and the biological target that leads to toxic effects.

Poisons can enter the body through several routes. The most common routes are ingestion, inhalation, and injection, though some poisons can also be absorbed through the skin. Once inside the body, poisons can act at the cellular level, interfering with the normal biochemical processes that sustain life. Depending on the type of poison, the effects can range from immediate death to prolonged illness followed by death, with varying degrees of physical suffering.

Many poisons target specific organs or systems within the body. For instance, neurotoxins such as cyanide or nerve agents act on the nervous system, blocking the enzymes responsible for neurotransmission and resulting in the cessation of vital functions such as breathing. Hemotoxins, on the other hand, target the blood, disrupting its ability to carry oxygen or causing catastrophic clotting disorders, as is seen with poisons like hemlock or snake venoms.

The liver plays a central role in the metabolism of poisons, attempting to detoxify the substances by converting them into less harmful metabolites through enzymatic reactions. However, in many cases, these metabolic processes can lead to the production of even more toxic compounds, which continue to damage tissues and organs. The kidneys are responsible for excreting many toxins, but prolonged exposure can lead to renal failure, compounding the effects of the poison.

The dose-response relationship is a fundamental principle of toxicology, stating that "the dose makes the poison." This concept, first articulated by Paracelsus in the 16th century, underscores the idea that even substances commonly regarded as harmless, such as water or salt, can become toxic when consumed in excessive amounts. Conversely, some poisons, such as botulinum toxin, are so potent that even minute quantities can result in death.

In forensic toxicology, understanding how these substances affect the body is essential for determining whether poisoning was the cause of death and identifying the specific poison responsible. Toxicologists work in collaboration with pathologists during autopsies, analysing blood, urine, tissue samples, and sometimes even hair to detect the presence of toxins and interpret their impact on the body.

Historical Cases of Poisoning

Some of the most notorious poisoning cases in history have shaped public perceptions of poison as a weapon and driven the advancement of forensic toxicology. Arsenic, for instance, earned the moniker "the inheritance powder" during the 18th and 19th centuries due to its widespread use in criminal acts. Tasteless, odourless, and difficult to detect with early forensic methods, arsenic was the poison of choice for those wishing to dispose of rivals or family members without drawing immediate suspicion.

One of the most infamous cases of arsenic poisoning was that of Mary Ann Cotton, a 19th-century Englishwoman who was convicted of murdering her husbands, children, and others with arsenic to collect on life insurance policies. Cotton's case highlighted the lethal potential of arsenic and the challenges forensic scientists faced in detecting it. Early toxicologists, including the famous French chemist Mathieu Orfila, developed tests to detect arsenic in biological samples, marking the beginning of modern forensic toxicology.

Cyanide, another highly toxic substance, has also been associated with several high-profile deaths. Cyanide acts quickly by inhibiting cytochrome c oxidase, an enzyme essential for cellular respiration. Without this enzyme, cells are unable to use oxygen to produce energy, leading to cellular asphyxiation and death within minutes. The cyanide poisoning of Jonestown, Guyana, in 1978, remains one of the most horrific examples of mass poisoning. Over 900 members of the Peoples Temple, a religious cult led by Jim Jones, died after ingesting cyanide-laced punch in a mass suicide-murder orchestrated by Jones. The speed and efficiency with which cyanide acts make it a particularly devastating poison.

Thallium, known as the "poisoner's poison," is another substance notorious for its use in criminal cases due to its slow and often subtle effects. In the 20th century, thallium gained attention in the case of Graham Young, a British man who, starting as a teenager, poisoned multiple family members and coworkers with thallium, studying the effects on his victims. Young's case underscored the dangers of poisons that act slowly, mimicking natural diseases and making detection difficult without detailed toxicological analysis.

Another famous historical case involved the mysterious death of Russian mystic Grigori Rasputin in 1916. Rasputin was reportedly poisoned with cyanide by political conspirators, though he survived the initial poisoning attempt. His eventual death, which involved additional methods of murder, remains one of history's most discussed assassination plots, illustrating the challenges in determining how multiple forms of violence interact in death.

These historical cases serve as milestones in the development of forensic toxicology, as each case presented unique challenges that required advancements in detection methods. Poisoners have often relied on their victims' ignorance of toxicology, but with each high-profile case, toxicologists have expanded their understanding of how poisons work and how they can be detected.

Detecting Poisons in the Body

The detection of poisons in the body requires sophisticated laboratory techniques and a deep understanding of how toxins interact with biological systems. Forensic toxicologists use a variety of methods to identify and quantify toxic substances in bodily fluids and tissues. These methods must be sensitive enough to detect even trace amounts of poison, as many substances can be lethal at low concentrations.

One of the most common techniques used in toxicology is gas chromatography-mass spectrometry (GC-MS). This method allows toxicologists to separate chemical compounds based on their physical properties and identify them by their mass-to-charge ratio. GC-MS is highly effective for detecting volatile compounds, such as alcohols, organic solvents, and some drugs. For poisons like cyanide, which are volatile and act quickly, GC-MS can provide rapid and definitive identification.

For non-volatile compounds, such as heavy metals like arsenic, lead, or thallium, atomic absorption spectroscopy (AAS) or inductively coupled plasma mass spectrometry (ICP-MS) is often used. These techniques are capable of detecting very low levels of metals in biological samples, which is crucial for cases where chronic exposure to low doses of poison may have occurred. AAS measures the absorption of light by atoms in a sample, providing a direct measure of the concentration of a particular metal. ICP-MS, on the other hand, uses plasma to ionize the sample and then measures the mass of the ions, offering highly sensitive detection even in complex biological matrices.

High-performance liquid chromatography (HPLC) is another essential tool in the toxicologist's arsenal, particularly for detecting drugs and other non-volatile organic compounds. HPLC separates compounds based on their interactions with a liquid mobile phase and a solid stationary phase, allowing for the detection of poisons that are less volatile or more complex in structure.

Immunoassay techniques, such as enzyme-linked immunosorbent assays (ELISA), are used to detect specific toxins or drugs based on their interaction with antibodies. These methods are particularly useful in cases of drug overdose, as they can quickly detect the presence of drugs like opioids, barbiturates, or benzodiazepines in blood or urine samples.

Forensic toxicologists also rely on post-mortem toxicology reports to determine the cause of death. During an autopsy, samples of blood, urine, liver, kidney, and sometimes hair or bone are collected for analysis. The choice of sample depends on the type of poison suspected and the time elapsed since death. For example, blood is ideal for detecting poisons that act quickly and are metabolized rapidly, while hair samples can provide a long-term record of exposure to certain toxins.

Toxicologists must also consider the possibility of contamination or environmental exposure to poisons, which can complicate the interpretation of toxicology results. In cases where decomposition has occurred, certain chemicals produced during the breakdown of tissues can mimic the presence of toxins, requiring careful analysis to avoid false positives.

How Poisons Cause Death: Mechanisms of Action

The mechanisms by which poisons cause death vary depending on the chemical properties of the substance and its target within the body. Broadly speaking, poisons disrupt the normal functioning of cells, tissues, or organs, leading to the failure of critical physiological systems. Poisons may act at the molecular level, interfering with enzymes, receptors, or ion channels, or they may cause direct damage to tissues by generating reactive oxygen species or inducing necrosis.

Neurotoxins, such as cyanide and organophosphates, target the nervous system by disrupting neurotransmission. Cyanide inhibits the enzyme cytochrome c oxidase, which is necessary for the production of ATP in the mitochondria. Without ATP, cells cannot produce the energy needed to sustain life, leading to rapid cell death. This mechanism is particularly devastating to tissues that have high energy demands, such as the heart and brain, leading to cardiac arrest and loss of brain function.

Organophosphates, which are found in certain pesticides and nerve agents, inhibit the enzyme acetylcholinesterase, leading to an accumulation of acetylcholine at nerve synapses. This causes continuous stimulation of muscles, glands, and the central nervous system, resulting in convulsions, respiratory failure, and death. The use of organophosphates in chemical warfare, as seen in the 1995 Tokyo subway sarin attack, underscores the lethal efficiency of neurotoxins and the challenges faced in treating exposed individuals.

Hemotoxins, such as those found in snake venom, affect the blood's ability to clot or carry oxygen. Some hemotoxins disrupt the blood coagulation cascade, leading to uncontrolled bleeding, while others destroy red blood cells, resulting in haemolytic anaemia and organ failure. Arsenic, which interferes with the production of ATP by inhibiting pyruvate dehydrogenase, also acts as a hemotoxin by causing widespread cellular dysfunction and multisystem organ failure.

The Role of Forensic Toxicology in Uncovering Poisonings

Forensic toxicology is an essential field in the investigation of suspicious deaths, particularly those involving poisons. The ability to detect and interpret the presence of toxic substances in the body is critical for establishing the cause of death and identifying the poison responsible. The history of poisoning cases has driven the evolution of toxicology as a scientific discipline, leading to the development of more sensitive and accurate methods for detecting poisons, even in cases where they are present in minute quantities.

The complexity of poisons and their diverse mechanisms of action require a deep understanding of chemistry, biology, and medicine. As new toxins are discovered and new methods of poisoning are developed, forensic toxicologists must continually adapt and refine their techniques to stay ahead of those who would use poison as a weapon. The historical and scientific significance of poisoning cases underscores the importance of this field in both criminal investigations and public health.

CHAPTER 18: DYING IN SPACE: THE SCIENCE OF DEATH IN EXTREME ENVIRONMENTS

The prospect of space travel has always been associated with adventure, discovery, and the pushing of human boundaries. As humanity moves closer to the reality of long-term space exploration and potential colonization of other planets, it becomes necessary to confront the physiological and existential challenges posed by the most unforgiving environment known to humankind—space. Amid the excitement of reaching beyond Earth's atmosphere lies an uncomfortable question: what happens to the human body in the event of death in space? In extreme environments where familiar Earth-bound rules no longer apply, the nature of dying, as well as the biological and physical consequences of death, take on entirely new dimensions.

Space is a vacuum, devoid of the air and atmospheric pressure essential for human life. It is a realm where the absence of gravity, the presence of high-energy radiation, and the lack of oxygen define a unique set of conditions that make survival for humans impossible without extensive technological assistance. The human body, which evolved under Earth's protective environment, faces immediate and severe threats in space, including the rapid onset of hypoxia, exposure to harmful radiation, and the physical effects of zero gravity. For decades, science fiction has grappled with the idea of death in space, but the realities of what happens to a person's body when exposed to such conditions are grounded in scientific principles that are only now becoming fully understood.

This chapter explores the various factors that contribute to the human experience of death in space, from the immediate physiological responses to the vacuum of space to the longer-term consequences of exposure to radiation and microgravity. Furthermore, it considers the practical challenges of dealing with human remains in space, particularly as long-term missions to Mars or beyond come closer to realization. Understanding death in space requires a detailed examination of how extreme environments affect the body and the scientific principles that govern these effects. In many ways, dying in space is a stark reminder of the fragility of the human body in the face of the cosmos.

The Immediate Effects of Exposure to the Vacuum of Space

One of the most well-known dangers associated with space is the vacuum, an environment completely devoid of atmospheric pressure. On Earth, the air we breathe exerts pressure on our bodies, maintaining equilibrium with the internal pressure of our biological systems. This balance is critical to our survival. In space, where there is no atmospheric pressure, this equilibrium is abruptly disrupted, causing rapid and catastrophic physiological effects.

When a human is exposed to the vacuum of space without protective equipment, death would occur in a matter of minutes, primarily due to the lack of oxygen and the dramatic pressure differential. The vacuum of space causes immediate hypoxia, or oxygen deprivation, leading to unconsciousness within 15 seconds. The brain, being the most oxygen-dependent organ, quickly ceases to function without a supply of oxygenated blood. Hypoxia is compounded by the vacuum's effect on the body's fluids. In a pressurized environment, liquids in the body, including blood, are kept in a liquid state. However, in a vacuum, the pressure drop allows these fluids to boil at much lower temperatures than they would on Earth. Although human skin and blood vessels are capable of withstanding some degree of pressure change, the lack of atmospheric pressure in space would cause the moisture in a person's mouth, eyes, and respiratory tract to vaporize almost instantly, causing extreme discomfort and rapid tissue damage.

Despite common depictions in popular media, the human body would not explode in space. Instead, the skin and underlying tissue would swell as gases expanded within the body's tissues. This phenomenon, known as ebullism, occurs when gas bubbles form within bodily fluids due to the drastic reduction in pressure. Ebullism would cause significant swelling, particularly in the hands and face, but the body's structural integrity would remain intact. However, the damage caused by gas expansion, coupled with hypoxia, would quickly lead to death if no immediate intervention occurred.

In addition to hypoxia and ebullism, exposure to the vacuum of space leads to severe thermal imbalances. Space, while cold in many respects, does not allow for heat transfer in the traditional sense. The vacuum prevents heat loss through convection, meaning that the body would lose heat only through radiation. A person exposed to space might initially experience extreme cold in areas directly facing away from the sun, but they would not freeze instantly as heat loss in a vacuum is a slower process than in an atmosphere. Conversely, areas of the body exposed to direct sunlight would heat up rapidly, as there is no atmosphere to filter the sun's radiation. These thermal extremes would exacerbate the already fatal conditions caused by hypoxia and ebullism.

It is worth noting that the human body can briefly survive exposure to space if rescued quickly. The longest known exposure of a human to near-vacuum conditions occurred during a 1965 test when a NASA technician was accidentally exposed to a vacuum chamber at approximately 120,000 feet of altitude. He lost consciousness in 15 seconds but was successfully revived after being exposed to air within 25 seconds. Such cases demonstrate that while space exposure is deadly, death is not instantaneous, and there remains a small window for survival in very limited circumstances.

The Impact of Radiation on the Human Body

Radiation in space poses a significant risk to both living astronauts and the bodies of the deceased. Earth's magnetic field and atmosphere shield living organisms from most of the harmful effects of cosmic radiation, but once beyond this protective layer, the intensity of radiation increases dramatically. Space is filled with high-energy particles, including protons, heavy ions, and electrons, originating from the sun and other cosmic sources. These particles can penetrate deep into human tissue, causing damage at the cellular and molecular levels.

For a living person, prolonged exposure to radiation in space can lead to both short-term and long-term health effects. Acute radiation sickness, characterized by nausea, vomiting, and fatigue, occurs after high doses of radiation exposure. In extreme cases, this can lead to death as radiation damages the cells lining the digestive tract and impairs the body's ability to regenerate tissue. Over the long term, radiation exposure increases the risk of cancer, as DNA within cells is damaged, leading to mutations and the uncontrolled growth of cells. This is a significant concern for astronauts on long-duration space missions, such as those planned for Mars, where radiation exposure over many months or years may exceed safe limits.

In the context of death in space, radiation continues to affect the body after death, though the impact is more relevant from a forensic and scientific standpoint. Radiation can break down tissues at the cellular level, causing gradual degradation of DNA and other biological molecules. This process complicates efforts to recover or analyse bodies exposed to space for extended periods, as the structural integrity of tissues may be compromised by radiation damage. Furthermore, the preservation of bodies in space is influenced by radiation in conjunction with other environmental factors, such as temperature and vacuum exposure.

In the case of future space missions, particularly those involving long-term colonization of other planets, managing radiation exposure will be a critical concern, not only for the living but also in the event of death. The risk of radiation-induced degradation means that any plans for space burials or long-term storage of human remains must account for the potentially damaging effects of cosmic radiation. Shielding from radiation may be necessary to preserve remains, whether for scientific study or for reasons of cultural significance.

Death in Microgravity: The Effects of Zero Gravity on the Body

Microgravity, a condition of near-weightlessness experienced in space, has profound effects on the human body, even in life. Astronauts who spend extended periods in microgravity environments experience muscle atrophy, bone density loss, and cardiovascular deconditioning, all of which result from the lack of gravitational force on the body's systems. In life, these effects can be mitigated through exercise and other countermeasures, but the physiological consequences of living in microgravity provide insight into what happens to the body after death in space.

When a person dies in microgravity, many of the usual post-mortem processes that occur on Earth, such as the settling of blood and fluids due to gravity (livor mortis), do not occur in the same way. In microgravity, the body's fluids remain suspended, dispersing more evenly throughout the body rather than pooling in the lower extremities. This alters the typical appearance of a body after death, as the usual signs of lividity (the purplish discolouration that occurs as blood settles in the veins and capillaries) are absent.

Rigour mortis, the stiffening of muscles after death, would still occur in space, as it is a process driven by the depletion of adenosine triphosphate (ATP) in muscle cells, causing them to contract. However, the lack of gravity may influence how rigor mortis manifests, particularly in terms of positioning. Without the force of gravity to hold the body in a fixed position, the limbs and torso may remain more flexible for a longer period before stiffening fully sets in.

Decomposition in space is another process affected by the absence of gravity and atmospheric pressure. On Earth, decomposition is driven by the action of bacteria, enzymes, and the natural breakdown of tissues as cells die. In space, where there is no atmosphere and extreme cold can preserve biological material, decomposition may be slowed significantly or halted altogether. The vacuum of space would rapidly desiccate the body, essentially mummifying it in a short period, provided it was not exposed to other environmental factors such as radiation or heat from the sun. The lack of microorganisms in space also means that the usual putrefaction caused by bacterial activity would not occur, further preserving the body in a relatively stable state for longer periods than would be expected on Earth.

In closed environments, such as a spacecraft or space station, where microgravity is present but atmospheric conditions are controlled, the

decomposition process would more closely resemble that on Earth, though with some differences due to the lack of gravitational effects on fluid movement and tissue settling. This raises important questions about how human remains would be managed in such environments, particularly on long-duration missions where the presence of a deceased crew member could pose a health risk to the living.

The Science of Space Burials: Challenges and Considerations

As space exploration advances, the prospect of space burials becomes increasingly relevant. The idea of burying or disposing of bodies in space may seem far-fetched but for missions to Mars or beyond, where the return of human remains to Earth may be impractical, the question of how to handle human remains in space must be addressed.

One possibility for space burials involves sending bodies into deep space, allowing them to drift away from Earth and other celestial bodies. This method would be relatively simple, requiring minimal resources beyond the energy needed to propel the body out of orbit. However, ethical considerations arise regarding the potential for human remains to drift indefinitely in space, particularly if future generations encounter these remains during their explorations. The cultural and psychological implications of abandoning human bodies to the void of space must also be considered.

Another option for managing human remains in space is

cremation, which would reduce the body to ashes that could either be stored aboard the spacecraft or released into space. Cremation in space, however, presents significant technical challenges. The process requires both oxygen and high temperatures, which are not readily available in space environments. Moreover, the release of particulate matter from cremation could pose risks to spacecraft systems, particularly if the ashes are not contained properly.

For missions to Mars or other planets, the burial of human remains on the surface may be a more viable option. Mars, with its thin atmosphere and extreme cold, would naturally preserve bodies for extended periods, similar to how the permafrost preserves organic material on Earth. However, radiation exposure on Mars is a concern, and any burial process would need to consider the potential for radiation to degrade the remains over time. Additionally, burial on another planet raises important ethical questions about contamination and the potential for introducing Earth-based microbes into extraterrestrial environments.

The concept of space burials also touches on cultural and religious traditions surrounding death. Different cultures have specific rituals and beliefs about the treatment of the dead, and these beliefs may influence how space agencies and future space travellers approach the subject of death in space. The development of space burial practices will likely require input from ethicists, religious leaders, and cultural anthropologists, in addition to scientists and engineers.

Death in Space and Its Implications for Human Exploration

As humanity ventures deeper into space, the inevitability of death in extreme environments must be considered. The physiological effects of exposure to the vacuum of space, radiation, and microgravity all present unique challenges to both the living and the deceased. The science of death in space is a reminder of the fragility of human life in the face of the vast and hostile cosmos.

The future of space exploration will require careful planning for how to manage death in space, whether through space burials, cremation, or other methods of dealing with human remains. The practical, ethical, and cultural implications of death in space will play a critical role in shaping how humanity approaches its exploration of the final frontier.

CHAPTER 19: THE BRAIN AFTER DEATH: WHAT WE KNOW SO FAR

The brain, a complex organ responsible for controlling every function of the human body, stands as the final frontier in understanding death. When the brain dies, it marks the irreversible cessation of life, but the journey towards that cessation is fraught with scientific intrigue. Brain death, while largely accepted in the medical community, still raises questions among scientists, ethicists, and the public about when a person truly dies. In contrast, cardiac death, marked by the stopping of the heart, has long been considered the quintessential marker of death. However, with the increasing understanding of brain function and its critical role in sustaining life, brain death has emerged as the focal point in discussions about human mortality.

What happens to the brain as it approaches death, and what transpires in its final moments, has captivated scientists for decades. In recent years, technological advances have allowed researchers to observe brain activity in unprecedented detail, challenging previous assumptions about the exact moment death occurs. There is now evidence suggesting that certain neural processes continue for minutes or even longer after the heart stops beating, leading to a profound re-examination of our understanding of brain death. This chapter delves into the science of brain death, exploring how the brain shuts down, the timeline of its final moments, and the lingering activity that occurs after clinical death. The debate over brain death versus cardiac death, once considered distinct, is now becoming more nuanced as scientific discoveries reveal a more complex relationship between these two markers of death.

The brain's decline begins long before death becomes apparent. The process of dying is not instantaneous but rather a progression of shutting down physiological systems, with the brain as the final arbiter of life and death. This chapter examines this journey, from the first signs of brain dysfunction to the moment when brain death is declared. Additionally, we will explore what scientific research has uncovered about the brain's activity after clinical death, a topic that has fascinated neuroscientists and contributed to the ongoing debate over the definition of death itself.

The Process of Brain Death: The Gradual Shutdown of Vital Functions

Brain death is a condition in which all brain activity has irreversibly ceased, leading to the permanent loss of consciousness, the ability to breathe independently, and the regulation of bodily functions. It is a state where the brain has lost all function, including that of the brainstem, which controls fundamental reflexes like breathing and maintaining heart rate. The onset of brain death can occur due to various causes, including traumatic brain injury, stroke, lack of oxygen (anoxia), or prolonged cardiac arrest. Whatever the cause, the progression towards brain death follows a predictable pattern of neurological decline, beginning with localized brain dysfunction and culminating in the global failure of the brain's structures.

The first sign of impending brain death is often a loss of consciousness, which occurs when the brain's higher cortical functions are compromised. This can be caused by swelling of the brain (cerebral oedema), which exerts pressure on the brainstem and other critical regions. As the brain swells, it compresses the blood vessels that supply oxygenated blood to the neurons, further exacerbating damage and leading to ischemia, a condition where brain tissue is deprived of oxygen. Ischemia quickly sets off a cascade of events that accelerate neuronal death, as the energy-dependent processes that maintain cellular integrity begin to fail. Neurons, the functional units of the brain, are particularly sensitive to oxygen deprivation, and without an adequate supply, they rapidly lose the ability to generate electrical impulses that facilitate communication across brain regions.

As ischemia spreads, areas of the brain responsible for regulating essential body functions begin to shut down. The brainstem, which governs autonomic functions like breathing, heart rate, and blood pressure, is among the last areas to be affected, but once compromised, it signals the final stage of the dying process. With the brainstem's failure, spontaneous breathing ceases, necessitating mechanical ventilation if the person is to be kept alive artificially. At this point, the individual enters a state of coma, characterized by the complete absence of consciousness and the inability to respond to stimuli. If the brainstem's functions cannot be restored, the individual will progress to brain death, marked by the cessation of all neurological activity.

Determining brain death is a rigorous process that involves a series of clinical tests to confirm the complete and irreversible loss of brain function. These tests, which are standard in most parts of the world, include checking for the absence of cranial nerve reflexes, such as the pupillary light reflex (where the pupils constrict in response to light), and the corneal reflex (blinking when the cornea is touched). The absence of these reflexes indicates brainstem dysfunction. Additionally, apnoea tests are conducted to confirm the absence of spontaneous breathing. During an apnoea test, the patient is removed from a ventilator for a brief period while being closely monitored. If carbon dioxide levels in the blood rise to a certain threshold without triggering an attempt to breathe, it is a clear indication that the brainstem is no longer functioning. Brain death is officially declared only after multiple rounds of testing, often supplemented by neuroimaging techniques such as electroencephalography (EEG) or cerebral angiography to further confirm the absence of brain activity.

The Final Moments of Brain Activity: Insights from Scientific Research

One of the most remarkable findings in recent neurological research is the observation that the brain continues to exhibit activity for a short period after death, challenging the traditional view that brain death is a sudden and total cessation of function. Instead, the dying brain appears to undergo a series of distinct physiological changes, with some neural networks continuing to fire for minutes after clinical death is declared. This discovery has fuelled ongoing discussions about the exact timing of death and the potential implications for medical decision-making.

Research has shown that when the heart stops beating, the brain does not immediately cease all activity. Instead, as the blood supply to the brain is cut off, neurons begin to fire rapidly, in what is sometimes referred to as a "brainstorm." This phenomenon is characterized by a surge of electrical activity as the brain attempts to maintain homeostasis in the face of declining oxygen levels. These electrical bursts may be a final, desperate attempt by the brain to restore normal function, but without oxygenated blood to sustain them, the neurons soon succumb to energy depletion, and widespread neuronal death follows.

One study, conducted by researchers at the University of Michigan, involved monitoring the brain activity of rats during induced cardiac arrest. The researchers found that in the moments following the cessation of the heart, the rats' brains exhibited a sudden spike in synchronized neural activity, followed by a rapid decline as brain function progressively shut down. The implications of these findings for human death are profound, as they suggest that the brain may remain active and even coordinated for a brief window of time after the heart has stopped. Although similar studies have yet to be replicated in humans, the existence of a post-cardiac arrest brain surge in other mammals indicates that the human brain may follow a similar trajectory.

Another significant area of research has explored the brain's ability to retain a level of consciousness or awareness in the immediate aftermath of cardiac arrest. Reports from survivors of cardiac arrest, who are successfully resuscitated, often describe out-of-body experiences or a sense of heightened awareness during the period in which they were clinically dead. While these experiences are subjective and difficult to verify, they raise intriguing questions about what happens to the brain during the early stages of death. Some neuroscientists hypothesize that these experiences may be related to the brain's final bursts of electrical activity, though the exact mechanisms remain poorly understood.

The possibility that the brain continues to exhibit structured activity after cardiac death has led to a reconsideration of how death is defined. Traditionally, cardiac death, marked by the stopping of the heart and the cessation of blood flow, was considered the definitive marker of death. However, the discovery that the brain can remain active for a short period post-cardiac death complicates this view, suggesting that death is not an instantaneous event but a process that unfolds over several minutes, with the final moments of brain activity representing the true endpoint.

Brain Death versus Cardiac Death: The Ongoing Debate

The distinction between brain death and cardiac death has been the subject of considerable debate within the medical community, particularly as advances in resuscitation technology have blurred the line between life and death. Cardiac death occurs when the heart stops beating, and blood flow to the brain and other vital organs is halted. This can lead to brain death if circulation is not quickly restored. However, with the advent of cardiopulmonary resuscitation (CPR) and defibrillation, many individuals who experience cardiac arrest are successfully revived, sometimes after several minutes without a heartbeat.

Brain death, on the other hand, is defined by the total and irreversible loss of brain function, including the brainstem. It is considered a more definitive marker of death because, unlike the heart, the brain cannot be revived once its neurons have died. The brain's reliance on a constant supply of oxygenated blood makes it uniquely vulnerable to damage, and once brain cells die, they cannot regenerate. This is why brain death, rather than cardiac death, has become the accepted criterion for legal death in many countries, particularly when organ donation is involved.

However, the distinction between brain death and cardiac death is not always clear-cut, particularly in cases of prolonged cardiac arrest. Some argue that brain death is an artificial construct, used primarily for medical ethics and organ transplantation, while cardiac death remains the true biological marker of death. Critics of the brain death standard point out that the heart can continue beating with the help of mechanical support, even after the brain has ceased functioning. In such cases, the individual is technically alive, even though their brain is irreversibly damaged.

Proponents of the brain death standard counter that the brain is the organ that defines human identity and consciousness. Once the brain has ceased to function, the individual has effectively lost all of the qualities that make them a person, even if their body can be maintained through artificial means. This view is supported by the fact that brain-dead individuals cannot breathe independently, regulate their body temperature, or respond to external stimuli. In this sense, brain death represents a more complete and irreversible form of death than cardiac arrest, which may still be reversible in some cases.

The debate over brain death versus cardiac death is further complicated by advances in medical technology that can artificially sustain bodily functions long after the brain has stopped functioning. Mechanical ventilation, for example, can keep the heart beating and the lungs oxygenating blood even in the absence of brain activity. In such cases, the individual may appear alive from a purely physiological perspective, but brain death has rendered them incapable of consciousness or recovery. This raises difficult ethical questions about how and when life support should be withdrawn, particularly when families are faced with the decision to end life-sustaining treatment for a brain-dead loved one.

Scientific Discoveries About Brain Activity After Death

One of the most striking discoveries in recent years is the observation of low-frequency brainwaves that persist after death. While these brainwaves are not indicative of consciousness, they suggest that the brain continues to process information, albeit at a reduced level, after clinical death has been declared. These low-frequency oscillations, which are known as delta waves, are typically associated with deep sleep or unconscious states. However, their presence after death raises important questions about the nature of brain activity in the final moments of life.

In 2018, a team of Canadian neuroscientists conducted a study in which they monitored the brain activity of patients who had been declared clinically dead. Remarkably, in one case, the researchers observed delta wave activity more than 10 minutes after the patient's heart had stopped beating. The significance of this finding is still being debated, as it is unclear whether these brainwaves represent any form of residual consciousness or simply the last vestiges of neurological function before the brain shuts down entirely.

These findings have also fuelled interest in the potential for brain resuscitation. While current medical technology is not capable of reviving a brain that has undergone prolonged oxygen deprivation, the discovery of post-mortem brain activity has led some researchers to explore the possibility of delaying or reversing brain death under certain conditions. For example, experiments with hypothermia have shown that cooling the brain can slow the process of neuronal death, allowing for a longer window of time in which resuscitation might be possible.

One of the most controversial areas of research in this field is the use of brain organoids, which are miniature, lab-grown versions of the human brain. These organoids are created from stem cells and exhibit many of the same structural and functional properties as the human brain, including the ability to generate electrical activity. While brain organoids are far from being fully developed brains, they offer a glimpse into the future of neuroscience and raise ethical questions about the potential for regenerating brain function after death.

The Brain's Final Frontier

The brain's role in death remains one of the most mysterious and scientifically compelling aspects of human mortality. As the organ that defines consciousness, identity, and life itself, the brain's gradual shutdown during death is a complex and multifaceted process that continues to challenge scientists and ethicists alike. While brain death is widely accepted as the definitive marker of death in modern medicine, new research into post-mortem brain activity suggests that death is not an instantaneous event but a process that unfolds over time.

The ongoing debate over brain death versus cardiac death reflects the evolving understanding of what it means to die, as advances in resuscitation technology and neuroscience push the boundaries of life and death. As scientists continue to explore the brain's final moments, the definition of death may become more fluid, raising profound questions about human identity, consciousness, and the limits of medical intervention.

Here is Chapter 20: Near-Death Experiences: What Science Says, written with a clinical and information-rich approach suitable for academic citation.

CHAPTER 20: NEAR-DEATH EXPERIENCES: WHAT SCIENCE SAYS

Near-death experiences (NDEs) have fascinated both scientists and the public for decades, straddling the line between personal anecdotes and scientific inquiry. These phenomena, which are commonly reported by individuals who have been close to death or have temporarily died and then been resuscitated, often involve vivid descriptions of events that defy conventional understanding. Accounts of NDEs include a wide variety of features, such as feelings of peace, detachment from the physical body, visions of a bright light or tunnel, and encounters with deceased loved ones or spiritual beings. While these experiences are often deeply transformative for those who report them, the scientific community remains divided over their interpretation.

NDEs are particularly challenging to study because of their subjective nature. They occur under conditions where scientific observation is typically not possible, such as during cardiac arrest, severe trauma, or coma. This lack of direct observation, coupled with the emotional and spiritual significance that many individuals attach to these experiences, makes it difficult to draw definitive conclusions. Nevertheless, over the past several decades, researchers in fields ranging from neuroscience to psychology have endeavoured to understand the mechanisms behind NDEs and to assess whether they can be explained by natural, physiological processes, or if they point to something beyond the material world.

This chapter explores the scientific study of near-death experiences, focusing on the neurological and psychological explanations that have been proposed. We will examine the recurring themes that characterize NDEs, such as tunnel vision, out-of-body experiences, and feelings of euphoria, and evaluate the research that seeks to explain these phenomena. By examining the available evidence, we aim to provide a balanced understanding of what science currently says about near-death experiences, without venturing into metaphysical speculation. Although many questions remain unanswered, the scientific investigation of NDEs continues to offer valuable insights into the workings of the brain and consciousness, particularly at the boundary between life and death.

Common Features of Near-Death Experiences

The experiences reported by individuals who have undergone NDEs are remarkably consistent, despite varying cultural, religious, and personal backgrounds. Most accounts describe a series of events that follow a general pattern, though the details can vary significantly from person to person. One of the most frequently reported features of NDEs is a sense of detachment from the physical body, often described as an out-of-body experience (OBE). During an OBE, individuals claim to observe their surroundings, sometimes even witnessing medical personnel attempting to resuscitate them, as though they were floating above their bodies.

Another common feature of NDEs is the sensation of moving

through a tunnel toward a bright light. This tunnel vision is often accompanied by a sense of acceleration and feelings of euphoria, peace, or love. Many individuals report encountering deceased relatives or spiritual entities, who may offer comfort or guidance during the experience. In some cases, individuals describe reaching a boundary or barrier, beyond which they cannot or should not pass, and then being told that it is not yet their time to die, prompting their return to life.

Feelings of time distortion are also frequently reported. Some individuals describe a sense of timelessness or the perception that time has slowed down or stopped altogether. Others recall experiencing a rapid review of their life, where key moments are replayed in vivid detail, often accompanied by an emotional or moral evaluation of their actions. This life review is one of the most intriguing aspects of NDEs, as it suggests that the brain is capable of accessing and processing vast amounts of autobiographical memory, even under conditions of extreme physiological stress.

Despite the similarities among NDE reports, the interpretation of these experiences varies widely. Some individuals view their NDEs as proof of an afterlife or spiritual realm, while others interpret them as psychological or neurobiological phenomena. This divergence in interpretation has fuelled ongoing debate among scientists, particularly in the fields of neuroscience, psychology, and religious studies. To understand these experiences from a scientific perspective, it is necessary to examine the physiological and neurological processes that occur during near-death states.

Neurological Explanations for Near-Death Experiences

The brain, under normal circumstances, is a highly organized and structured organ, with various regions responsible for different cognitive and physiological functions. However, when the body is under extreme stress—such as during cardiac arrest, trauma, or oxygen deprivation—this delicate balance is disrupted. During these moments, the brain is deprived of the oxygen and glucose it needs to function, leading to widespread neuronal dysfunction. Many researchers believe that near-death experiences are the result of the brain's response to these extreme conditions, as it enters a hyperactive or disorganized state in its final moments before shutting down.

One of the most prominent neurological theories regarding NDEs is that they are the result of a lack of oxygen to the brain, a condition known as cerebral hypoxia. During cardiac arrest or other life-threatening events, the brain's oxygen supply is severely compromised, leading to the rapid deterioration of brain function. Hypoxia can cause hallucinations, confusion, and altered states of consciousness, which may account for many of the features associated with NDEs, such as tunnel vision, euphoria, and OBEs. The tunnel effect, for example, has been linked to the loss of peripheral vision caused by the gradual failure of the retina, which is highly sensitive to oxygen levels.

Another key area of interest for neuroscientists is the temporal lobe, a region of the brain that plays a critical role in memory, emotion, and sensory processing. The temporal lobe is particularly susceptible to disruption during states of hypoxia or extreme stress. Some researchers have suggested that stimulation of the temporal lobe, either through electrical activity or chemical imbalances, may trigger the vivid imagery, life reviews, and out-of-body sensations reported in NDEs. In particular, the work of Dr. Michael Persinger, a neuroscientist who conducted experiments on temporal lobe stimulation, demonstrated that electrical stimulation of this region could produce experiences similar to NDEs, including the sensation of a presence or spiritual being.

Research into the role of brain chemistry has also provided insights into the possible mechanisms behind NDEs. Under conditions of extreme stress, the brain releases a cascade of neurotransmitters, including endorphins, serotonin, and dopamine, which are associated with feelings of pleasure, euphoria, and dissociation. These neurochemical changes may explain why many individuals report feelings of peace and joy during their NDEs, despite being on the brink of death. Additionally, the release of ketamine-like substances produced by the brain during traumatic events may induce dissociative states, leading to the perception of an OBE.

One neurological hypothesis posits that NDEs result from a failure of the brain's self-modelling system. This system is responsible for generating a cohesive sense of self, integrating sensory inputs from the body with higher-order cognitive functions. In extreme situations, such as during cardiac arrest or severe trauma, the brain's ability to maintain this self-model may break down, leading to the perception of separation from the physical body, or an OBE. This theory is supported by research into OBEs induced in laboratory settings, where individuals have reported similar sensations after disruptions to their brain's self-modelling processes.

While these neurological explanations provide plausible mechanisms for many of the features observed in NDEs, they are not without limitations. For instance, some individuals report NDEs occurring under conditions where brain function is presumed to be severely impaired or non-existent, such as during deep anaesthesia or cardiac arrest lasting several minutes. These reports challenge the idea that NDEs are solely the result of abnormal brain activity, prompting some researchers to explore other possibilities.

Psychological Perspectives on Near-Death Experiences

In addition to neurological explanations, psychological theories have been proposed to account for the subjective nature of

NDEs. From a psychological standpoint, NDEs may represent the brain's attempt to cope with the imminent threat of death by generating comforting or protective imagery. The human mind, when confronted with overwhelming fear or trauma, often employs defence mechanisms to reduce anxiety and protect the individual from psychological harm. NDEs may be an example of such a mechanism, offering individuals a sense of peace and reassurance in their final moments.

One psychological theory suggests that NDEs are a form of depersonalization or dissociation, where the mind detaches from the physical body to avoid the pain or fear associated with dying. Dissociative experiences are common in situations of extreme stress or trauma, and they can lead to feelings of unreality, detachment from the body, and altered perceptions of time. The brain's response to near-death situations may involve a similar dissociative process, allowing individuals to experience their dying moments from a distance, as though they were observing rather than participating in their death.

Another psychological explanation for NDEs is that they are constructed from an individual's pre-existing beliefs, expectations, and cultural background. Research has shown that the content of NDEs often reflects the religious or cultural beliefs of the individual, suggesting that these experiences may be influenced by cognitive processes related to memory and imagination. For example, individuals from Christian backgrounds often report seeing religious figures such as Jesus or angels during their NDEs, while individuals from other religious traditions may encounter figures or symbols relevant to their own beliefs. This suggests that NDEs are shaped, at least in part, by the individual's internal world, including their spiritual and cultural framework.

The life review phenomenon, in which individuals report seeing their life flash before their eyes, may also have psychological roots. From a cognitive perspective, the life review could be seen as the brain's attempt to process a vast amount of autobiographical memory in a short period. In moments of extreme stress, the brain may prioritize emotionally significant memories, leading to a rapid review of key life events. This process could be driven by the brain's survival instinct, as it attempts to find meaning or resolution in the face of impending death.

The psychological interpretation of NDEs also extends to their long-term effects on individuals. Many people who experience NDEs report profound changes in their attitudes toward life and death, often developing a stronger sense of spirituality, a reduced fear of death, and a greater appreciation for life. These transformative effects may be a result of the emotional intensity of the experience, combined with the individual's interpretation of its meaning. Some psychologists argue that the positive changes reported by NDE survivors are consistent with post-traumatic growth, a phenomenon in which individuals emerge from traumatic experiences with a renewed sense of purpose and resilience.

Despite the compelling nature of psychological explanations for NDEs, they do not fully account for the more objective aspects of these experiences, such as cases where individuals report perceiving events or details that they could not have known from their physical vantage point. These veridical NDEs, in which individuals accurately describe events that occurred while they were clinically dead or unconscious, continue to challenge both psychological and neurological theories.

Veridical Near-Death Experiences: A Challenge to Scientific Explanation

One of the most intriguing aspects of NDE research is the phenomenon of veridical NDEs, where individuals report knowledge of events or information that they could not have obtained through normal sensory channels. These accounts often involve details of medical procedures, conversations between doctors and nurses, or descriptions of objects or events that were outside the individual's line of sight during their NDE. Proponents of the view that NDEs represent evidence of consciousness beyond the brain frequently cite these cases as proof that the mind can exist independently of the body, at least temporarily.

Perhaps the most famous example of a veridical NDE comes from the case of Pam Reynolds, a woman who underwent a rare surgical procedure in 1991 to treat a brain aneurysm. During the operation, Reynolds' body was cooled to a near-freezing temperature, her heartbeat was stopped, and her brain activity was reduced to nearly zero. Despite being clinically dead for several minutes, Reynolds later reported experiencing an OBE during which she observed the surgical team working on her body. She accurately described the tools used during the procedure and recounted specific details of conversations between the surgeons, even though she had been unconscious and her brain was not functioning.

Cases like Pam Reynolds' have sparked intense debate within the scientific community. Some researchers argue that veridical NDEs can be explained by residual brain activity or the brain's ability to reconstruct events based on limited sensory input. Others suggest that these experiences represent a form of unconscious memory, where the individual is able to recall sensory information that was processed by the brain at a subliminal level, even though they were not consciously aware of it at the time. However, critics of these explanations point out that in many veridical NDEs, the individual's brain was either severely compromised or entirely inactive, raising doubts about the ability of the brain to generate these experiences.

Despite the controversy surrounding veridical NDEs, they remain a compelling area of research. To address the question of whether consciousness can exist independently of the brain, some scientists have proposed conducting experiments in which hidden objects or images are placed in hospital rooms, visible only from a vantage point above the patient's body. If individuals who experience OBEs during cardiac arrest or surgery can describe these hidden objects, it would provide strong evidence in favour of the view that consciousness can persist beyond brain activity. While preliminary studies have been conducted, definitive evidence has yet to be obtained.

What Science Says About Near-Death Experiences

Near-death experiences remain one of the most enigmatic and controversial subjects in modern science. While significant progress has been made in understanding the neurological and psychological mechanisms that may underlie these phenomena, many aspects of NDEs continue to defy explanation. The brain's response to life-threatening situations, particularly in the moments before death, reveals much about how consciousness is constructed and how it may unravel under extreme stress.

Neurological theories suggest that NDEs are the product of abnormal brain activity, triggered by hypoxia, neurotransmitter release, and the breakdown of the brain's self-modelling system. Psychological explanations point to the role of dissociation, cultural beliefs, and cognitive processes in shaping the content of NDEs. However, the persistence of veridical NDEs and the transformative effects reported by survivors suggest that these experiences are more than just hallucinations or the brain's final bursts of activity. While science has provided valuable insights into the nature of NDEs, the full scope of these experiences remains a mystery.

As research into NDEs continues, new discoveries may offer further clarity about the nature of consciousness, death, and the boundaries between the two. For now, near-death experiences occupy a unique space at the intersection of science, philosophy, and personal belief, challenging us to reconsider what it means to die and what, if anything, lies beyond.

CHAPTER 21: CRYONICS: FREEZING THE BODY AFTER DEATH

Cryonics, the practice of freezing human bodies after death in the hope of future revival, occupies a controversial space at the intersection of science, ethics, and speculative futurism. It offers an extraordinary promise: that one day, advances in medical technology may enable the reanimation of individuals who have died from currently incurable conditions, thereby granting them a second chance at life. To its proponents, cryonics represents the ultimate extension of life-saving medicine, a means of circumventing biological death until such a time when it can be reversed. To its detractors, it is an impractical and unproven concept, more akin to science fiction than reality, fraught with insurmountable scientific and ethical challenges.

At its core, cryonics is built on the premise that biological death is not an absolute event but rather a process. Advocates of cryonics argue that when the heart stops beating and the brain ceases to function, the body does not immediately reach a state of irreversible death. Instead, they claim that if the body can be preserved at extremely low temperatures quickly enough, the cellular and molecular structures that define life could be maintained indefinitely, awaiting a future where advanced medical science can repair the damage caused by disease, ageing, and the freezing process itself.

This chapter explores the scientific basis for cryonics, as well as the significant technical, ethical, and logistical hurdles that must be overcome for cryonic preservation to ever become a viable option for life extension. The practice of cryonics remains deeply speculative, and no human body preserved through this method has ever been successfully revived. Nevertheless, advances in cryobiology, neuroscience, and regenerative medicine continue to push the boundaries of what is scientifically conceivable, suggesting that while cryonics is far from mainstream medicine, it is not entirely outside the realm of future possibility.

The Science of Cryopreservation: Halting Biological Decay

The central objective of cryonics is to preserve the human body after death by freezing it at temperatures so low that cellular and molecular activity slows to a near standstill. The scientific principles underpinning cryonics are derived from the field of cryobiology, the study of how living organisms respond to extremely low temperatures. Cryobiology has made significant strides in recent decades, particularly in the successful preservation of individual cells, tissues, and even small organs at sub-zero temperatures. However, scaling these techniques to the level of whole-body preservation remains an immense challenge.

The primary challenge in cryonics is avoiding the damage caused by ice crystal formation during the freezing process. When water freezes, it expands and forms sharp crystals that can puncture cell membranes and disrupt the intricate molecular structures within tissues. This ice-induced damage is one of the main reasons why simple freezing of the human body is not a viable means of preservation. To counteract this, cryonics employs a process known as vitrification, in which biological tissues are cooled to very low temperatures in the presence of cryoprotectants—chemical agents that prevent ice formation by turning cellular water into a glass-like state rather than a crystalline one.

Vitrification, when done correctly, can prevent the catastrophic damage caused by ice crystals, but it is not without its limitations. The cryoprotectants used in vitrification are toxic at high concentrations, and while they help preserve the structural integrity of cells and tissues, they can cause damage in other ways, such as disrupting normal biochemical processes or introducing oxidative stress. Moreover, the freezing process itself can cause mechanical stress on the tissues, leading to fractures or other forms of physical damage. These technical challenges must be addressed before cryonics can be considered a viable means of preserving the body in a condition that would allow for future revival.

Another critical concern is the preservation of the brain. The brain is the seat of consciousness, identity, and memory, and if cryonics is to succeed in restoring life, the brain must be preserved in such a way that these essential aspects of personhood can be recovered. Neuroscientists and cryobiologists are particularly focused on how to preserve the brain's delicate neural networks and synaptic connections, which encode memories and cognitive functions. If these structures are irreparably damaged during the freezing or storage process, even future medical technology may be unable to revive the person in a meaningful sense.

Despite these challenges, there have been promising developments in the field of cryobiology. Recent experiments have demonstrated that vitrified tissues can be rewarmed and restored to a functional state, at least on a cellular level. For example, researchers have successfully vitrified and thawed small samples of brain tissue without significant loss of structure or function. However, scaling these methods to whole organs, let alone entire bodies, is still beyond the reach of current science. The prospect of freezing and reviving a human being remains speculative, but ongoing research in areas such as nanotechnology and tissue regeneration offers some hope that the barriers to successful cryonic revival could eventually be overcome.

The Cryonics Process: From Death to Freezing

For cryonics to have any chance of success, the preservation process must begin as soon as possible after clinical death is declared. Time is of the essence, as biological decay begins almost immediately after the heart stops beating. Brain cells, in particular, are highly sensitive to oxygen deprivation and begin to die within minutes. Therefore, cryonics protocols are designed to intervene swiftly, ideally within minutes of cardiac arrest, to minimize cellular damage.

The cryonics process typically begins with the stabilization of the body to ensure that oxygenated blood continues to circulate, preventing immediate cell death. This is achieved through mechanical means, such as cardiopulmonary support and ventilation, which artificially sustain the body's vital functions. Once stabilized, the body is cooled with ice to lower its temperature gradually. Cooling slows metabolic processes, buying time for the next steps in the preservation process.

After initial cooling, the body undergoes a process called perfusion, during which the blood is replaced with a cryoprotectant solution. Cryoprotectants are essential for preventing ice crystal formation during freezing, as they inhibit the crystallization of water and allow the body's tissues to vitrify. The perfusion process is delicate and must be performed with precision, as improper perfusion can lead to incomplete cryoprotection, resulting in localized ice formation and damage. Additionally, the toxicity of cryoprotectants remains a significant concern, and researchers are constantly seeking to improve the chemical compositions used in cryonic preservation.

Once perfusion is complete, the body is gradually cooled to the temperature of liquid nitrogen, approximately -196 degrees Celsius. At this temperature, metabolic activity ceases almost entirely, and biological decay is effectively halted. The body is then stored in a cryostat, a specialized container filled with liquid nitrogen that maintains the body at cryogenic temperatures indefinitely.

Cryonics organizations, such as Alcor Life Extension Foundation and the Cryonics Institute, are responsible for performing this procedure and maintaining the bodies in long-term cryogenic storage. These organizations face significant logistical challenges, including ensuring a constant supply of liquid nitrogen, monitoring the condition of stored bodies, and dealing with the legal and ethical complexities of handling human remains. The storage of cryopreserved bodies requires meticulous attention to detail and ongoing maintenance, as any disruption in the cooling process could lead to irreversible damage.

Cryonics organizations also face legal challenges, particularly regarding the timing of cryopreservation. In most jurisdictions, cryonics can only begin after legal death has been declared, which typically means that the heart has stopped beating and the person is considered clinically dead. However, by this point, some biological deterioration may have already occurred, particularly in the brain. Ideally, cryonics advocates would prefer to begin the preservation process before significant damage occurs, but current laws do not permit this. Some proponents of cryonics argue for the redefinition of legal death to include the concept of "information-theoretic death," where a person is not considered truly dead until the brain's information—such as memories and personality—has been irretrievably lost.

The Ethical and Legal Challenges of Cryonics

Cryonics raises numerous ethical questions, many of which centre on the fundamental nature of life and death. One of the most significant ethical concerns is the treatment of the dead, particularly in societies where cultural and religious beliefs play a critical role in how the deceased are honoured and remembered. For many, the idea of freezing a body to reanimate it in the future runs counter to deeply held beliefs about the finality of death and the sanctity of human remains. In some cultures, death is seen as a natural transition to another state of being, whether it be an afterlife, reincarnation, or spiritual liberation. Cryonics, by contrast, seeks to intervene in this process, effectively postponing death until future technology can restore life.

The notion of reanimating the dead also raises concerns about personal identity and the continuity of consciousness. If cryonics were to succeed in restoring life to a cryopreserved individual, would the person who emerges from the process be the same individual who was originally preserved? This question touches on philosophical debates about the nature of the self and what constitutes personal identity. Some argue that as long as the brain's neural architecture is preserved, along with the memories and personality encoded within it, the individual's identity will remain intact. Others contend that even minor disruptions to the brain's structure or function could result in a fundamentally different person emerging from the process, raising ethical concerns about the potential loss of self.

Legal challenges to cryonics are equally significant. The preservation and handling of human remains are subject to strict regulations in most countries, and cryonics occupies a grey area in many legal systems. In the United States, for example, cryonics is classified as a form of post-mortem care, similar to burial or cremation. However, because cryonics involves the preservation of the body with the intent of future revival, it is not subject to the same regulatory oversight as traditional medical procedures. This has led to a lack of standardized protocols and oversight, with different cryonics organizations operating under varying levels of scrutiny.

One of the most pressing legal questions surrounding cryonics is the issue of consent. Cryonics is typically undertaken as a voluntary procedure, with individuals signing up for cryopreservation long before their death. However, questions arise when a person is cryopreserved without explicit consent, either because they were incapacitated at the time of death or because their wishes were unclear. This has led to legal battles over the control of cryopreserved bodies, particularly when family members disagree about whether cryonics should have been pursued.

In addition to questions of consent, cryonics raises concerns about the potential for exploitation. Cryonics services are expensive, with the cost of whole-body preservation often reaching hundreds of thousands of dollars. This has led to accusations that cryonics organizations are preying on vulnerable individuals, offering them false hope in exchange for exorbitant fees. Critics argue that without concrete evidence that cryonics can work, it is unethical to charge individuals large sums of money for a speculative and unproven procedure.

The Future of Cryonics: Scientific and Technological Prospects

While cryonics remains speculative and controversial, ongoing advances in science and technology continue to push the boundaries of what might be possible in the future. The development of nanotechnology, in particular, has been touted by cryonics advocates as a potential game-changer. Nanotechnology involves the manipulation of matter at the atomic or molecular scale, and it holds promise for the development of molecular machines capable of repairing damage at the cellular level. In theory, such machines could be used to repair the damage caused by the cryopreservation process, restoring frozen tissues to a functional state.

One of the most ambitious ideas proposed by cryonics enthusiasts is the concept of molecular repair, in which nanobots or other advanced technologies could be used to rebuild damaged tissues, replace lost cells, and even reverse the effects of aging. This idea is based on the principle that if the brain's neural networks can be preserved in a sufficiently intact state, future technology might be able to restore the individual's memories, personality, and consciousness. While this vision remains far from realization, research into regenerative medicine and tissue engineering continues to advance, offering glimpses of what may be possible in the future.

Another area of interest is the potential for brain emulation or "mind uploading." This concept, which is closely related to cryonics, involves scanning the brain's structure in such detail that it could be replicated in a computer, creating a digital copy of the individual's consciousness. Advocates of this idea argue that if the physical brain can be preserved long enough for future technology to develop the capacity for detailed brain mapping, it might be possible to "upload" a person's mind into a computer, thereby achieving a form of digital immortality. While this idea is highly speculative, it represents one of the many futuristic possibilities that have emerged from the study of cryonics and life extension.

Despite these technological prospects, significant obstacles remain. The challenges of reversing cryopreservation, repairing cellular damage, and restoring full brain function are immense, and there is no guarantee that these obstacles will ever be overcome. Nevertheless, the scientific community continues to explore related fields, such as organ cryopreservation for transplantation and the use of cryoprotectants in medical treatments, which could yield valuable insights for cryonics research.

The Promise and Perils of Cryonics

Cryonics represents one of the most ambitious and controversial ideas in the quest to extend human life. It offers the tantalizing prospect of transcending biological death, preserving the body in a state of suspended animation until future technology can reverse the aging process and cure currently fatal diseases. However, the practice of cryonics is fraught with scientific, ethical, and logistical challenges, and its success is far from guaranteed.

The science of cryopreservation has made significant strides, particularly in the preservation of cells, tissues, and small organs, but applying these techniques to whole-body preservation remains an enormous challenge. The ethical and legal implications of freezing human bodies for potential future revival are equally complex, touching on fundamental questions about life, death, identity, and consent.

As research into cryobiology, nanotechnology, and regenerative medicine advances, the possibility of successful cryonic revival may become more plausible. However, for now, cryonics remains an experimental and speculative field, driven more by hope and futuristic vision than by concrete scientific evidence. Whether cryonics will ultimately succeed in its goal of bringing the dead back to life remains one of the most intriguing and uncertain questions in the science of death.

CHAPTER 22: ORGAN DONATION: LIFE AFTER DEATH

Organ donation represents one of the most significant and transformative medical advances of modern times. The ability to take viable organs from a deceased individual and transplant them into another person, thus extending life and restoring health, stands as a remarkable testament to the power of medicine to transcend the finality of death. The process of organ transplantation, however, is complex, both medically and ethically. From the precise moment organs are harvested to the intricate procedures involved in transplantation, the science of organ donation is at the cutting edge of medical technology and bioethics. Furthermore, organ donation challenges our understanding of death, as it allows parts of one individual to continue functioning within another after the donor has passed away.

At its core, organ donation depends on the recognition that death is not always an instantaneous event. Although the heart may stop beating and the brain may cease functioning, many of the body's organs remain viable for a limited period, provided they are properly preserved and transplanted in a timely manner. These organs—such as the heart, kidneys, liver, lungs, and corneas—can be surgically removed from the deceased donor and transplanted into recipients whose organs have failed due to disease or injury. In many cases, this process can save lives, offering hope to those who have exhausted all other medical options.

Yet, organ donation is not without its ethical complexities. The decision to donate one's organs after death raises profound questions about autonomy, consent, and the nature of personhood. Moreover, the medical and logistical challenges of organ transplantation, including matching donors and recipients, preserving organs during transport, and preventing organ rejection, require careful coordination between numerous medical professionals and facilities. Despite these challenges, organ donation remains one of the most powerful ways in which the death of one person can bring life to another.

This chapter delves into the scientific, ethical, and logistical dimensions of organ donation, exploring how organs are harvested and transplanted, the medical innovations that have made this practice possible, and the ethical debates surrounding organ donation and transplantation. Through this exploration, we aim to provide a comprehensive understanding of how organ donation allows life to continue after death, both biologically and symbolically.

The Science of Organ Donation: Harvesting and Preservation

The success of organ donation relies heavily on the ability to harvest and preserve viable organs after death. This process begins the moment a potential donor is declared legally and medically dead, typically under the definition of brain death, where all brain activity has ceased and is considered irreversible. Brain death is distinct from cardiac death, where the heart stops beating, and is preferred in cases of organ donation because it allows the body's organs to remain perfused with oxygenated blood, thereby maintaining their viability until they can be removed.

Once brain death has been confirmed, medical professionals begin the process of harvesting the donor's organs. Time is of the essence in this procedure, as organs begin to deteriorate rapidly once the body's physiological functions cease. The first step involves carefully monitoring and maintaining the donor's body to ensure that oxygenation and circulation are preserved until the organs can be removed. This is typically done in an operating room setting, where the donor is kept on mechanical ventilation to keep the organs oxygenated and functional.

The actual process of organ harvesting, known as procurement, is a meticulously coordinated surgical procedure. Surgeons work with precision to remove the organs while minimizing any damage to the surrounding tissues. The heart, liver, kidneys, lungs, pancreas, intestines, and corneas are among the most commonly harvested organs, each requiring specific techniques to ensure their safe removal. Once removed, the organs are placed in sterile containers filled with a preservation solution designed to minimize cellular damage and prevent the formation of ice crystals that could damage the tissues. The organs are then stored at cold temperatures, typically on ice, to slow metabolic activity and preserve their function until they can be transplanted into the recipient.

The window of time in which an organ remains viable after removal from the donor's body is limited and varies depending on the organ. For example, the heart and lungs must typically be transplanted within four to six hours of procurement, while the liver and kidneys can remain viable for up to 12 to 24 hours. Advances in preservation techniques, such as the use of specialized preservation solutions and portable organ perfusion devices, have extended these time limits, allowing for longer transport times and increasing the chances of successful transplantation.

One of the most significant challenges in organ preservation is the prevention of ischemia-reperfusion injury. This type of injury occurs when an organ is deprived of oxygen (ischemia) during the time it is removed from the donor's body and then suddenly re-exposed to oxygenated blood during transplantation (reperfusion). Ischemia-reperfusion injury can lead to inflammation and tissue damage, reducing the likelihood of a successful transplant. Researchers are actively working to develop new preservation methods, such as normothermic perfusion, which involves continuously pumping oxygenated blood through the organ at normal body temperatures, thereby reducing the risk of ischemia-reperfusion injury and improving organ viability.

The preservation of organs is not limited to those harvested after death. In some cases, living donors can provide organs for transplantation, most commonly kidneys and portions of the liver. Living donation offers several advantages over deceased donation, including shorter wait times for recipients and better organ function post-transplant. However, living donation also carries risks for the donor, and careful ethical considerations must be made to ensure that the decision to donate is voluntary and informed.

The Transplantation Procedure: Matching Donors and Recipients

Successful organ transplantation depends on more than just the procurement and preservation of organs; it also requires a careful matching process to ensure compatibility between the donor and recipient. The human immune system is highly attuned to recognizing foreign tissues, and when an organ from another individual is introduced into the body, the recipient's immune system may perceive the transplanted organ as an invader, attacking it in a process known as rejection. To minimize the risk of rejection, donors and recipients must be carefully matched based on several key factors.

The first and most important factor in matching donors and recipients is blood type. The ABO blood group system, which classifies individuals into blood types A, B, AB, or O, plays a crucial role in determining compatibility. Transplanting an organ from a donor with an incompatible blood type can trigger a severe immune response, leading to immediate and catastrophic organ rejection. Therefore, blood type matching is one of the first steps in the organ allocation process.

In addition to blood type, human leukocyte antigen (HLA) matching is another critical factor in transplantation. HLAs are proteins found on the surface of cells that help the immune system distinguish between the body's own cells and foreign cells. Each person has a unique combination of HLAs, and the more similar the HLA profiles of the donor and recipient, the less likely the recipient's immune system is to reject the transplanted organ. While a perfect HLA match is ideal, it is not always possible, especially given the limited availability of donor organs. In many cases, immunosuppressive medications are used to reduce the recipient's immune response and allow for successful transplantation even with less-than-perfect matches.

Once a suitable donor-recipient match is identified, the transplantation procedure can begin. The recipient is prepared for surgery, which involves removing the failed organ and replacing it with the healthy donor organ. Depending on the type of organ being transplanted, the surgery can be complex and lengthy, requiring careful coordination between multiple surgical teams. For example, heart and lung transplants often involve delicate vascular connections and the precise reconnection of blood vessels to ensure proper function. Liver transplants require the removal of the diseased liver and the attachment of the donor liver to the bile ducts and blood vessels.

After the organ is transplanted, the recipient must be closely monitored for signs of rejection or other complications. Rejection remains one of the most significant risks following transplantation, as the recipient's immune system may attack the transplanted organ despite immunosuppressive treatment. To reduce this risk, recipients are typically placed on a lifelong regimen of immunosuppressive drugs, which weaken the immune system's ability to recognize and attack the donor organ. While these medications are effective at preventing rejection, they also increase the recipient's susceptibility to infections and other immune-related conditions.

Despite these challenges, organ transplantation has a high success rate, particularly for certain organs such as kidneys and livers. Advances in surgical techniques, immunosuppressive therapies, and post-transplant care have significantly improved outcomes for transplant recipients, allowing many individuals to lead healthy, productive lives after receiving a donated organ.

The Ethical Complexities of Organ Donation

While organ donation has the potential to save lives, it also raises a host of ethical questions. One of the most fundamental ethical concerns is the issue of consent. Organ donation typically requires the donor, or their family, to provide informed consent before the organs can be harvested. In many countries, individuals can choose to become organ donors by registering their consent while they are still alive, often through driver's licenses or national donor registries. However, in the absence of explicit consent, the decision to donate often falls to the donor's next of kin, who may be faced with difficult decisions in the midst of grief.

Different countries take varying approaches to the issue of consent. Some countries, such as the United States, operate under an "opt-in" system, where individuals must actively register to become organ donors. Others, such as Spain and France, have adopted an "opt-out" system, where individuals are presumed to consent to organ donation unless they have explicitly stated otherwise. Opt-out systems tend to have higher rates of organ donation, as they reduce the burden on families to make decisions in the immediate aftermath of death. However, these systems also raise concerns about autonomy and whether individuals should be presumed to consent to such a significant decision without explicit agreement.

Another ethical issue concerns the allocation of donated organs. The demand for transplantable organs far exceeds the supply, leading to difficult questions about how organs should be distributed among those in need. In most countries, organ allocation is based on a combination of medical factors, such as the severity of the recipient's condition, the likelihood of success, and the time spent on the waiting list. However, these criteria can lead to difficult decisions when multiple individuals are equally eligible for a transplant. In some cases, factors such as age, lifestyle, and social support may also be considered, raising concerns about fairness and the potential for bias.

The issue of living donation presents additional ethical complexities. While living donors can provide life-saving organs, such as kidneys, to recipients, the decision to donate is not without risks. Living donors must undergo surgery to remove the donated organ, which carries the possibility of complications, including infection, bleeding, and long-term health consequences. Ensuring that living donors are fully informed of these risks and that their decision to donate is voluntary is critical to maintaining ethical standards in transplantation.

Organ trafficking and "transplant tourism" present some of the most troubling ethical issues in organ donation. In some parts of the world, desperate individuals may be exploited by organ traffickers, who offer financial compensation in exchange for organs. These illicit practices often take advantage of vulnerable populations and undermine the ethical foundations of organ donation. Transplant tourism, where wealthy individuals travel to countries with fewer regulations to purchase organs from impoverished donors, further exacerbates these ethical concerns. International efforts to combat organ trafficking and promote ethical donation practices are ongoing, but the issue remains a significant challenge in the field of transplantation.

Life After Death: The Continuing Impact of Organ Donation

The most profound aspect of organ donation is its ability to extend life beyond the death of the donor. When a person donates their organs, they provide others with the opportunity to live, in some cases transforming multiple lives through a single donation. This concept of life after death is both biological and symbolic, as the donor's organs continue to function in another body, offering recipients the chance to regain their health and independence.

The impact of organ donation on recipients is often life-changing. For individuals with end-stage organ failure, transplantation offers the possibility of a return to normal life, free from the limitations and suffering imposed by their condition. Kidney transplantation, for example, allows recipients to escape the burden of dialysis, while heart and lung transplants offer hope to those with severe cardiovascular or respiratory disease. For many recipients, organ donation represents a new lease on life, enabling them to pursue personal and professional goals that were previously unattainable.

The symbolic significance of organ donation extends beyond the recipients themselves. For the families of donors, the knowledge that their loved one's organs have gone on to save the lives of others can provide comfort in the face of loss. In some cases, donor families and transplant recipients develop lasting relationships, united by the shared experience of organ donation. These connections underscore the profound and enduring impact that organ donation can have, not only on individual lives but on entire communities.

Organ donation also plays a critical role in advancing medical science. Transplantation offers researchers unique opportunities to study the effects of organ function and failure, as well as the immune system's response to foreign tissues. Advances in transplantation have led to important breakthroughs in immunology, regenerative medicine, and the treatment of chronic diseases. The continued study of organ donation and transplantation holds the promise of further medical innovations that could benefit future generations.

Despite these successes, challenges remain in ensuring that organ donation is accessible to all who need it. The shortage of available organs means that many individuals die while waiting for a transplant, highlighting the need for increased awareness and participation in organ donation programs. Efforts to expand the pool of eligible donors, including public education campaigns and reforms to donation policies, are essential to addressing this gap and ensuring that more lives can be saved through organ transplantation.

The Legacy of Organ Donation

Organ donation is one of the most remarkable ways in which death can give rise to new life. Through the transplantation of organs from deceased or living donors, individuals facing life-threatening illnesses can receive a second chance at life, allowing them to experience renewed health and vitality. The science of organ donation, from the harvesting and preservation of organs to the matching and transplantation process, represents a triumph of medical innovation, while the ethical considerations surrounding consent, allocation, and autonomy underscore the complexity of this life-saving practice.

Beyond its scientific and ethical dimensions, organ donation holds deep symbolic meaning. It demonstrates the interconnectedness of human life, as the organs of one individual continue to function within another, carrying on a legacy of life beyond death. The profound impact of organ donation on recipients, donor families, and society at large highlights the enduring significance of this medical miracle.

As medical technology continues to advance, and as efforts to promote ethical and equitable organ donation practices gain momentum, the potential for organ transplantation to transform lives will only grow. The legacy of organ donation will continue to be written, not only in the lives it saves but in the ongoing contributions it makes to the field of medicine and the collective understanding of life, death, and the human body.

CHAPTER 23: THE ROLE OF RELIGION AND SCIENCE IN DEATH

Death is an inevitable phenomenon that has preoccupied human societies for millennia, not only as a biological process but also as a profound philosophical and existential event. Across cultures, death is more than just the cessation of life; it is intertwined with questions of morality, the afterlife, and the continuity of existence. Religion and science, two powerful systems of thought, have both sought to explain the mystery of death, albeit through fundamentally different lenses. While religious beliefs often interpret death within the context of an afterlife or a metaphysical continuation of the self, science views death as the culmination of physiological decline, where life ceases in measurable, empirical terms, and the process of decomposition begins.

These two approaches—religious and scientific—are not necessarily mutually exclusive, but they do provide contrasting perspectives. Religion often addresses the spiritual and moral dimensions of death, offering explanations about what happens to the soul or consciousness after physical death, while science explores the mechanisms by which the body ceases to function and eventually decomposes. The intersection of these perspectives creates a rich tapestry of interpretations, as religious beliefs about resurrection or reincarnation intersect with scientific explanations of biological decay.

This chapter examines the role of religion and science in shaping humanity's understanding of death. It explores religious views on the afterlife, resurrection, and the immortality of the soul, as well as how these beliefs align —or conflict—with the scientific understanding of death and decomposition. Through this exploration, the chapter seeks to illuminate how both religion and science contribute to broader societal conceptions of mortality, and how they shape cultural responses to the inevitability of death.

Religious Perspectives on Death and the Afterlife

Religious traditions have long provided frameworks for understanding death, often positing that physical death is not the final cessation of existence, but rather a transition to another realm or state of being. These views vary widely across cultures and religious systems, but they often share a common emphasis on the persistence of the self, whether in the form of an immortal soul, a reincarnated spirit, or a resurrected body. The concept of an afterlife is central to many religious worldviews, shaping rituals surrounding death and providing moral and existential meaning to human life.

In Christianity, for example, death is viewed as a passage from earthly existence to eternal life. Christian theology teaches that the soul persists after death, with its ultimate fate determined by divine judgment. Believers in Christ are promised resurrection and eternal life in heaven, while those who reject salvation may face eternal separation from God in hell. Central to Christian beliefs about death is the doctrine of the resurrection of the body, as exemplified by the resurrection of Jesus Christ. This belief in bodily resurrection distinguishes Christianity from other traditions that focus solely on the immortality of the soul.

In Islam, similar themes emerge. Death is seen as a temporary separation of the soul from the body, with the soul continuing to exist in a state known as barzakh until the Day of Judgment. At that time, according to Islamic teachings, all individuals will be resurrected, their souls reuniting with their bodies to face judgment. Those who have lived righteous lives will be rewarded with eternal paradise, while the wicked will be condemned to eternal punishment. Like Christianity, Islam places great emphasis on the resurrection of the body, though the specifics of the afterlife and judgment differ between the two faiths.

Hinduism and Buddhism, by contrast, adopt a different view of death, centred on the cycle of reincarnation. In these traditions, death is not the end of existence but part of a continuous cycle of birth, death, and rebirth known as samsara. According to Hindu beliefs, the soul (atman) is eternal and undergoes numerous reincarnations, with each new life shaped by the karma accumulated in previous lives. Liberation from this cycle, known as moksha, represents the ultimate spiritual goal, where the soul is freed from the bonds of physical existence and attains union with the divine.

Buddhism also teaches that existence is marked by impermanence and that death is a natural part of the cycle of suffering known as dukkha. However, rather than positing the existence of a permanent soul, Buddhism teaches the doctrine of anatman—the belief that there is no enduring self. Instead, the process of reincarnation is driven by the continuity of consciousness and karma. The ultimate goal in Buddhism is nirvana, the cessation of desire and the end of the cycle of rebirth, which leads to liberation from suffering.

These religious perspectives on death all share a common feature: they provide a framework for understanding human mortality about something beyond the physical body. Whether through resurrection, reincarnation, or the attainment of spiritual liberation, these beliefs offer hope that death is not the final end of existence but a transition to a different, often higher, state of being. These views contrast sharply with the scientific understanding of death, which focuses on the irreversible cessation of biological function.

The Scientific Understanding of Death: Cessation and Decomposition

In contrast to the metaphysical explanations offered by religious traditions, the scientific perspective on death is grounded in the study of biology and the observable processes that occur when an organism ceases to live. From a scientific standpoint, death is the point at which the body's essential systems—such as the cardiovascular, respiratory, and nervous systems—cease to function, leading to the permanent loss of consciousness and the inability to sustain life. This definition has been further refined in medical contexts, where brain death, marked by the irreversible loss of all brain activity, is often considered the definitive marker of death.

The human body is a highly complex system that relies on the coordinated functioning of multiple organs and tissues to sustain life. At the moment of death, this intricate balance collapses. The heart stops beating, cutting off the supply of oxygenated blood to the brain and other vital organs. Without oxygen, cells rapidly begin to die, leading to the shutdown of critical systems. The brain, being highly dependent on oxygen, is among the first organs to be affected. Within minutes of cardiac arrest, brain cells begin to die, resulting in the permanent loss of consciousness and cognitive function.

Following death, the body undergoes a series of predictable physiological changes, known as the stages of decomposition. These stages are well-documented in forensic science and are essential for understanding how the body returns to the environment after death. Decomposition begins almost immediately as cells break down due to a lack of oxygen, triggering a process called autolysis, where enzymes within the cells start to digest surrounding tissues. This is followed by putrefaction, the phase in which bacteria and other microorganisms begin to break down the body's tissues, producing gases that cause the body to bloat and emit strong odours.

As decomposition progresses, the body's soft tissues liquefy, and the skeleton is gradually exposed. Eventually, under the right environmental conditions, the body is reduced to skeletal remains. The timeline of decomposition varies widely depending on factors such as temperature, humidity, and the presence of scavengers, but the process is inevitable and irreversible in all cases. Scientific research into decomposition has yielded valuable insights into forensic investigations, particularly in determining the time of death and identifying remains.

From a biological perspective, death represents the irreversible cessation of an organism's ability to maintain homeostasis —the balance of internal conditions necessary for survival. Once this balance is disrupted, life cannot be sustained, and the body undergoes a natural process of decay. There is no scientific evidence to support the existence of an afterlife or the persistence of consciousness after death, as these concepts fall outside the realm of observable, empirical phenomena. Nevertheless, the search for meaning in death remains a powerful driving force behind both religious beliefs and scientific inquiry, even as these two approaches diverge in their interpretations.

The Intersection of Religion and Science: Conflicting and Complementary Views

The relationship between religion and science, particularly in the context of death, is often portrayed as adversarial, with each offering fundamentally different answers to the question of what happens after death. However, the intersection between these two fields is more nuanced than simple conflict. While science and religion approach death from distinct epistemological frameworks—one empirical, the other metaphysical—there are areas of overlap where the two perspectives engage with one another in meaningful ways.

One area of intersection is the concept of brain death, which has become the accepted medical standard for determining death in many countries. Brain death, defined as the complete and irreversible loss of all brain function, including in the brainstem, is a concept that emerged from advances in medical technology, particularly the development of ventilators and life-support systems that can keep the heart and lungs functioning even after the brain has ceased to operate. This medical definition of death has raised ethical and religious questions, particularly for traditions that emphasize the continued presence of the soul or spirit within the body.

For example, in some branches of Judaism, the definition of death is traditionally associated with the cessation of breathing and heartbeat. The introduction of brain death as a medical criterion for death has led to debates within the Jewish community about whether it aligns with religious teachings. Some rabbinical authorities have accepted brain death as a legitimate definition of death, while others have rejected it, arguing that as long as the heart continues to beat, the individual cannot be considered fully dead. This tension illustrates the challenges that arise when scientific definitions of death come into contact with religious beliefs.

Similarly, in Islam, where the soul is believed to leave the body at the time of death, questions have been raised about the legitimacy of brain death as a marker of death. Islamic scholars have debated whether brain death is sufficient to declare a person dead or whether cardiac death is the only acceptable criterion. These debates reflect broader concerns about the ethical implications of organ donation, end-of-life care, and the use of life-support technologies, which often hinge on differing interpretations of what it means to die.

Despite these areas of conflict, there are also points of convergence between religious and scientific perspectives on death. Many religious traditions recognize the importance of scientific advances in prolonging life and easing the suffering of the dying. Palliative care, which focuses on providing comfort and dignity to those at the end of life, is an area where religious and scientific values often align. Both approaches emphasize the importance of compassion, care, and respect for the individual during the dying process, even as they differ in their ultimate explanations of death and what follows.

Furthermore, some religious traditions have embraced aspects of scientific discovery in their understanding of the afterlife. For instance, certain interpretations of Eastern religions, such as Buddhism and Hinduism, have found resonance with scientific concepts like entropy and the conservation of energy. These traditions often emphasize the impermanence of life and the cyclical nature of existence, which can be seen as compatible with the scientific view of the universe as a system governed by cycles of energy transfer and transformation. While these connections are largely metaphorical, they offer a bridge between scientific and religious understandings of death.

Resurrection, Reincarnation, and Scientific Possibilities

One of the most intriguing areas of intersection between religion and science is the concept of resurrection, reincarnation, and the possibility of extending life through scientific means. While religious beliefs about resurrection and reincarnation are rooted in metaphysical claims about the soul and its journey after death, recent advances in biotechnology and cryonics have raised the possibility of reviving individuals after death through purely scientific processes.

The idea of resurrection is central to several religious traditions, most notably Christianity, where the resurrection of Jesus Christ serves as the foundation for the belief in life after death. In Christian theology, resurrection is not simply the continuation of life after death but the transformation of the individual into a new, perfected form, free from the limitations of the physical body. This concept contrasts with the scientific understanding of death, where the decomposition of the body is irreversible, and there is no known mechanism by which life can be restored after brain death has occurred.

However, advances in fields such as cryonics, regenerative medicine, and brain-computer interfaces have led some to speculate about the possibility of scientific "resurrection." Cryonics, the process of freezing the body after death with the hope that future technology will be able to revive it, offers a potential, albeit highly speculative, means of circumventing death. While cryonics remains an unproven and controversial practice, its proponents argue that it aligns with the religious concept of resurrection by offering the possibility of a second life through scientific intervention.

Similarly, the concept of reincarnation, central to Hinduism and Buddhism, finds an interesting parallel in emerging technologies such as brain emulation and artificial intelligence. The idea of transferring an individual's consciousness into a digital medium or a new body raises questions about the continuity of identity and the nature of the self, themes that are also explored in religious teachings on reincarnation. While the technological feasibility of such processes remains speculative, they illustrate how science is beginning to explore questions that were once the exclusive domain of religion.

Bridging the Divide Between Religion and Science in Death

Religion and science offer different, though often complementary, frameworks for understanding death. While science focuses on the empirical aspects of biological decline, decomposition, and the cessation of life, religion provides meaning and context for what comes after death, offering hope, comfort, and a sense of continuity beyond the physical body. These two perspectives can, at times, seem irreconcilable, particularly when religious beliefs about the afterlife or the soul conflict with scientific understandings of brain death and decomposition.

However, the divide between religion and science is not absolute. As this chapter has explored, there are areas of intersection where religious and scientific perspectives engage in dialogue, particularly around the definition of death, ethical questions surrounding life support and organ donation, and the possibility of extending life through technology. Both religion and science seek to answer fundamental questions about the nature of existence, and while their answers may differ, they both play an essential role in shaping humanity's response to death.

In the ongoing quest to understand death, the insights provided by both religion and science will continue to evolve, offering new perspectives on one of life's most enduring mysteries. Whether through the metaphysical promise of an afterlife or the empirical study of biological processes, death remains a central focus of human inquiry, guiding how societies respond to mortality and the unknown.

CHAPTER 24: THE FUTURE OF DEATH: EMERGING TECHNOLOGIES AND RESEARCH

The future of death is no longer confined to the inevitable biological end of human life as we currently understand it. With rapid advances in biotechnology, artificial intelligence, and life sciences, the traditional concept of death is being challenged and redefined. These emerging technologies offer new possibilities for extending life, delaying death, or even transcending it altogether. From life extension research to genetic manipulation and the potential for artificial intelligence to alter the boundaries between life and death, the frontier of mortality is expanding in ways that may soon disrupt long-held assumptions.

The concept of death has traditionally been rooted in biology, defined by the cessation of vital functions—most notably, the failure of the heart and brain. However, new developments in medical science suggest that death may be reversible or, at the very least, preventable for longer periods than ever before. Research into life extension, regenerative medicine, and advanced biotechnologies holds the potential to significantly extend human lifespan, while artificial intelligence promises to alter how we conceptualize identity, consciousness, and mortality itself.

This chapter explores cutting-edge research and technologies that are reshaping our understanding of death. From efforts to manipulate the human genome to extend life, to the use of AI in medical decision-making and potential digital immortality, these advances offer a glimpse into a future where death is no longer the final frontier. However, these innovations are accompanied by significant ethical concerns, including questions about inequality, the societal impact of radically extended lifespans, and the moral implications of altering the fundamental processes of life and death.

Life Extension: The Quest for Longevity

Efforts to extend human life have fascinated scientists and philosophers for centuries, but recent advances in biotechnology and medicine are bringing the goal of life extension closer to reality. At the forefront of this research are interventions aimed at slowing or reversing the ageing process. Aging, once seen as an unavoidable consequence of biological decline, is now being studied as a treatable condition. Research into the molecular and genetic pathways that regulate ageing is shedding light on how cells age, and how these processes might be manipulated to extend lifespan.

One of the most promising areas of life extension research involves the study of telomeres, the protective caps at the ends of chromosomes that shorten with each cell division. Telomere shortening is associated with cellular ageing, as the loss of telomeric DNA eventually leads to cell senescence, a state in which cells lose their ability to divide and function properly. Researchers have hypothesized that by preserving or lengthening telomeres, it may be possible to delay the onset of ageing and the diseases associated with it, such as cancer, cardiovascular disease, and neurodegenerative disorders.

In recent years, scientists have successfully extended the lifespan of laboratory animals by manipulating the activity of telomerase, an enzyme that helps maintain telomere length. While the extension of the human lifespan through telomere manipulation is still in its early stages, the potential for therapeutic interventions targeting telomeres offers a promising avenue for future research. However, telomerase activation must be approached cautiously, as overactive telomerase is linked to the development of cancer. This underscores the complexity of balancing life extension with the prevention of age-related diseases.

In addition to telomere research, another major focus of life extension science is caloric restriction and its effects on longevity. Studies on various organisms, including mice, flies, and worms, have shown that reducing caloric intake can significantly extend lifespan, possibly by reducing metabolic stress and slowing the accumulation of cellular damage. These findings have led to human trials exploring the potential for caloric restriction or caloric restriction mimetics—drugs that replicate the effects of caloric restriction without requiring a reduction in food intake—to delay ageing and extend a healthy lifespan. Though the evidence in humans is still preliminary, the field represents a potential path to delaying the onset of age-related decline.

Emerging technologies in regenerative medicine are also contributing to the quest for life extension. Stem cell research, which explores the use of pluripotent cells to regenerate damaged tissues, offers the possibility of rejuvenating ageing organs or even replacing them entirely. Recent breakthroughs in induced pluripotent stem cells (iPSCs) have allowed scientists to reprogram adult cells into a pluripotent state, which could be used to regenerate tissues or grow new organs tailored to the patient's genetic makeup. These advancements in tissue regeneration raise the possibility of repairing age-related damage at a cellular level, potentially prolonging life by maintaining organ function well into old age.

While the science of life extension offers exciting possibilities, it also raises profound ethical questions. If technologies emerge that can significantly extend human life, who will have access to them? Will these therapies be available to all, or only to the wealthy and privileged? Moreover, the extension of life has implications for population growth, resource distribution, and the environment. If individuals live significantly longer, societal structures such as retirement, healthcare, and family life would need to be reimagined, and the cultural implications of altering the human lifespan would be profound.

Genetic Manipulation and the Future of Mortality

The manipulation of the human genome is another area of research that holds significant implications for the future of death and life extension. Advances in genetic engineering technologies, particularly CRISPR-Cas9, have made it possible to edit specific genes with unprecedented precision. This has opened the door to the potential treatment of genetic diseases, but it also raises the possibility of using genetic manipulation to enhance longevity or prevent the biological processes that lead to death.

CRISPR-Cas9, a gene-editing tool that allows scientists to cut and replace sections of DNA, has revolutionized the field of genetics. Its potential applications are vast, from correcting mutations that cause diseases to enhancing physical and cognitive abilities. In the context of life extension, CRISPR offers the possibility of directly altering genes associated with ageing, disease resistance, and metabolism. For example, researchers have identified several genes, such as FOXO3 and SIRT1, that are linked to longevity and resistance to age-related diseases. By targeting these genes, it may be possible to slow ageing and extend life.

Another area of genetic research relevant to mortality is the study of senescent cells, which accumulate in tissues as organisms age. Senescent cells no longer divide and can release harmful compounds that damage neighbouring cells, contributing to tissue degeneration and inflammation. By targeting these senescent cells for removal—a process known as senolysis—researchers hope to mitigate the effects of ageing and extend lifespan. Early studies in mice have shown that removing senescent cells can improve health and extend lifespan, and human trials of senolytic therapies are currently underway.

The potential for genetic manipulation to alter human mortality is not without ethical concerns. The possibility of germline editing—making genetic changes that can be passed down to future generations—raises questions about the long-term consequences of altering the human genome. Critics argue that germline editing could lead to unintended genetic consequences, as well as the possibility of "designer babies" whose genetic traits are selected by parents, leading to new forms of inequality and social division. The ethics of enhancing human life through genetic manipulation, as opposed to treating disease, also remain contentious, as society grapples with the implications of tampering with fundamental biological processes.

The potential for genetic manipulation to extend life and prevent age-related death represents a dramatic shift in how society approaches mortality. While the ability to edit the human genome offers the promise of preventing or curing fatal diseases, it also forces society to confront difficult questions about what it means to live a natural life and whether death is an essential part of the human experience. As these technologies develop, the balance between extending life and maintaining the integrity of human biology will be at the forefront of ethical debates.

Artificial Intelligence and Digital Immortality

One of the most speculative yet fascinating areas of research into the future of death involves artificial intelligence (AI) and the concept of digital immortality. While death has traditionally been understood as the permanent cessation of biological life, advances in AI and computational neuroscience are challenging the notion that consciousness and identity are confined to the physical body. Some researchers believe that it may one day be possible to transfer or replicate human consciousness in a digital medium, creating a form of digital immortality.

The concept of mind uploading, where the contents of an individual's brain are transferred into a computer, is rooted in the belief that consciousness arises from the complex interactions of neurons and can therefore be simulated in a digital environment. This idea, while still speculative, has gained traction as advances in AI, machine learning, and brain-computer interfaces have accelerated. If the structure and function of the brain could be mapped in sufficient detail, it might be possible to create a digital replica of an individual's mind, allowing for the continuation of their thoughts, memories, and identity in a non-biological form.

The development of neural interfaces—devices that allow direct communication between the brain and computers—offers a potential pathway toward this goal. Neural interfaces are already being used in experimental settings to restore movement in paralyzed individuals or to control prosthetic limbs with the mind. As these technologies improve, researchers hope to expand their capabilities to include the transfer of more complex cognitive processes, potentially leading to the ability to replicate or upload consciousness.

However, the concept of digital immortality raises profound philosophical and ethical questions. What would it mean to replicate a person's consciousness in a digital medium? Would the digital version be considered the same person, or merely a copy? If consciousness can be transferred, does this constitute a form of immortality, or is it a fundamentally different kind of existence? These questions challenge long-standing assumptions about identity, selfhood, and the nature of life and death.

The potential for AI to alter our understanding of death extends beyond the realm of mind uploading. AI is increasingly being used in medicine to assist with diagnosis, treatment planning, and even end-of-life care. Machine learning algorithms can analyse vast amounts of data to predict disease progression and optimize treatment strategies, potentially delaying death by improving medical outcomes. In the future, AI may play an even greater role in managing the complex factors that contribute to death, from identifying early signs of fatal diseases to predicting the likelihood of recovery in critically ill patients.

While the idea of digital immortality remains speculative, it highlights the extent to which AI and computational technologies are reshaping our understanding of death. As these technologies evolve, they will continue to challenge the boundaries between life and death, forcing society to confront new ethical dilemmas about the nature of existence and the meaning of mortality.

The Ethical Implications of Emerging Technologies

The rapid pace of technological advancement in life extension, genetic manipulation, and artificial intelligence brings with it a host of ethical concerns. These technologies have the potential to radically alter the human experience, but they also raise questions about fairness, inequality, and the consequences of disrupting the natural processes of life and death.

One of the primary ethical concerns surrounding life extension technologies is access. If therapies that extend lifespan become available, there is a significant risk that they will be accessible only to the wealthy and privileged, exacerbating existing social inequalities. The development of life extension technologies could lead to a society where the wealthy live significantly longer than the rest of the population, further entrenching divisions in wealth, health, and opportunity. Ensuring equitable access to life-extending treatments will be a critical challenge as these technologies become available.

In addition to issues of access, the extension of human life raises questions about the societal and environmental consequences of longer lifespans. If individuals are able to live significantly longer, or even achieve immortality, what impact will this have on population growth, resource consumption, and the environment? The human population is already placing immense strain on the planet's resources, and longer lifespans could exacerbate these challenges. Society will need to grapple with the ethical implications of extending life in a world that is already facing significant ecological and social pressures.

The use of genetic manipulation to enhance human life also presents ethical challenges, particularly in the context of germline editing. While somatic gene editing, which targets non-reproductive cells, is generally considered acceptable for treating diseases, germline editing affects reproductive cells and can be passed down to future generations. This raises concerns about the potential for unintended genetic consequences and the possibility of creating inequalities between those who have access to genetic enhancements and those who do not. The ethical debate surrounding germline editing highlights the tension between the desire to enhance human life and the need to protect future generations from the consequences of tampering with the human genome.

Finally, the concept of digital immortality and the potential for mind uploading raise existential and philosophical questions about the nature of identity and consciousness. If consciousness can be replicated in a digital form, does this constitute a continuation of the self, or is it a new entity entirely? The idea of digital immortality challenges long-held beliefs about the finality of death and the continuity of identity, forcing society to reconsider what it means to live, die, and persist after death.

A New Frontier in the Understanding of Death

The future of death is poised to be radically transformed by emerging technologies and scientific research. Advances in life extension, genetic manipulation, and artificial intelligence are challenging traditional definitions of mortality and offering new possibilities for delaying, preventing, or even transcending death. These innovations hold great promise for improving human health and extending lifespan, but they also raise profound ethical and philosophical questions that society must address.

As we move into this new frontier, it will be essential to balance the desire to extend life with the need to protect the values of equity, fairness, and respect for the natural processes of life and death. The technologies explored in this chapter offer a glimpse into a future where death may no longer be inevitable, but they also remind us of the complexity of altering the fundamental nature of human existence.

The ongoing exploration of life extension, genetic

manipulation, and digital immortality will continue to push the boundaries of what is possible, reshaping our understanding of mortality and challenging the very concept of death. As science advances, it will be necessary to engage in thoughtful and inclusive discussions about the ethical implications of these technologies, ensuring that the future of death benefits all of humanity.

CHAPTER 25: THE LEGAL SIDE OF DEATH: ESTATES, WILLS, AND RIGHTS

The death of an individual not only marks the cessation of biological life but also triggers a complex series of legal processes that govern the distribution of the deceased's assets, the resolution of debts, and the handling of personal rights, including those related to digital assets and intellectual property. The legal intricacies that follow death can have profound consequences for the deceased's heirs, beneficiaries, and estate administrators. The drafting of wills, the management of estates, and the legal rights surrounding the deceased's body are all areas in which the law plays a critical role. Furthermore, the rise of digital technology and the proliferation of online accounts, social media profiles, and other virtual assets have introduced new legal challenges related to digital estate management and posthumous rights.

The law's role in death is both pragmatic and protective, designed to ensure that an individual's wishes are honoured after death, that their property is distributed fairly, and that disputes among heirs or creditors are resolved according to established legal principles. At the same time, legal frameworks around death are constantly evolving, particularly as modern society becomes increasingly digitized and as questions arise about the posthumous management of digital legacies.

This chapter explores the legal complexities that arise after death, from the writing of wills and the management of estates to the evolving legal landscape surrounding digital assets and posthumous rights. By examining the legal principles that govern the disposition of an individual's property and the handling of their rights after death, this chapter provides a comprehensive overview of the legal side of death in the modern age.

The Role of Wills in Estate Planning

A will, also known as a last will and testament, is one of the most important legal documents in estate planning, outlining how a person's assets are to be distributed after their death. They will also provide instructions for appointing guardians for minor children, naming an executor to manage the estate, and designating beneficiaries who will inherit property. Without a legally valid will, a person's estate is subject to the default rules of intestacy, a legal framework that dictates how assets are distributed when there is no will in place. These rules vary by jurisdiction but generally prioritize close family members, often leading to outcomes that may not align with the deceased's wishes.

The drafting of a will is governed by several legal requirements, including capacity, formality, and voluntariness. In most jurisdictions, the person making the will, known as the testator, must be of sound mind and capable of understanding the nature and consequences of the document they are creating. This is referred to as testamentary capacity. The will must also be executed by specific formalities, such as being signed by the testator in the presence of witnesses. Failure to meet these requirements can result in the will being invalidated, leaving the estate to be distributed according to intestacy laws.

One of the key functions of a will is to designate an executor, who is responsible for administering the estate and ensuring that the terms of the will are carried out. The executor's duties include gathering the deceased's assets, paying debts and taxes, and distributing the remaining property to the beneficiaries. The executor must act by fiduciary principles, meaning they are legally obligated to act in the best interests of the estate and its beneficiaries. This role is often complex and requires navigating legal, financial, and administrative tasks, especially when disputes arise among heirs or when the estate is subject to substantial tax liabilities.

Wills can also include provisions for the management of digital assets, an area of increasing importance as more individuals accumulate significant digital footprints. Many jurisdictions now allow individuals to designate a digital executor, someone tasked with managing online accounts, social media profiles, and digital assets after death. However, the legal treatment of digital assets remains inconsistent, and without specific instructions in a will, it may be difficult for heirs to access or manage these assets.

Despite the importance of having a will, many individuals die without one, leaving their estate to be distributed according to the laws of intestacy. Intestacy laws prioritize spouses, children, and other close relatives, but they may not reflect the deceased's relationships or preferences. For instance, intestacy laws typically do not recognize unmarried partners, stepchildren, or close friends as legal heirs, which can result in unintended consequences for those who die without a will. Moreover, intestacy can lead to complex legal disputes among family members, particularly in cases where the distribution of assets is contentious.

For these reasons, estate planning and the drafting of a legally sound will are critical steps in ensuring that a person's wishes are honoured after death. Beyond the division of property, wills provide an opportunity for individuals to shape their legacy and make provisions for the people and causes that matter most to them. Wills can also help mitigate potential legal disputes, offering clarity and guidance to family members and reducing the likelihood of contentious litigation after death.

Managing Estates: Probate and the Administration of Assets

Once a person dies, the legal process of managing their estate begins, a procedure known as probate. Probate is the formal judicial process through which a will is validated, the deceased's assets are inventoried, and their debts and taxes are settled before the remaining assets are distributed to beneficiaries. The probate process varies by jurisdiction, but it typically involves the executor or estate administrator filing the will with the court and providing an inventory of the estate's assets and liabilities.

Probate can be a lengthy and complex process, particularly for large estates or those with significant debts or tax obligations. One of the executor's first responsibilities is to identify and gather the deceased's assets, which may include real estate, bank accounts, investments, personal property, and business interests. The executor must also identify any debts owed by the estate, such as mortgages, loans, credit card balances, and outstanding taxes. These debts must be paid before the estate can be distributed to beneficiaries, and the executor is responsible for ensuring that creditors are notified and allowed to make claims against the estate.

In some cases, probate can be avoided or simplified through the use of estate planning tools such as trusts, joint ownership arrangements, or beneficiary designations. A trust is a legal arrangement in which a trustee holds property on behalf of beneficiaries, allowing the assets to be transferred outside of probate. By placing assets into a trust, individuals can avoid the time and expense of probate and ensure that their property is distributed according to their wishes with minimal court involvement. Similarly, assets held in joint ownership or with designated beneficiaries, such as life insurance policies or retirement accounts, can pass directly to the surviving owner or designated beneficiaries without going through probate.

However, not all estates qualify for simplified probate procedures, and in many cases, the process can become contentious if there are disputes among heirs or creditors. For example, if a will is contested—whether on the grounds of fraud, undue influence, or lack of testamentary capacity—the probate process can be delayed as the court resolves the dispute. Similarly, if the estate is insolvent, meaning that the deceased's debts exceed their assets, the executor must carefully prioritize payments to creditors according to legal requirements, which can further complicate the administration process.

One of the most significant challenges in estate administration is the potential for estate taxes, also known as inheritance or death taxes, depending on the jurisdiction. These taxes can represent a substantial liability for large estates, particularly those that include valuable real estate, businesses, or investment portfolios. In the United States, for example, federal estate taxes apply to estates that exceed a certain threshold, though many states have additional estate or inheritance taxes. The executor must ensure that all applicable taxes are paid before the estate is distributed, and failure to do so can result in legal penalties.

The complexity of estate administration underscores the importance of comprehensive estate planning. While probate is an essential legal process for many estates, it can be burdensome, costly, and time-consuming. Effective estate planning, including the use of wills, trusts, and other legal tools, can simplify the administration of assets, reduce the likelihood of disputes, and minimize the financial and emotional burden on surviving family members.

Legal Rights Over Bodies: Burial, Cremation, and Posthumous Wishes

The legal rights surrounding the handling of a deceased person's body are governed by both statutory law and cultural norms. Upon death, the question of who has the legal right to determine the disposition of the body—whether through burial, cremation, or other means—becomes a critical issue. In many jurisdictions, the individual's expressed wishes regarding their final disposition are given legal weight, but in the absence of clear instructions, this responsibility typically falls to the next of kin.

The right to control the disposition of the body can be a source of legal disputes, particularly when family members disagree about how the deceased should be laid to rest. For example, disputes can arise between a spouse and children from a previous marriage, or among siblings who have different religious or cultural beliefs about burial practices. To prevent such disputes, individuals can specify their preferences in a legal document, such as a will or a letter of instruction. These preferences can include not only the method of disposition but also details such as the location of burial, the type of ceremony, and whether the individual wishes to be cremated or buried by religious customs.

In some jurisdictions, laws have been enacted to allow individuals to designate a specific person, known as an agent or representative, to make decisions about the disposition of their body. This designation can be made in advance through a legal document known as a disposition of remains form. By designating a trusted agent, individuals can ensure that their posthumous wishes are respected and that disputes among family members are minimized.

The legal status of human remains is also subject to regulation, particularly when it comes to organ donation, autopsy, and posthumous medical research. Organ donation, which allows individuals to donate their organs for transplantation after death is governed by specific legal frameworks, such as the Uniform Anatomical Gift Act in the United States. Individuals can express their consent to organ donation through a donor registry or by specifying their wishes in a will or driver's license. In many jurisdictions, next of kin also have the right to authorize or refuse organ donation on behalf of the deceased.

The handling of a deceased person's body is further complicated by legal requirements related to autopsies and forensic investigations. In cases where the cause of death is unclear or suspicious, a legal autopsy may be required to determine the circumstances of death. Autopsies are typically ordered by a medical examiner or coroner, and while family members can object, their wishes may be overridden by legal necessity.

In modern times, new legal questions have emerged regarding the handling of digital remains, particularly in cases where individuals express posthumous wishes regarding their online presence. For example, individuals may wish to have their social media profiles deleted, memorialized, or managed by a designated person after death. However, the legal treatment of digital remains varies by platform and jurisdiction, and the enforceability of posthumous digital rights remains a developing area of law.

Digital Assets and Posthumous Rights in the Digital Age

As society becomes increasingly reliant on digital technology, the management of digital assets and posthumous rights has become an important aspect of estate planning. Digital assets include a wide range of online accounts and properties, such as email accounts, social media profiles, cloud storage, cryptocurrency, intellectual property, and domain names. The legal status of these assets after death remains a relatively new area of law, and the treatment of digital assets in estate planning can vary significantly depending on the platform and jurisdiction.

One of the challenges in managing digital assets after death is the lack of standardized laws governing access to these assets. In many cases, digital platforms have their own policies for managing accounts after death, which may or may not align with the wishes of the deceased or their heirs. For example, some social media platforms allow users to designate a "legacy contact" who can manage the account after death, while others automatically delete accounts after a period of inactivity. In some jurisdictions, laws have been enacted to give estate executors the right to access and manage digital assets, but these laws are still evolving.

The management of digital assets raises several legal and ethical questions. For example, should heirs have access to the deceased's private communications, such as email or social media messages? How should intellectual property, such as digital artwork or writings, be managed and distributed after death? These questions are further complicated by privacy concerns and the potential for misuse of digital information.

Cryptocurrency, an increasingly popular form of digital asset, presents unique challenges in estate planning. Unlike traditional financial accounts, cryptocurrency is typically stored in digital wallets protected by private keys. If the private key is lost or inaccessible after death, the cryptocurrency may be irretrievable. To ensure that cryptocurrency is properly transferred to beneficiaries, individuals must take steps to include detailed instructions in their estate plans, such as providing access to digital wallets and private keys.

The rise of digital assets has also led to new legal debates about posthumous rights, particularly in the context of intellectual property and digital legacies. For example, artists, writers, and content creators who publish their work online may wish to specify how their intellectual property is handled after death. This could include designating heirs to manage royalties, copyrights, or licenses, as well as determining how unfinished or unpublished works should be treated.

Posthumous rights also extend to the question of digital immortality—the possibility that an individual's digital presence could continue to exist indefinitely after death. Advances in artificial intelligence and machine learning have led to the creation of digital avatars or chatbots that can simulate a deceased person's voice, personality, and interactions. While these technologies offer new possibilities for preserving a digital legacy, they also raise ethical concerns about consent, privacy, and the commercialization of the deceased's likeness or identity.

Conclusion: Navigating the Legal Complexities of Death

The legal processes that follow death are essential to ensuring that a person's wishes are honoured, their assets are distributed fairly, and their rights are respected. From the drafting of wills and the administration of estates to the handling of digital assets and posthumous rights, the law plays a crucial role in shaping how society manages death. As new technologies and digital platforms emerge, the legal landscape surrounding death continues to evolve, presenting both opportunities and challenges for individuals seeking to manage their legacies.

The complexity of legal issues surrounding death underscores the importance of careful estate planning. By drafting clear and legally valid wills, designating executors, and addressing the management of digital assets, individuals can help ensure that their wishes are respected and that their loved ones are spared unnecessary legal disputes. At the same time, society must continue to grapple with the ethical and legal questions raised by new technologies, particularly as digital assets and artificial intelligence reshape the boundaries of life, death, and posthumous rights.

CHAPTER 26: THE SCIENCE OF AUTOPSY: REVEALING THE CAUSE OF DEATH

Autopsies, long regarded as a fundamental tool in forensic pathology, are vital in revealing the cause of death in cases where it is sudden, suspicious, or unexplained. Far from a mere post-mortem examination, the autopsy is a meticulous scientific process that combines anatomical, physiological, and toxicological analysis to determine how and why an individual died. It serves as a critical element in both medical and legal investigations, providing clarity in cases where the circumstances surrounding death are unclear, and often offering closure to families of the deceased.

The role of autopsies has evolved alongside advances in medical science, with modern forensic techniques allowing pathologists to uncover even the most obscure causes of death. While the practice of examining the deceased dates back millennia, contemporary autopsies benefit from cutting-edge technologies such as toxicology screening, advanced imaging, and genetic analysis, which provide a more comprehensive understanding of the factors leading to death.

This chapter offers a comprehensive overview of the autopsy process, from the initial external examination to the final determination of the cause and manner of death. By delving into the scientific methods employed by forensic pathologists, the chapter elucidates how the autopsy remains an indispensable tool in the investigation of death, shedding light on the circumstances that may otherwise remain concealed.

The Purpose and Types of Autopsies

An autopsy, also known as a post-mortem examination, serves several key purposes. It is performed to determine the cause of death, identify any diseases or injuries that may have contributed to death, and provide information that may be used in legal or medical investigations. Autopsies are conducted in a variety of contexts, ranging from routine medical examinations of hospital deaths to complex forensic investigations involving criminal activity. The findings of an autopsy can play a crucial role in court cases, insurance claims, and public health initiatives.

There are two primary types of autopsies: clinical autopsies and forensic autopsies. Clinical autopsies, also referred to as hospital or medical autopsies, are typically performed on patients who die under medical care, especially when the cause of death is unknown or when further information is needed to understand the progression of a disease. These autopsies are often requested by physicians or family members to gain insight into the underlying medical conditions that led to death. Clinical autopsies provide valuable information for medical research and education, allowing healthcare professionals to learn from previously unrecognized diseases or complications.

In contrast, forensic autopsies are conducted under the authority of a medical examiner or coroner in cases where death is sudden, unexpected, or the result of violence, injury, or poisoning. The primary goal of a forensic autopsy is to establish the cause and manner of death, which may be classified as natural, accidental, suicidal, homicidal, or undetermined. Forensic pathologists—physicians specializing in legal medicine—conduct these autopsies, often working closely with law enforcement agencies to provide crucial evidence in criminal investigations.

Regardless of the type, the autopsy process follows a systematic approach, beginning with the external examination of the body, followed by the internal examination, and concluding with laboratory analyses. Each step contributes to the overall understanding of how the individual died, and in many cases, the findings of the autopsy can influence legal, medical, and public health outcomes.

The External Examination: Clues on the Surface

The autopsy process begins with a thorough external examination of the body, which can reveal critical information about the events leading up to death. This step is particularly important in forensic autopsies, where visible injuries or abnormalities may provide immediate clues regarding the cause of death. For example, bullet wounds, stab marks, and bruises are often the first indicators of violent or suspicious death, while signs of rigour mortis, livor mortis, and decomposition offer valuable insights into the time and circumstances of death.

The external examination is conducted in a well-lit and sterile environment, where the pathologist carefully documents the condition of the body. This documentation typically includes the body's general appearance, including height, weight, and any distinguishing features such as tattoos, scars, or birthmarks. The pathologist also notes the presence of medical devices, such as pacemakers or surgical implants, which may provide relevant information about the deceased's medical history.

A key aspect of the external examination is the assessment of livor mortis and rigour mortis, which are post-mortem changes that can offer clues about the timing of death. Livor mortis, or post-mortem lividity, refers to the pooling of blood in the lower parts of the body due to gravity after the heart stops beating. The colour and distribution of lividity can help estimate the time of death and indicate whether the body has been moved post-mortem. For instance, fixed lividity in a particular position suggests that the body remained in that position for several hours after death.

Rigour mortis, the stiffening of the body's muscles after death, is another important factor in estimating the post-mortem interval (PMI). Rigour mortis typically begins within a few hours of death, reaching its peak stiffness at around 12 hours and gradually dissipating over the next 24 to 48 hours. By assessing the degree of muscle stiffness, the pathologist can estimate the time since death, which can be crucial in determining the sequence of events leading to death.

The external examination also includes an assessment of any visible trauma, such as abrasions, lacerations, and contusions. These injuries can offer important information about how the individual died and whether foul play is involved. For example, defensive wounds on the hands or forearms may indicate that the deceased attempted to fend off an attacker, while patterned injuries—such as tyre marks or the imprint of a weapon—can help reconstruct the circumstances of an assault or accident.

Beyond trauma, the external examination can reveal signs of medical conditions that contributed to death. For example, jaundice (yellowing of the skin) may indicate liver disease, while cyanosis (a bluish discolouration of the skin) suggests respiratory or circulatory failure. In cases of suspected drug overdose, needle marks, track marks, or other signs of intravenous drug use may be observed.

Once the external examination is complete, the pathologist moves on to the internal examination, where the body's organs and tissues are carefully dissected and analysed for further clues about the cause of death.

The Internal Examination: Exploring the Body's Systems

The internal examination, often referred to as the dissection, is the core of the autopsy process. During this phase, the pathologist opens the body to examine the internal organs and tissues for signs of disease, trauma, or other abnormalities that may have contributed to death. This part of the autopsy is conducted with meticulous care, as it is critical to accurately identify the physiological mechanisms that led to the cessation of life.

The internal examination begins with a Y-shaped incision that extends from the shoulders to the sternum and down to the pubic bone, allowing the pathologist to access the chest and abdominal cavities. The skin and soft tissues are carefully reflected, exposing the rib cage and internal organs. The pathologist then systematically removes and examines each organ, starting with the thoracic cavity (which contains the heart and lungs) and moving to the abdominal cavity (which contains the liver, stomach, intestines, and other digestive organs).

Examination of the cardiovascular system is one of the most critical aspects of the internal autopsy, particularly in cases where the cause of death is suspected to be heart disease or a related condition. The pathologist carefully dissects the heart, examining its chambers, valves, and coronary arteries for signs of atherosclerosis, myocardial infarction (heart attack), or structural defects. The coronary arteries are often opened to assess for blockages or plaques that could have led to a fatal cardiac event. Heart disease remains one of the leading causes of death worldwide, and the autopsy can provide valuable insights into undiagnosed or untreated cardiovascular conditions.

The respiratory system is examined next, with the pathologist inspecting the lungs for signs of disease, trauma, or environmental factors that may have caused respiratory failure. Conditions such as pneumonia, chronic obstructive pulmonary disease (COPD), or pulmonary embolism can be identified through the examination of lung tissue. In cases of suspected asphyxiation or drowning, the presence of fluid, foam, or foreign objects in the airways can confirm the cause of death.

The digestive system is also examined for signs of gastrointestinal disease, perforation, or obstruction. The pathologist may find evidence of ulcers, tumours, or infections that contributed to death. In cases of poisoning or overdose, the contents of the stomach are analysed for the presence of toxic substances, which may provide critical evidence in determining the cause of death.

The liver and kidneys, as vital organs responsible for filtering toxins from the body, are thoroughly examined for signs of disease or dysfunction. Liver disease, including cirrhosis or fatty liver disease, can often be identified through changes in the organ's appearance, while kidney failure may be indicated by scarring or other structural abnormalities. These organs play a key role in the body's metabolic processes, and their examination can provide important clues about the deceased's health and the factors that led to death.

The brain is one of the final organs to be examined during the autopsy, as it requires careful removal from the skull. The pathologist opens the skull by making an incision around the scalp and using a specialized saw to remove the top portion of the skull. The brain is then gently removed for examination. Neurological conditions such as stroke, bleeding, or traumatic brain injury may be identified through the examination of the brain's structures. In cases of sudden, unexplained death, the brain's condition can offer insights into the role of neurological factors in the fatal event.

Forensic Techniques: Toxicology, Histology, and DNA Analysis

Beyond the physical examination of the body's organs and tissues, modern autopsies rely heavily on forensic techniques such as toxicology, histology, and DNA analysis to uncover critical details about the cause of death. These laboratory analyses complement the findings of the external and internal examinations, providing a deeper understanding of the factors that contributed to death.

Toxicology is one of the most important forensic tools in the investigation of sudden or suspicious deaths, particularly those involving drugs, alcohol, or poisoning. During the autopsy, samples of blood, urine, and tissue are collected and sent to a toxicology laboratory for analysis. The toxicologist screens these samples for the presence of substances such as narcotics, prescription medications, alcohol, and poisons. The concentration of these substances in the blood or tissues can provide valuable information about whether the individual died from an overdose, poisoning, or the toxic effects of a substance.

In cases of drug overdose, toxicology results can help determine whether the death was accidental, intentional, or the result of drug interactions. For example, high concentrations of opioids, benzodiazepines, or other central nervous system depressants in the bloodstream may indicate a fatal overdose. At the same time, the presence of multiple drugs may suggest polypharmacy —a dangerous combination of medications that can lead to unintended death.

Histology is another critical forensic technique used in autopsies, involving the microscopic examination of tissues to identify diseases, infections, or other cellular abnormalities that are not visible to the naked eye. Tissue samples from the heart, lungs, liver, kidneys, and other organs are examined under a microscope by a histopathologist, who looks for signs of inflammation, infection, or cancer. Histological analysis can confirm the presence of diseases such as pneumonia, myocarditis, or cancer, which may have contributed to death. In cases of suspected trauma, histology can also reveal microscopic evidence of injury, such as haemorrhaging or tissue damage.

DNA analysis is often employed in forensic autopsies, particularly in cases involving unidentified bodies or criminal investigations. DNA samples can be collected from the deceased's tissues and compared to DNA databases or family members to establish identity. In cases of violent crime, DNA analysis can also be used to match biological evidence, such as hair, blood, or skin cells, to the perpetrator. DNA technology has revolutionized forensic science, providing a powerful tool for solving complex cases and bringing closure to families.

In addition to toxicology, histology, and DNA analysis, modern autopsies may also employ advanced imaging technologies such as CT scans and MRI, which allow pathologists to examine the body's internal structures in great detail without the need for extensive dissection. These imaging techniques are particularly useful in cases of trauma, where fractures, internal bleeding, or foreign objects may be present. Post-mortem imaging, often referred to as virtual autopsy, is becoming an increasingly valuable tool in forensic investigations, offering a non-invasive method for visualizing the body's internal injuries and abnormalities.

Determining the Cause and Manner of Death

The ultimate goal of the autopsy is to determine the cause and manner of death. The cause of death refers to the specific medical condition or injury that led to the cessation of life, while the manner of death categorizes the circumstances surrounding the death, such as natural, accidental, suicidal, homicidal, or undetermined. The findings of the autopsy, combined with the results of forensic analyses, allow the pathologist to make an informed determination about how and why the individual died.

In cases of natural death, the cause may be related to chronic diseases such as heart disease, cancer, or respiratory failure. For example, the autopsy may reveal that the individual died of a myocardial infarction (heart attack) due to atherosclerosis, or from respiratory failure due to advanced lung disease. In cases of accidental death, the autopsy may uncover evidence of trauma, such as blunt force injuries from a car accident or drowning.

Suicidal and homicidal deaths are often more complex, requiring careful analysis of injuries, toxicology results, and the circumstances surrounding death. For example, in cases of suicide, the pathologist may find evidence of self-inflicted wounds, drug overdose, or hanging. In cases of homicide, the autopsy can provide critical evidence for law enforcement, such as the type of weapon used, the nature of the injuries, and the sequence of events leading to death.

In some cases, the manner of death may be classified as undetermined, particularly when the available evidence is inconclusive or when multiple factors contributed to the death. For example, in cases where the deceased had both a chronic illness and a traumatic injury, it may be difficult to determine which factor was the primary cause of death.

The Autopsy as a Vital Tool in Death Investigation

The science of autopsy remains one of the most essential tools in death investigation, providing critical insights into the causes and circumstances of death. Through a combination of external and internal examination, forensic techniques, and laboratory analysis, the autopsy allows pathologists to uncover the medical and physiological factors that led to death, often solving mysteries that would otherwise remain unsolved.

As forensic technology continues to advance, the autopsy will remain at the forefront of death investigation, offering invaluable information for medical, legal, and public health purposes. Whether in the context of sudden, suspicious, or unexplained deaths, the autopsy serves as a bridge between life and death, revealing the hidden truths that lie beneath the surface.

CHAPTER 27: HISTORICAL PLAGUES AND EPIDEMICS: DEATH ON A LARGE SCALE

Throughout human history, plagues and pandemics have been responsible for some of the most catastrophic death events, shaping the course of civilizations and transforming medical knowledge. These large-scale outbreaks of disease have had profound social, political, and economic impacts, often forcing societies to confront mortality on an unprecedented scale. While modern medicine has mitigated the effects of many infectious diseases, historical plagues such as the Black Death, and the Spanish Flu, and more recent outbreaks like HIV/AIDS and COVID-19 continue to serve as reminders of humanity's vulnerability to biological forces.

Plagues and pandemics are unique in their ability to affect large populations rapidly and indiscriminately. Unlike localized outbreaks, these events transcend geographic and social boundaries, claiming lives across classes, ethnicities, and political systems. The sheer scale of death that accompanies pandemics disrupts entire societies, upending economies, altering political structures, and forcing innovations in medical science and public health. Moreover, the psychological and cultural consequences of mass death linger long after the disease has been eradicated, influencing everything from art and literature to religious practices and societal values.

This chapter examines some of the most significant plagues and pandemics in history, focusing on their biological, social, and historical implications. From the devastation of the Black Death in the 14th century to the global spread of the Spanish Flu in 1918, these events highlight the intersection of disease, society, and medicine. By exploring how mass death has shaped societies, we gain insight into how pandemics have driven advances in medical understanding, public health infrastructure, and social organization.

The Black Death: Unleashing Death Across Medieval Europe

The Black Death, also known as the Bubonic Plague, stands as one of the most infamous and deadly pandemics in human history. Sweeping through Europe between 1347 and 1351, the Black Death claimed an estimated 25 to 50 million lives, amounting to nearly one-third of Europe's population at the time. The pandemic was caused by the bacterium Yersinia pestis, which was transmitted through fleas that infested black rats. The rapid spread of the disease, combined with the limited medical knowledge of the period, contributed to its staggering death toll.

The Black Death presented with a range of symptoms, most notably the appearance of painful, swollen lymph nodes—known as buboes—along with fever, chills, and necrosis of the skin. As the disease progressed, it often led to septicaemia or pneumonia, both of which were invariably fatal in the absence of effective treatment. In addition to the bubonic form, Yersinia pestis could also cause pneumonic plague, which spreads directly from person to person through respiratory droplets, increasing the potential for widespread infection.

The biological devastation wrought by the Black Death had profound social and economic consequences. Entire villages were wiped out, and the sudden loss of such a large portion of the population led to labour shortages, contributing to the breakdown of feudal systems. The scarcity of workers increased wages for surviving labourers, leading to shifts in social power dynamics. The decimation of local economies and trade networks, combined with widespread fear and uncertainty, destabilized political structures and weakened religious institutions, which had been unable to protect from the disease.

From a medical standpoint, the Black Death highlighted the limitations of medieval medicine, which relied heavily on religious and supernatural explanations for disease. At the time, the prevailing theory of illness was based on the imbalance of the four humours—blood, phlegm, yellow bile, and black bile—and treatments often included bloodletting, herbal remedies, and other ineffective methods. Without an understanding of germ theory or the role of vectors in disease transmission, medieval physicians were ill-equipped to combat the plague, leading to high mortality rates and the proliferation of misguided attempts to prevent or cure the disease.

The long-term effects of the Black Death on European society were profound. The massive loss of life forced the surviving population to rethink their relationship with mortality, leading to shifts in religious and philosophical thought. The plague's impact on the economy contributed to the decline of feudalism and the rise of a more market-based economy, while its devastation of urban centres led to new approaches in urban planning, sanitation, and public health. In many ways, the Black Death catalysed the later developments of the Renaissance and the eventual emergence of modern medical practices.

The Spanish Flu of 1918: A Modern Pandemic

While the Black Death is often considered the most devastating pandemic in medieval history, the Spanish Flu of 1918 stands as the deadliest pandemic of the modern era. Unlike the Black Death, which primarily affected Europe, the Spanish Flu was a global pandemic, infecting approximately one-third of the world's population and causing an estimated 50 to 100 million deaths. What made the Spanish Flu particularly lethal was its ability to spread rapidly across continents in the aftermath of World War I, facilitated by troop movements and global transportation networks.

The Spanish Flu was caused by the H1N1 strain of the influenza virus, which originated in birds before mutating to infect humans. While influenza is a common seasonal virus, the 1918 strain was unusually virulent, and it disproportionately affected young, healthy adults—a demographic typically less vulnerable to severe outcomes from influenza. The virus triggered an overreaction of the immune system, known as a cytokine storm, which caused widespread inflammation and damage to lung tissue, often leading to pneumonia and death. This immune response was particularly deadly in those with strong immune systems, which is why so many otherwise healthy individuals succumbed to the disease.

The symptoms of the Spanish Flu were severe and progressed rapidly. Patients often developed high fevers, body aches, and a characteristic "heliotrope cyanosis"—a purplish-blue discolouration of the skin due to lack of oxygen. In many cases, death occurred within days of symptom onset, particularly in individuals who developed secondary bacterial infections, such as pneumonia. Hospitals and healthcare facilities were quickly overwhelmed by the number of cases, and the lack of effective treatments or vaccines exacerbated the crisis.

The social and political effects of the Spanish Flu were significant, particularly in the context of the post-World War I era. The pandemic coincided with the demobilization of troops and the resettlement of populations, leading to widespread social unrest and economic instability. The high mortality rate, particularly among young adults, left a lasting demographic impact, with many families losing primary breadwinners and communities experiencing population declines. Governments were largely unprepared for a pandemic of this scale, and public health responses varied widely, with some cities implementing strict quarantine measures and others resisting such interventions.

From a medical perspective, the Spanish Flu underscored the importance of public health infrastructure and the need for coordinated responses to global health crises. While germ theory was well-established by 1918, the mechanisms of influenza transmission were not fully understood, and the development of antiviral drugs and vaccines remained decades away. The pandemic prompted a renewed focus on medical research, leading to advances in virology and immunology that would later inform the development of influenza vaccines.

The Spanish Flu also served as a turning point in global health governance, laying the groundwork for the establishment of international health organizations such as the World Health Organization (WHO). The pandemic demonstrated the need for global cooperation in disease surveillance, research, and response, as no nation was immune from the effects of the virus. The legacy of the Spanish Flu continues to influence modern public health policies, particularly in the context of pandemic preparedness and response strategies.

Other Significant Plagues and Epidemics: Shaping Medical Knowledge

While the Black Death and the Spanish Flu are among the most well-known pandemics in history, numerous other plagues and epidemics have had significant impacts on society and medical understanding. One such event was the Justinian Plague, which struck the Byzantine Empire in the 6th century and is believed to be the first recorded outbreak of the same bacterium, Yersinia pestis, that would later cause the Black Death. The Justinian Plague contributed to the weakening of the Byzantine Empire and had lasting effects on European and Mediterranean history.

Another critical pandemic was the Third Cholera Pandemic (1846–1860), which was part of a series of cholera outbreaks that ravaged Europe, Asia, and the Americas during the 19th century. Cholera, caused by the bacterium Vibrio cholerae, spreads through contaminated water and food, leading to severe diarrhoea, dehydration, and death if untreated. The third cholera pandemic was particularly important for the development of public health measures, as it prompted physician John Snow to identify contaminated water as the source of the disease, laying the foundation for modern epidemiology and public health sanitation efforts.

The 20th century saw the emergence of other notable epidemics, such as HIV/AIDS, which began in the 1980s and continues to affect millions globally. Unlike pandemics characterized by rapid onset and high mortality over a short period, HIV/AIDS is a slow-moving epidemic that initially spread undetected for years. The virus attacks the immune system, leading to acquired immunodeficiency syndrome (AIDS), which leaves individuals vulnerable to opportunistic infections. The response to the HIV/AIDS epidemic transformed global public health, leading to significant advances in virology, antiviral treatments, and global health funding.

More recently, the COVID-19 pandemic, caused by the novel coronavirus SARS-CoV-2, has reshaped the world in unprecedented ways. First detected in late 2019, COVID-19 quickly spread globally, leading to widespread morbidity and mortality. While the development of vaccines and antiviral treatments has helped mitigate the virus's impact, the pandemic has highlighted both the strengths and weaknesses of global health systems, as well as the importance of pandemic preparedness. COVID-19 has also underscored the role of social, political, and economic factors in shaping public health responses, with countries adopting varying strategies to manage the crisis.

The Social and Medical Impacts of Large-Scale Death Events

The biological devastation caused by plagues and pandemics is only part of the story. These events have profound social, political, and economic implications that extend far beyond the immediate loss of life. In many cases, pandemics have accelerated shifts in social structures, economies, and political systems, often serving as catalysts for change.

For example, the labour shortages caused by the Black Death contributed to the decline of feudalism in Europe, as surviving workers were able to demand higher wages and better working conditions. Similarly, the devastation of the Spanish Flu disrupted economies and reshaped social norms, as communities struggled to cope with the high mortality rates among young, working-age adults. In both cases, the sheer scale of death forced societies to adapt, leading to lasting changes in economic and social systems.

Pandemics have also played a key role in advancing medical knowledge. The study of infectious diseases, epidemiology, and public health has often been driven by the need to respond to large-scale outbreaks. For example, the cholera pandemics of the 19th century led to significant advances in public health infrastructure, including the development of sanitation systems, clean water supplies, and waste management practices. Similarly, the HIV/AIDS epidemic spurred the development of antiviral therapies and global health initiatives aimed at preventing the spread of infectious diseases.

In many cases, pandemics have also led to changes in cultural and religious practices. The Black Death, for instance, caused widespread religious and philosophical introspection, as people sought to understand why such devastation had befallen them. Some turned to religious zeal, believing the plague was divine punishment, while others became disillusioned with the church's inability to protect them. These shifts in religious belief and practice had long-lasting effects on European culture, contributing to the intellectual movements that followed.

Lessons from History and the Role of Plagues in Shaping Societies

Historical plagues and epidemics are a reminder of the fragile balance between human society and the natural world. While modern medicine has made significant strides in preventing and controlling infectious diseases, the threat of pandemics remains ever-present. The lessons of the Black Death, the Spanish Flu, and more recent pandemics underscore the importance of preparedness, global cooperation, and public health infrastructure in mitigating the impact of future outbreaks.

The study of historical pandemics not only provides insight into the biological and medical aspects of disease but also highlights the social, political, and cultural transformations that accompany large-scale death events. By understanding the historical and contemporary responses to plagues, we gain a deeper appreciation for the resilience of human societies and how death on a massive scale continues to shape the trajectory of civilizations.

CHAPTER 28: MASS GRAVES: SCIENCE AND DISCOVERY IN ARCHAEOLOGY

Mass graves, the final resting places of multiple individuals buried together, have long been of interest to archaeologists and forensic scientists due to the wealth of information they provide about past societies, conflicts, and disasters. Whether ancient burial sites or modern-day war zones, these graves are often the result of significant social or political upheavals, environmental catastrophes, or systematic violence, such as genocide. The scientific investigation of mass graves involves a multidisciplinary approach that combines archaeology, forensic anthropology, and historical analysis to uncover the stories behind these sites.

The study of mass graves serves several critical purposes. In cases of modern atrocities, such as war crimes or acts of genocide, forensic scientists play a crucial role in identifying victims, establishing timelines, and providing evidence for legal proceedings. For ancient mass graves, archaeologists seek to understand the cultural, environmental, or political contexts that led to the deaths and subsequent burials of large numbers of people. Advances in archaeological and forensic techniques, including the use of remote sensing, DNA analysis, and isotopic testing, have revolutionized the field, allowing researchers to piece together complex narratives from these burial sites.

This chapter examines the scientific methodologies used to uncover and analyse mass graves, focusing on both historical and contemporary examples. By exploring the techniques that archaeologists and forensic scientists employ, we gain insight into how these burial sites are studied to determine the causes and contexts of death, as well as the broader implications for understanding human behaviour, conflict, and mortality.

The Archaeology of Mass Graves: Uncovering History Beneath the Surface

Mass graves have been discovered across the globe, ranging from the burial pits of ancient civilizations to the graves left in the wake of modern conflicts. In each case, the discovery of a mass grave represents both a challenge and an opportunity for archaeologists. On one hand, these graves often contain large numbers of human remains, sometimes with little preservation due to the conditions of burial. On the other hand, the careful excavation and analysis of these sites can reveal invaluable information about the societies that produced them.

The discovery of a mass grave typically begins with the identification of a potential site, which may be prompted by historical records, eyewitness accounts, or accidental discovery. In modern forensic investigations, such as those conducted by international tribunals in post-conflict zones, satellite imagery and aerial surveys are often used to identify disturbed ground that may indicate the presence of a mass burial. In the case of ancient mass graves, researchers may rely on a combination of historical documents, geographic features, and archaeological surveys to locate sites.

Once a potential mass grave site is identified, archaeologists and forensic experts begin the painstaking process of excavation. This process is governed by strict protocols to ensure that the remains are preserved and that the context of the burial is maintained. Excavation typically involves the careful removal of soil layer by layer, with detailed documentation of the location and orientation of each body. In many cases, archaeologists use tools such as trowels, brushes, and sieves to carefully remove dirt from around the bones, ensuring that fragile skeletal remains are not damaged in the process.

One of the key goals of the excavation is to determine the layout and structure of the grave. This includes identifying whether the bodies were buried simultaneously or in successive layers, whether they were buried in an orderly manner or hastily disposed of, and whether there are any signs of ritual or symbolic behaviour associated with the burial. The arrangement of the bodies can provide important clues about the circumstances of death. For example, a mass grave containing bodies buried in an orderly fashion, with evidence of grave goods, may suggest a communal burial after a natural disaster, whereas bodies disposed of haphazardly may indicate violence or mass execution.

In many cases, archaeologists also look for evidence of trauma or disease on the skeletal remains. Signs of blunt force trauma, sharp force injuries, or projectile wounds can provide direct evidence of violence, while evidence of infectious diseases, such as lesions caused by tuberculosis or syphilis, can offer insights into past epidemics. In some cases, the presence of certain types of grave goods or personal items can also help archaeologists identify the individuals buried in the grave or shed light on their social status, occupation, or ethnic background.

Once the excavation is complete, the skeletal remains are

carefully documented and transported to a laboratory for further analysis. At this stage, forensic anthropologists and bioarchaeologists play a critical role in analysing the bones to determine the age, sex, ancestry, and health status of the individuals buried in the grave. By examining skeletal markers, such as the development of bones and teeth, scientists can estimate the age of the deceased at the time of death. Similarly, certain morphological features of the skull and pelvis can provide clues about an individual's biological sex.

Forensic Anthropology and the Analysis of Mass Graves

Forensic anthropology is the application of physical anthropology to the analysis of human remains in a legal context, and it is particularly critical in the investigation of mass graves. Forensic anthropologists work alongside archaeologists to help identify victims, establish cause and manner of death, and provide evidence for criminal investigations, especially in cases of war crimes and genocide. The analysis of mass graves often requires the careful examination of skeletal trauma, pathology, and post-mortem alterations to the body, providing insights into how the individuals died and how their bodies were treated after death.

One of the first steps in the forensic analysis of a mass grave is the estimation of the minimum number of individuals (MNI) buried at the site. This is a critical calculation, as it provides a baseline figure for the number of victims, particularly in cases where the remains are commingled or fragmented. Forensic anthropologists achieve this by counting the most repeated skeletal elements—such as the number of femurs or skulls—ensuring that no individual is counted more than once. This process helps investigators estimate the scale of the mass death event, which is often a critical piece of evidence in legal contexts.

In many cases, the analysis of skeletal trauma plays a central role in determining the cause of death in mass graves. Forensic anthropologists examine the bones for evidence of perimortem injuries—those that occurred at or near the time of death. Common types of trauma found in mass graves include blunt force trauma (e.g., from clubbing or falls), sharp force trauma (e.g., from knives or machetes), and projectile trauma (e.g., from bullets or shrapnel). In cases of mass violence or war crimes, the pattern and distribution of trauma on the bones can provide crucial evidence about how the victims were killed. For example, gunshot wounds to the skull or chest may indicate execution-style killings, while defensive injuries on the forearms or hands suggest that the individuals attempted to protect themselves during an attack.

In addition to trauma, forensic anthropologists often look for signs of disease or malnutrition that may have contributed to death. This is particularly important in cases where mass graves are the result of famine, epidemics, or forced labour camps. For example, the presence of Harris lines—transverse lines visible on X-rays of long bones—can indicate periods of growth interruption due to malnutrition during childhood, while enamel hypoplasia on the teeth can also signal periods of stress or illness. These markers provide important context for understanding the broader social and environmental conditions that contributed to mass death.

Post-mortem alterations to the body, such as burning, dismemberment, or burial in unusual positions, are also of interest to forensic anthropologists. These alterations may provide clues about how the bodies were treated after death, which can offer insights into the intentions of those responsible for the burial. In some cases, post-mortem treatment of bodies may reflect attempts to conceal the crime, as seen in instances where bodies are buried in shallow graves or subjected to burning to destroy evidence.

Modern War Zones and Mass Grave Investigations

In contemporary contexts, mass graves are often associated with war crimes, genocide, and political violence. The investigation of these graves requires a delicate balance between archaeological rigour and the legal needs of criminal investigations. Modern mass graves, particularly those uncovered in post-conflict zones, present a unique set of challenges, as the remains are often heavily degraded, commingled, or intentionally concealed.

One of the most well-known examples of modern mass graves is the Bosnian War, during which mass graves were uncovered following the genocide in Srebrenica in 1995. Forensic scientists working with the International Criminal Tribunal for the former Yugoslavia (ICTY) played a critical role in uncovering and documenting these graves, providing key evidence in the prosecution of war criminals. The excavation of mass graves in Srebrenica revealed the remains of thousands of men and boys who had been systematically executed and buried in large pits. Forensic analysis of the skeletal remains, combined with DNA testing, allowed investigators to identify many of the victims and establish a timeline of events leading up to their deaths.

Another significant investigation of modern mass graves occurred in the aftermath of the Rwandan Genocide in 1994, during which an estimated 800,000 people were killed over the course of 100 days. Many of the victims were buried in mass graves, some of which were later exhumed by forensic teams working with international human rights organizations. The forensic investigation of these graves revealed evidence of extreme violence, including machete wounds, bullet holes, and evidence of torture. In addition to identifying victims, the forensic analysis helped to establish patterns of killing and provided crucial evidence for the prosecution of those responsible for the genocide.

In these modern cases, DNA analysis has become one of the most important tools for identifying victims and linking perpetrators to the crime. By comparing DNA samples from the remains with DNA samples from living relatives, forensic scientists are able to positively identify individuals who would otherwise remain anonymous.

This technology has revolutionized the field of forensic anthropology, allowing for the identification of victims even in cases where the remains are severely degraded or fragmented.

The investigation of modern mass graves is not only a scientific endeavour but also a moral and legal one. Forensic scientists working in these contexts often face the difficult task of balancing their role as impartial investigators with the need to provide closure to families and communities. In many cases, the discovery and identification of mass grave victims play a critical role in the process of transitional justice, helping societies recover from the trauma of violence and providing evidence for legal proceedings aimed at holding perpetrators accountable.

Ancient Mass Graves: Archaeology and Cultural Insights

While the investigation of modern mass graves is often driven by legal and humanitarian concerns, the excavation of ancient mass graves provides a window into past societies, shedding light on the social, political, and environmental factors that led to large-scale death events. These graves are often the result of warfare, epidemics, or natural disasters, and they offer valuable insights into how past civilizations responded to crises.

One of the most famous examples of an ancient mass grave is the Tollense Valley battlefield in northern Germany, which dates back to the Bronze Age (around 1200 BCE). Discovered in 1996, the site contains the remains of more than 100 individuals who died in what is believed to be a large-scale battle. The excavation of the site revealed evidence of violent trauma, including skull fractures, arrow wounds, and broken bones, indicating that the individuals died in combat. The discovery of the Tollense Valley battlefield has provided archaeologists with rare insights into the nature of warfare during the Bronze Age, suggesting that large-scale, organized conflicts may have been more common during this period than previously thought.

Another significant ancient mass grave is the Plague of Athens burial pit, which dates back to the 5th century BCE. During the Peloponnesian War, a devastating plague swept through the city of Athens, killing an estimated one-third of the population. Excavations of the mass grave associated with this plague revealed the remains of hundreds of individuals who were buried hastily, likely due to the overwhelming number of deaths. The discovery of this grave has provided archaeologists with valuable information about the social and political impact of the plague on ancient Athens, as well as clues about the possible identity of the disease that caused the outbreak.

Ancient mass graves are not limited to sites of warfare or epidemic. Some graves may reflect cultural practices of human sacrifice, ritual killings, or responses to natural disasters. For example, the discovery of sacrificial mass graves in the Moche civilization of Peru, dating to around 500 CE, revealed the remains of individuals who had been killed as part of a ritual sacrifice to appease the gods. The analysis of the skeletal remains, combined with evidence from Moche art and iconography, suggests that these individuals were captured warriors who were sacrificed during religious ceremonies. The discovery of these graves has provided archaeologists with new insights into the religious and social dynamics of the Moche culture.

The Scientific and Human Significance of Mass Graves

The study of mass graves is a multidisciplinary endeavour that combines the rigour of archaeological excavation with the precision of forensic analysis. These graves, whether ancient or modern, serve as powerful reminders of the human capacity for violence, as well as the resilience of societies in the face of tragedy. By uncovering the stories buried within these graves, scientists not only reveal the causes and contexts of death but also contribute to our broader understanding of human history and behaviour.

Whether used to prosecute war criminals or to gain insights into ancient civilizations, the investigation of mass graves is a critical tool in the ongoing quest to understand the complexities of death on a large scale. As forensic technology continues to evolve, the ability to identify victims, establish timelines, and reconstruct events from the past will only improve, providing new opportunities to uncover the hidden narratives buried beneath the surface.

CHAPTER 29: EUTHANASIA: THE SCIENCE AND ETHICS OF CHOOSING DEATH

Euthanasia, often referred to as "assisted dying" or "mercy killing," is one of the most complex and controversial issues in modern medicine and bioethics. It encompasses the practice of intentionally ending a life to relieve suffering, particularly in cases of terminal illness, extreme pain, or incurable conditions. As medical science has advanced, so too has the ability to extend life through life-sustaining treatments, even when quality of life may be severely diminished. This has brought the question of when and how it is ethically permissible to intervene in the dying process to the forefront of legal, medical, and philosophical debates.

Euthanasia exists on a spectrum of end-of-life care decisions, from withholding or withdrawing life-sustaining treatments to active intervention to cause death. The scientific aspects of euthanasia involve understanding pain management, palliative care, and the medical mechanisms of hastening death. Ethical considerations revolve around autonomy, the sanctity of life, and the physician's role in the death process. Meanwhile, legal frameworks surrounding euthanasia vary significantly around the world, reflecting divergent cultural, religious, and societal values.

This chapter explores euthanasia from multiple angles, focusing on the science of end-of-life care, the ethical debates surrounding the right to die, and the diverse legal frameworks that govern euthanasia and assisted dying globally. Through an examination of these perspectives, the chapter aims to provide a comprehensive understanding of how society navigates the difficult choices that arise when death is imminent and suffering is profound.

The Science of Euthanasia: Understanding the Biological Process

At its core, euthanasia involves intervening in the biological process of death. There are two primary forms of euthanasia: active euthanasia and passive euthanasia. Active euthanasia involves the direct administration of substances, typically lethal doses of medication, to cause death. Passive euthanasia, on the other hand, entails withholding or withdrawing life-sustaining treatments, such as ventilators, feeding tubes, or medications, allowing the individual to die naturally from their underlying condition.

The medical management of euthanasia, particularly active euthanasia, relies on a combination of pharmacological agents that induce death in a controlled and painless manner. Typically, the process involves the administration of barbiturates or other sedatives to induce unconsciousness, followed by drugs that halt respiratory and cardiac function. One of the most common drugs used in euthanasia is sodium pentobarbital, a barbiturate that depresses the central nervous system, causing sedation and respiratory depression, which ultimately leads to death. In some protocols, muscle relaxants such as pancuronium bromide may be administered to suppress breathing further, ensuring a swift and peaceful death.

In the case of physician-assisted suicide, a related but distinct practice, the patient self-administers the lethal medication prescribed by a doctor. The role of the physician in this scenario is to provide the means for death while allowing the patient to take the final action. This practice is legal in some countries and U.S. states, where it is often referred to as "medical aid in dying" (MAID).

Palliative care, which focuses on relieving symptoms and improving quality of life for patients with life-limiting illnesses, plays a critical role in the euthanasia debate. Palliative care physicians are experts in managing pain, shortness of breath, anxiety, and other distressing symptoms at the end of life. Many who oppose euthanasia argue that with appropriate palliative care, suffering can be alleviated to the point where euthanasia becomes unnecessary. However, supporters of euthanasia contend that even with the best palliative care, some patients experience intractable suffering that cannot be fully controlled by medication or other treatments. For these individuals, euthanasia may be seen as the most humane option for ending their pain.

The concept of refractory suffering—pain or other symptoms that cannot be adequately controlled despite exhaustive medical efforts—is often central to the decision to pursue euthanasia. Conditions such as advanced cancer, amyotrophic lateral sclerosis (ALS), and end-stage chronic obstructive pulmonary disease (COPD) are examples of illnesses where patients may seek euthanasia due to the relentless progression of symptoms despite palliative care interventions. These conditions often bring prolonged physical suffering, emotional distress, and a sense of loss of dignity, prompting some patients to express a desire to hasten death.

The medical mechanisms involved in euthanasia must be precise to ensure a peaceful and controlled death, with minimal distress for both the patient and the family. Physicians who administer euthanasia or assist in dying must have specialized training in end-of-life care to navigate the medical, ethical, and legal complexities of this process.

Ethical Debates Surrounding Euthanasia: Autonomy, Dignity, and the Role of Physicians

The ethical debates surrounding euthanasia are complex, involving deeply held values about life, death, and individual autonomy. At the heart of the euthanasia debate is the question of whether individuals have the right to choose the manner and timing of their death, especially when faced with terminal illness or intractable suffering. This right to die is often framed as an extension of personal autonomy, the principle that individuals have the right to make decisions about their bodies and lives, free from external interference.

Proponents of euthanasia argue that allowing individuals to choose euthanasia is an expression of respect for autonomy, particularly when the alternative is prolonged suffering or a loss of dignity. In this view, euthanasia is seen as a compassionate response to suffering, offering patients control over the end of their lives and the opportunity to die with dignity on their terms. Supporters also emphasize the importance of quality of life, arguing that when life becomes unbearable due to pain, disability, or loss of independence, individuals should have the right to end their suffering.

Another key ethical consideration is the concept of dignity. Many patients who seek euthanasia express concerns about losing their dignity as their disease progresses. For example, individuals with advanced neurodegenerative diseases may fear becoming completely dependent on others for basic functions, such as eating, toileting, or bathing, which they perceive as an intolerable loss of autonomy and dignity. In these cases, euthanasia is seen as a way to preserve dignity by allowing individuals to avoid the final stages of their illness, where they may feel dehumanized by their physical decline.

Opponents of euthanasia, however, raise serious ethical objections based on the sanctity of life. From this perspective, life is considered inherently valuable, regardless of the quality of life or the presence of suffering. Opponents argue that deliberately ending a life, even with the patient's consent, undermines the fundamental value of human life and opens the door to a slippery slope where vulnerable individuals—such as the elderly, disabled, or mentally ill—may feel pressure to choose death rather than burden their families or society.

The role of the physician in euthanasia is also a major point of ethical contention. Traditionally, the medical profession has adhered to the principle of non-maleficence, which asserts that physicians should do no harm. For many, this principle is incompatible with euthanasia, as it involves the deliberate termination of life. Critics argue that the role of physicians should be to provide care, comfort, and healing, not to facilitate death. This position is often rooted in the Hippocratic Oath, which historically forbids physicians from engaging in practices that intentionally end life.

However, those who support euthanasia argue that the principle of beneficence—the obligation to alleviate suffering—can justify physician involvement in euthanasia. In this view, when suffering is so severe that it cannot be adequately relieved by medical treatments, euthanasia may be seen as an act of mercy. Moreover, the ethical principle of patient autonomy supports the idea that physicians should respect the patient's wishes regarding their death, particularly when they are competent to make such decisions.

The debate over euthanasia is also influenced by cultural and religious beliefs. In many religious traditions, life is viewed as sacred, and only a higher power has the authority to decide when a life should end. For example, in Catholicism, euthanasia is explicitly condemned as a violation of the sanctity of life, while other religious traditions may also oppose the practice based on similar principles. However, some secular societies prioritize individual rights and autonomy, leading to more permissive attitudes toward euthanasia.

Legal Frameworks: Euthanasia Around the World

The legal status of euthanasia varies widely around the world, reflecting the diverse cultural, ethical, and religious values of different societies. While some countries have legalized euthanasia or physician-assisted dying, others maintain strict prohibitions against the practice. In many cases, the legality of euthanasia is shaped by ongoing public debates, court rulings, and legislative efforts to balance individual rights with broader societal concerns.

In countries where euthanasia is legal, such as the Netherlands, Belgium, Luxembourg, and Canada, strict legal frameworks govern the practice. These frameworks typically include safeguards to ensure that euthanasia is only performed in cases where the patient meets specific criteria, such as having a terminal illness, experiencing unbearable suffering, and making a voluntary and well-considered request for euthanasia. For example, in the Netherlands, the Termination of Life on Request and Assisted Suicide (Review Procedures) Act of 2002 allows euthanasia and physician-assisted suicide under stringent conditions. The patient must be suffering unbearably without the prospect of improvement, and the physician must ensure that the request is voluntary and well-informed. The decision must also be reviewed by an independent physician, and the procedure is subject to oversight by regional review committees.

In Belgium, euthanasia has been legal since 2002 for adults and was extended to minors in 2014, making it the first country to allow euthanasia for children under certain conditions. Belgian law requires that the patient be in a medically futile condition, with unbearable physical or psychological suffering that cannot be alleviated. The decision to proceed with euthanasia must involve consultation with multiple physicians, and the patient must provide explicit consent.

Canada legalized medical assistance in dying (MAID) in 2016, following a landmark Supreme Court ruling in 2015 that struck down the country's ban on physician-assisted dying. Under Canadian law, eligible individuals must have a serious and incurable illness, be in an advanced state of irreversible decline, and experience intolerable suffering. The law was further expanded in 2021 to allow individuals whose natural death is not reasonably foreseeable to access MAID under certain circumstances, although additional safeguards are in place for these cases.

In contrast, other countries have taken a more restrictive approach to euthanasia. In many jurisdictions, euthanasia remains illegal, and individuals who assist in the death of another person may face criminal charges. For example, the United Kingdom prohibits both euthanasia and assisted suicide, with the Suicide Act of 1961 criminalizing the act of assisting or encouraging another person to end their life. Those found guilty of assisting suicide can face up to 14 years in prison. Despite ongoing public debate and calls for reform, euthanasia remains a contentious issue in the UK, with opponents citing concerns about potential abuses and the protection of vulnerable individuals.

In the United States, the legal landscape of euthanasia and assisted dying is complex, with laws varying by state. While euthanasia remains illegal throughout the country, several states have legalized physician-assisted suicide, including Oregon, Washington, California, Vermont, Colorado, and the District of Columbia. These states have enacted "Death with Dignity" laws that allow terminally ill patients to obtain and self-administer life-ending medication, provided they meet specific criteria. Oregon's Death with Dignity Actpassed in 1997, was the first law of its kind in the U.S., and it has served as a model for similar legislation in other states.

The legal status of euthanasia continues to evolve, with ongoing debates about the ethical, medical, and legal implications of allowing individuals to choose death. In some countries, public opinion has shifted in favour of legalizing euthanasia, particularly as medical advancements prolong life in cases of severe suffering. However, the legal frameworks that govern euthanasia must carefully balance respect for individual autonomy with protections for vulnerable individuals, ensuring that the practice is conducted safely and ethically.

The Future of Euthanasia: Medical Advances and Ethical Challenges

As medical science continues to advance, new technologies and treatments may further complicate the euthanasia debate. Innovations in palliative care, pain management, and life-sustaining treatments may offer new ways to alleviate suffering, potentially reducing the demand for euthanasia. At the same time, developments in artificial intelligence, robotics, and biotechnology may raise new ethical questions about the role of technology in end-of-life care and the decision to pursue euthanasia.

For example, the rise of artificial intelligence (AI) in healthcare has the potential to revolutionize end-of-life care by providing more personalized and precise treatments for pain and symptom management. AI algorithms could help physicians predict which patients are likely to benefit from certain interventions, allowing for more targeted and effective care. However, the integration of AI into end-of-life decision-making also raises concerns about the depersonalization of care and the potential for technology to override human judgment in matters of life and death.

Another emerging issue is the use of advanced life-sustaining technologies, such as ventricular assist devices (VADs) and extracorporeal membrane oxygenation (ECMO), which can prolong life in cases of severe heart or lung failure. While these technologies offer hope for patients who may otherwise die, they also raise ethical questions about when it is appropriate to withdraw life-sustaining treatments and whether patients should have the right to request euthanasia in cases where their quality of life is severely diminished.

The future of euthanasia will also be shaped by evolving societal attitudes toward death, autonomy, and the value of life. As more countries and states consider legalizing euthanasia, the ethical and legal frameworks surrounding end-of-life care will continue to be debated and refined. Ultimately, the question of whether individuals should have the right to choose death will remain one of the most challenging and deeply personal issues in medicine and bioethics.

Navigating the Complexities of Euthanasia

Euthanasia represents a profound intersection of medical science, ethics, and law. It raises difficult questions about autonomy, dignity, suffering, and the role of physicians in the dying process. As medical advancements continue to extend life, the debate over euthanasia is likely to intensify, with advocates and opponents offering competing visions of what it means to die with dignity and compassion.

The legal status of euthanasia varies widely around the world, reflecting the diverse cultural, religious, and ethical values of different societies. While some countries have embraced euthanasia as a means of relieving suffering, others remain staunchly opposed to the practice, citing concerns about the sanctity of life and the protection of vulnerable individuals.

As the science and ethics of euthanasia continue to evolve, the challenge for society will be to navigate these complexities in a way that respects both individual autonomy and the broader moral and ethical concerns that surround the decision to end life. The future of euthanasia will depend on ongoing dialogue between patients, physicians, lawmakers, and society at large, as we continue to grapple with the difficult questions that arise at the intersection of life and death.

CHAPTER 30: THE FINAL FRONTIER: THE PHILOSOPHICAL AND SCIENTIFIC MYSTERY OF WHAT HAPPENS AFTER DEATH

Death, the final event in the life of every living organism, remains one of the greatest mysteries of human existence. While science can explain the biological processes that occur when the body ceases to function, the question of what happens after death—if anything—has long been a subject of philosophical, theological, and scientific inquiry. Human curiosity about the afterlife, reincarnation, and the nature of consciousness transcends cultures and epochs, as people have sought to understand whether death marks the definitive end of existence or the beginning of something beyond.

The exploration of death and the afterlife encompasses a wide range of perspectives, from religious doctrines that describe heavenly realms, reincarnation, or spiritual rebirth, to scientific theories about consciousness and its cessation. While much of the debate about the afterlife remains speculative and beyond the reach of empirical science, advances in neuroscience, quantum theory, and the study of near-death experiences (NDEs) have sparked renewed interest in what happens when life ends.

This chapter explores the major philosophical, theological, and scientific perspectives on the afterlife, reincarnation, and the nature of consciousness. By examining these diverse viewpoints, the chapter seeks to illuminate the profound questions that arise when we confront the reality of death and the possibility of what, if anything, lies beyond.

Theological Perspectives on the Afterlife: Heaven, Hell, and Rebirth

Religious beliefs about the afterlife are among the most deeply rooted and widely varied perspectives on what happens after death. These beliefs often provide comfort to the living by offering a vision of continued existence or ultimate justice beyond the grave. The concept of the afterlife is central to many of the world's major religions, including Christianity, Islam, Hinduism, and Buddhism, each of which presents a distinct view of what happens after death.

In Christianity, the afterlife is traditionally framed as a binary destination: heaven or hell. According to Christian theology, the soul is judged based on its actions during life, and those who have lived by God's will are rewarded with eternal life in heaven, a place of peace, joy, and union with God. In contrast, those who have sinned and failed to repent are condemned to hell, a realm of punishment and suffering. The belief in resurrection, exemplified by the resurrection of Jesus Christ, is a central tenet of Christian eschatology, with the promise of bodily resurrection at the end of time, when souls will be reunited with their bodies in either eternal glory or eternal damnation.

Islam shares similar themes, with a strong emphasis on divine judgment after death. In Islam, the soul enters a state known as barzakh—an intermediate phase between death and the final judgment—where it awaits the resurrection. On the Day of Judgment, individuals will be judged by Allah based on their deeds, and their eternal fate will be determined. The righteous are granted entry into paradise (Jannah), a garden of eternal bliss, while the sinful are consigned to hell (Jahannam), a place of torment. The Islamic afterlife is both physical and spiritual, with the resurrection of the body playing a key role in the final judgment.

In contrast to the Abrahamic traditions, Hinduism and Buddhism emphasize the cycle of reincarnation, known as samsara, where the soul is continually reborn into new bodies based on its karma—actions and decisions made in previous lives. In Hinduism, the ultimate goal is to achieve liberation (moksha) from the cycle of birth, death, and rebirth, at which point the soul attains union with the divine. The path to moksha involves living per one's dharma (duty) and accumulating good karma. In Buddhism, the concept of nirvana represents liberation from samsara and the cessation of suffering. Unlike Hinduism, Buddhism teaches that there is no permanent self or soul (anatman), and liberation is the realization of the impermanence of all things.

While these theological perspectives provide varied and intricate descriptions of the afterlife, they all share a common belief that death is not the end but a transition to a new state of existence. Whether through resurrection, judgment, or reincarnation, these religious frameworks offer answers to the existential questions that arise when we contemplate death and the fate of the soul.

Philosophical Perspectives: The Nature of Consciousness and the Self

Philosophical inquiry into death and the afterlife often centres on the nature of consciousness and the self, raising profound questions about personal identity, the continuity of existence, and the possibility of survival after death. For millennia, philosophers have grappled with whether the mind, soul, or consciousness can persist beyond the death of the body, or whether death represents the permanent cessation of all subjective experience.

One of the most enduring philosophical debates about death concerns dualism versus materialism. Dualism, famously articulated by the philosopher René Descartes, posits that the mind and body are distinct entities, with the mind (or soul) capable of existing independently of the body. Descartes' mind-body dualism suggests that while the body is a physical entity subject to decay and death, the mind is an immaterial substance that may continue to exist after the body's demise. This view is compatible with many religious beliefs about the afterlife, which hold that the soul survives death and moves on to another realm of existence.

In contrast, materialism asserts that consciousness is a product of the brain's physical processes and that when the brain ceases to function, consciousness ceases as well. According to this view, often associated with modern neuroscience, death is the end of all subjective experience. The philosopher David Hume, for example, argued that the self is a bundle of perceptions that arise from sensory experiences and that when the brain dies, the perceptions that constitute the self are extinguished. Materialists contend that there is no evidence for the existence of a soul or consciousness separate from the brain, and thus, any notion of life after death is purely speculative.

However, even within materialist frameworks, there are interesting debates about personal identity and the nature of consciousness. The philosopher Derek Parfit, for example, challenged traditional notions of identity, arguing that personal identity is not as important as the continuity of psychological experiences and memories. According to Parfit, what matters is not whether the same "self" persists over time, but whether there is psychological continuity between past, present, and future experiences. This perspective raises intriguing questions about what it would mean to survive death—whether through reincarnation, resurrection, or other means—if the continuity of experiences, rather than the preservation of a single, unchanging self, is what constitutes personal identity.

Another philosophical question concerns the meaning of death and whether it should be feared. Existential philosophers like Martin Heidegger and Jean-Paul Sartre have argued that death gives life meaning by imposing a finite limit on existence. For Heidegger, death is a fundamental aspect of human existence, forcing individuals to confront their mortality and live authentically in light of the inevitability of death. Sartre, in his existentialist framework, viewed death as the ultimate limit of human freedom—an event that renders all human projects and aspirations meaningless in the long run. Yet, for both thinkers, the awareness of death is not something to be feared but rather embraced as part of the human condition.

On the other hand, Epicurean philosophers, such as Epicurus himself, famously argued that death is nothing to be feared because it is simply the cessation of experience. According to the Epicurean view, "where death is, we are not; and where we are, death is not," meaning that because we do not experience death directly, it is not something that can cause suffering. From this perspective, the fear of death is irrational because it is based on the mistaken belief that we can somehow experience non-existence.

While philosophy does not offer definitive answers about what happens after death, it provides valuable frameworks for thinking about personal identity, consciousness, and the meaning of death. Whether one subscribes to a dualist view of the soul or a materialist understanding of consciousness, philosophical inquiry invites deep reflection on the nature of existence and the ultimate mystery of death.

Scientific Perspectives: Near-Death Experiences and the Study of Consciousness

The scientific exploration of what happens after death is inherently limited by the boundaries of empirical investigation. Unlike the physical processes of death, which can be observed and measured, the subjective experience of death—if any—remains beyond the reach of current scientific tools. Nevertheless, advances in neuroscience, the study of near-death experiences (NDEs), and ongoing research into the nature of consciousness have opened up new avenues for understanding the end of life and what might happen afterwards.

Near-death experiences are one of the most intriguing phenomena associated with the mystery of death. NDEs are typically reported by individuals who have come close to death or have been resuscitated after clinical death. These experiences often include vivid perceptions of light, a sense of peace or euphoria, encounters with deceased loved ones, and an out-of-body sensation. In some cases, individuals report travelling through a tunnel or experiencing a life review, where they relive key moments from their past.

While NDEs are often interpreted as evidence of an afterlife, many scientists approach these experiences from a physiological and neurological perspective. One theory suggests that NDEs are the result of anoxia or hypoxia, a lack of oxygen in the brain, which can cause hallucinations, disorientation, and vivid mental imagery. Other

researchers propose that NDEs may be linked to the release of endorphins or other neurochemicals that produce feelings of euphoria and calm during moments of extreme stress or trauma. Ketamine, a dissociative aesthetic, has been shown to induce similar experiences, leading some to speculate that the brain's chemical response to trauma may be responsible for NDEs.

Despite these physiological explanations, NDEs remain a subject of scientific fascination because of the consistency of certain reports and the fact that they often occur in individuals who have been declared clinically dead. Studies conducted by researchers such as Dr. Raymond Moody and Dr. Sam Parnia have sought to document and analyse NDEs, but the phenomenon remains controversial. Critics argue that NDEs do not provide conclusive evidence of an afterlife, but rather reflect the brain's final moments of activity before death.

Beyond the study of NDEs, ongoing research into the nature of consciousness has raised important questions about whether consciousness can persist after the death of the body. Neuroscience generally holds that consciousness is a product of brain activity, specifically the interactions between neurons and the electrical and chemical signals they generate. However, some scientists and philosophers have speculated about the possibility of consciousness existing independently of the brain, citing the enigmatic nature of consciousness itself.

The field of quantum mechanics has also contributed to the debate about consciousness and death, with some researchers proposing that consciousness may be related to quantum processes occurring at the subatomic level. The quantum mind hypothesis, while speculative, suggests that consciousness might involve quantum coherence or entanglement, processes that are not fully understood and may not be bound by the same physical limitations as the brain. Proponents of this theory argue that consciousness could theoretically exist outside of the brain in some form, raising the possibility of survival after death. However, these ideas remain highly controversial and have not been substantiated by empirical evidence.

While science has yet to provide definitive answers about what happens after death, the study of consciousness, NDEs, and quantum theory continues to push the boundaries of our understanding of the mind and its relationship to the body. As research into these areas progresses, it may offer new insights into one of the most enduring mysteries of human existence.

The Ultimate Mystery: Unanswered Questions and Future Research

Despite centuries of philosophical inquiry, religious speculation, and scientific investigation, the question of what happens after death remains unanswered. For many, the uncertainty surrounding death is a source of fear or anxiety, while for others, it is an invitation to explore the deeper mysteries of existence. While religious traditions offer varied and often comforting visions of the afterlife, the lack of empirical evidence leaves the question open to interpretation and debate.

Advances in neuroscience, physics, and technology may eventually provide new tools for understanding the nature of consciousness and its relationship to death. Ongoing research into brain activity at the time of death, the phenomenon of NDEs, and the potential quantum basis of consciousness could yield new insights into whether consciousness can persist beyond the body. However, even with these advances, the subjective experience of death may remain beyond the reach of scientific observation, leaving open the possibility that some aspects of the afterlife may forever remain in the realm of philosophy and theology.

In the end, the mystery of what happens after death is as much a reflection of the human desire for meaning and purpose as it is a scientific or philosophical question. Whether one believes in an afterlife, reincarnation, or the cessation of consciousness, the search for answers about death reveals as much about the nature of life as it does about the nature of death itself.

The Final Frontier of Human Inquiry

The mystery of what happens after death has captivated human imagination for millennia, inspiring countless religious, philosophical, and scientific explorations. While religious traditions provide comforting narratives about the afterlife, reincarnation, or spiritual transformation, scientific inquiry focuses on the biological and neurological processes that occur at the end of life. Despite these diverse perspectives, the question of whether consciousness persists after death remains one of the greatest unanswered questions of human existence.

As our understanding of the brain and consciousness evolves, new possibilities for exploring the nature of death may emerge. However, the mystery of death will likely continue to provoke debate, reflection, and wonder for generations to come. The final frontier of human inquiry, death challenges us to confront the limits of knowledge and to contemplate the unknown with curiosity and humility.

EPILOGUE: THE SILENCE AFTER

Death has been an omnipresent shadow in human existence, its certainty both feared and revered. Throughout history, it has shaped our religions, our philosophies, our scientific endeavours, and even the way we live. In this book, we have explored death in its multifaceted complexity—from its biological inevitability to its cultural significance, from the legal frameworks we use to define its boundaries to the profound mysteries that arise when life slips into the unknown. Death is, at once, the ultimate equalizer and the great unknown.

What we leave behind, and how we understand death, reflects our deepest desires and our greatest fears. Is death a transition, a gateway to another realm of existence, or simply the cessation of the self—a return to the silence from which we emerged? For some, death is the final release from suffering; for others, it is a threshold that promises renewal or eternal life. The truth is, we do not know for certain. Our understanding is limited by the same frailties that make us mortal—our finite cognition, the limitations of language, and the constraints of our scientific tools.

In many ways, death compels us to live with uncertainty. It challenges our quest for definitive answers and forces us to grapple with the possibility that some questions may never be resolved. Yet, it is in this uncertainty that we find meaning. The brevity of life sharpens our focus on what matters most—the relationships we cultivate, the experiences we cherish, and the legacies we leave behind.

Science has allowed us to peer ever deeper into the processes of death, uncovering the mechanisms by which the body and mind shut down. We have learned to delay death through medical intervention and to alleviate the suffering that often accompanies it. But as we push the boundaries of life and death, we are reminded of the ethical, philosophical, and spiritual dimensions that cannot be quantified or explained through data alone. Death is not just a scientific event; it is a deeply personal and profoundly human experience.

As we stand at the intersection of knowledge and mystery, it is worth considering how we might approach death—not with fear, but with a sense of acceptance and curiosity. What lies beyond may be unknown, but perhaps the act of living with full awareness of our mortality can enrich the time we are given. Death, in all its inevitability, teaches us to value life, to seek connection, and to find purpose in the fleeting moments we share.

In the end, death is not simply the cessation of life; it is the silence that frames it. It is in this silence that we are invited to reflect on what it means to have lived. Our questions about death remain unanswered, but perhaps they do not need to be. It is enough to know that death, like life, is part of the same continuum—one cannot exist without the other. To live is to accept the presence of death, and in that acceptance, we may find peace, even if the silence after is unknowable.

REFERENCES

1. Blum, D. (2010). The Poisoner's Handbook: Murder and the Birth of Forensic Medicine in Jazz Age New York. Penguin Books.

2. Doughty, C. (2017). From Here to Eternity: Traveling the World to Find the Good Death. W.W. Norton & Company.

3. Fitzharris, L. (2017). The Butchering Art: Joseph Lister's Quest to Transform the Grisly World of Victorian Medicine. Scientific American / Farrar, Straus and Giroux.

4. Gawande, A. (2014). Being Mortal: Medicine and What Matters in the End. Metropolitan Books.

5. Halber, D. (2014). The Skeleton Crew: How Amateur Sleuths Are Solving America's Coldest Cases. Simon & Schuster.

6. Humphries, S. (2013). Dissolving Illusions: Disease, Vaccines, and The Forgotten History. CreateSpace Independent Publishing Platform.

7. Johnston, S. I. (1999). Restless Dead: Encounters Between the Living and the Dead in Ancient Greece. University of California Press.

8. Kean, S. (2014). The Tale of the Dueling Neurosurgeons: The History of the Human Brain as Revealed by True Stories of Trauma, Madness, and Recovery. Little, Brown and Company.

9. Lane, N. (2015). The Vital Question: Energy, Evolution, and the Origins of Complex Life. W.W. Norton & Company.

10. Maples, W. R. (1995). Dead Men Do Tell Tales: The Strange

and Fascinating Cases of a Forensic Anthropologist. Broadway Books.

11. Melinek, J., & Mitchell, T. J. (2014). Working Stiff: Two Years, 262 Bodies, and the Making of a Medical Examiner. Scribner.

12. Nichols, T. (2017). The Death of Expertise: The Campaign Against Established Knowledge and Why it Matters. Oxford University Press.

13. Pollard, T. (2015). The Secrets of the Lazarus Club. Canongate Books.

14. Parnia, S. (2014). Erasing Death: The Science That Is Rewriting the Boundaries Between Life and Death. HarperOne.

15. Roach, M. (2006). Spook: Science Tackles the Afterlife. W.W. Norton & Company.

16. Skloot, R. (2010). The Immortal Life of Henrietta Lacks. Crown Publishing Group.

17. Tyson, N. D. (2007). Death by Black Hole: And Other Cosmic Quandaries. W.W. Norton & Company.

ACKNOWLEDGEMENTS

I would like to express my deepest gratitude to everyone who has supported the creation of this book. My sincere thanks go to my family for their unwavering encouragement and patience during the long hours of research and writing. Without your understanding and belief in this project, this book would not have been possible.

A special thanks to my colleagues and mentors in the medical and academic communities, whose insights and expertise have shaped my understanding of life, death, and the science that binds them. Your guidance and thought-provoking conversations were invaluable in crafting the content of this book.

I would also like to acknowledge the authors and researchers whose work has inspired this exploration of death in its many forms. Their contributions to the fields of medicine, philosophy, and forensic science have laid the foundation for much of the discussion within these pages.

Finally, my heartfelt thanks go to the team at Irene Minds for their dedication to bringing this book to life. Your support in the editing, production, and publishing processes has been instrumental in making this vision a reality.

Thank you all.

— Dr. Bhaskar Bora

COPYRIGHT INFORMATION

© 2024 by Dr. Bhaskar Bora

All rights reserved. No part of this book may be reproduced, distributed, or transmitted in any form or by any means, including photocopying, recording, or other electronic or mechanical methods, without the prior written permission of the publisher, except in the case of brief quotations embodied in critical reviews and certain other non-commercial uses permitted by copyright law.

Published by Irene Minds
First Edition: 2024

DISCLAIMER

This book is intended for informational and educational purposes only. While every effort has been made to ensure the accuracy and completeness of the information contained herein, the author and publisher make no representations or warranties regarding the content's suitability for any particular purpose. This book is not intended to serve as medical, legal, or professional advice.

Readers should consult qualified professionals regarding specific issues related to death, dying, and end-of-life care. The views and opinions expressed in this book are those of the author and do not necessarily reflect the views of any organizations or institutions with which the author may be affiliated.

The inclusion of any case studies, historical events, or referenced materials is for illustrative purposes only and does not imply endorsement or factual accuracy beyond the cited sources. The author and publisher disclaim any liability for any actions taken based on the information presented in this book.

Printed in Great Britain
by Amazon